Ethnic Marketing

Accepting the Challenge of Cultural Diversity

Guilherme D. Pires

and

P. John Stanton

THOMSON
™

Australia • Canada • Mexico • Singapore • Spain • United Kingdom • United States

Ethnic Marketing

Copyright © Thomson Learning 2005

For more information, contact Thomson Learning, High Holborn House, 50/51 Bedford Row, London, WC1R 4LR or visit us on the World Wide Web at: http://www.thomsonlearning.co.uk

British Library Cataloguing-in-Publication Data
A catalogue record for this book is available from the British Library

ISBN 1–86152–996–1

First edition 2005

Typeset by Graphicraft Limited, Hong Kong
Printed in Hong Kong by C&C Offset Printing Co. Ltd.

To my parents, who would have been very proud. To my children, who I hope will be very proud. But especially to Maria Clara, my wife, whose patience knows no bounds.

Guilherme Pires

To my parents, who were ahead of Australian times, and my wonderful wife, Patricia.

John Stanton

Contents

List of tables

List of figures

List of exhibits

Preface

There is growing evidence that the cultural and ethnic diversity of many advanced and newly industrializing economies is increasing and that ethnic minorities, rather than disappearing into a melting pot of national cultural homogeneity, are seeking to maintain their identity. While policy makers, sociologists and demographers consider the causes and consequences, business has been slow to recognize and seize the opportunities created by this growth and reawakening occurring within national borders.

Potential marketing opportunities are often cited but the prescriptions offered for targeting ethnic groups as consumers are diverse, often lacking in rigour and failing to convey both the potholes and the opportunities involved in the process. A systematic exposition of how to develop an effective marketing strategy targeting ethnic groups within a country has been lacking. *Ethnic Marketing* seeks to fill this gap. It is concerned to recognize the importance that individual ethnic groups and their institutions can have for marketing. Hence, the focus is on the ethnic group and the challenges and opportunities that ethnic groups represent. This focus, and the application of segmentation, targeting and positioning principles, distinguishes ethnic marketing in focus and scope from international cross-cultural marketing and multicultural marketing.

We have endeavoured to provide a text that clearly defines the field of study, that argues the case for targeting ethnic groups and explains a process for doing so, while also providing supporting evidence. As such, the text is intended for other marketing academics seeking to influence their approach to teaching domestic marketing in a culturally diverse education environment, marketing practitioners and businesses seeking better ways of reaching their diverse potential customers, as well as advanced marketing students in postgraduate and undergraduate courses.

Introduction to ethnic marketing

1.1 Chapter objectives

This chapter explains the concept of ethnicity and ethnic groups and the reasons why businesses should and can target them in culturally diverse countries. Ethnic marketing is defined and its field of study separated from other forms of marketing. The emergence of ethnic minorities as a permanent characteristic of many advanced economies is explained and linked to marketing. A snapshot of the extent of cultural diversity in advanced and emerging markets is provided, with particular emphasis placed on North America, Europe and Australasia. The chapter then maps the path this book follows for developing an ethnic marketing strategy.

This book is intended to provide the reader with both an introduction to the emerging field of ethnic marketing and an appreciation of how an ethnic marketing strategy can be developed to target and win the loyalty of ethnic minority consumers. Ethnic marketing is growing in importance as marketers seek to develop strategies that target the growing and culturally diverse markets emerging in many advanced economies. By the time you have completed reading this book we hope we will have explained what ethnic marketing is, where and how it can be used and illustrated the significant opportunities for its application, as well as the outcomes it can afford. Like all emerging fields of research and application, differences of opinion exist and this diversity of views needs to be acknowledged in any book seeking to portray the development of ethnic marketing.

1.2 Introduction to the concept of ethnicity

Not surprisingly, ethnicity will be a recurring theme throughout this book. Before defining ethnic marketing a brief look at the concept of ethnicity is necessary. Because it is an intended basis for data collection and because of the wide research conducted to arrive at a definition, the definition used in constructing the *Australian Standard Classification of Cultural and Ethnic Groups* [ASCCEG] (ABS, 2000) is a useful starting point. The difficulty for ASCCEG was to define ethnicity in a way that was both useful and generally acceptable, a difficulty that marketers will also confront.

The term 'ethnicity' refers to the shared identity or similarity of a group of people on the basis of one or more characteristics, including the following:

- a long shared history, the memory of which is kept alive;
- a cultural tradition, including family and social customs, sometimes religiously based;
- a common geographic origin;
- a common language (not necessarily limited to that group);
- a common literature, written or oral;
- a common religion;
- being a minority (often with a sense of being oppressed); and,
- being racially conspicuous.

This list was drawn from a House of Lords report, *Patterns of Prejudice* (United Kingdom, 1983), which leads to a definition of an ethnic group. The key factor in defining an ethnic group is that the group regards itself, and is regarded by others, as a distinct community by virtue of certain characteristics (listed above), not all of which have to be present in a group.

ASCCEG then needed to confront how such groups could be identified in terms of the listed characteristics. The two broad approaches were self-perceived group identification and a historically determined approach, with ASCCEG justifying the use of self-perceived group identification. Marketers seeking to target markets on the basis of ethnicity have a useful introduction to the concept in ASCCEG.

1.3 The development of ethnic marketing

Open a marketing textbook, whether domestically or internationally focused, and it is unlikely the glossary will contain the term ethnic marketing. That is because it is an emerging approach to segmenting and targeting markets that focuses on meeting the needs and wants of particular groups of consumers – ethnic minority consumers – rather than treating them as a part of a large integrated market.

Ethnic marketing arises from the growing recognition by marketers that marketing to ethnic minority consumers as if they were indistinguishable from other consumers may often ignore differences in communications preferences and consumption behaviour. Developing a value proposition that better meets the needs and preferences of ethnic minority consumers can be a way of winning customers and holding their loyalty.

Marketing research into ethnic minority consumers has a relatively long history. Cui (2001) traces marketing research on American ethnic minorities back to 1932, showing an increasing volume especially since the 1990s, with a heavy emphasis on the differences between the consumption behaviour of ethnic minorities and the consumption behaviour of mainstream consumers. These differences provide the opportunities for ethnic marketing to become a more effective approach to communicate with, supply and satisfy minority ethnic consumers than the alternatives encompassed in the marketing approaches used in domestic marketing, global marketing, or a weaker form of ethnic marketing often called multicultural marketing.

Domestic marketing

Market segmentation, seeking to group consumers who are alike based on some important common characteristics likely to influence their decision-making and consumer behaviour, is a cornerstone of modern marketing strategy. Determining the most suitable variables with which to identify markets that a business can target occupies both domestic and international marketers. Demographic, psychographic, geographic and benefit dimensions are widely used. While demographic variables may include ethnicity, ethnicity is rarely used as a basis for segmentation although it may be a relevant

characteristic of the population being marketed to. If not ignored, it is generally placed in the too-hard basket.

When explaining how to market to a domestic market, most marketing
texts in Western economies will tend to ignore cultural diversity based on
ethnicity. At most, ethnicity is treated as a marginally useful, highly qualified
segmenting variable. Culture and subcultures are important influences on
consumer behaviour but culture is given far more attention in the development of international marketing strategies than domestically. Segmenting by
subculture – identifying groups of people with common shared value systems,
common life experiences and in the same situation – is a widely used method
of segmenting that leads to identification of various demographic groups
such as teenagers, preteens and gays. But rarely is ethnicity used to segment
a market domestically.

Widely used marketing texts show similarities in the consideration given to
ethnicity. Subcultures 'usually develop from a basic dimension of race, religion or nationality', and 'it is these which tend to have the most influence on
consumer behaviour' (Baker, 1998: 124). The concept of ethnic group is not
directly acknowledged. Kotler *et al.* (1998) are similarly circumspect. Cultural
factors are claimed to exert the major influence on consumer behaviour
(p. 193), but subcultures are emphasized as the basis for segmentation, especially international segmentation (pp. 310, 788). For domestic marketing,
ethnic diversity is not defined other than by reference to overseas migration
leading to many 'national groups', each with specific wants and different
buying habits (p. 113), that can provide a rationale for micro-marketing.
Although in both texts segmentation focuses on subculture, the elements of
an ethnic group differ: Kotler *et al.* interchange ethnicity and nationality;
Baker cites nationality, race and religion as possible determinants.

More recent texts provide a similar limited recognition of ethnicity.
McColl-Kennedy and Kiel (2000) argue that subcultures provide a qualified
basis for segmentation, with 'nationality' groups used interchangeably with
'ethnic groups' (p. 93). Even more confusing, 'ethnic origin (birthplace)' is
referred to as a segmentation variable while examples cited conflate race,
nationality and birthplace (p. 244). Miller and Layton (2000) acknowledge
the existence of 'ethnic markets' within a national boundary (p. 205). While
they identify subcultures as the relevant focus for segmentation, national
origin, ethnic groups and race are used interchangeably and it is 'ethnic
origin' that is 'useful for segmenting the market for some products' (pp. 141,
205). There is no basis for assuming these concepts define the same segment.

In general, while there is a growing acknowledgement of cultural diversity
and the potential for using subcultures as a segmenting variable within
domestic economies, marketers have not sought to address when and how to
reach ethnic minority consumers other than through mainstream marketing
methods.

International and global marketing

The case for the importance of cultural differences in international marketing is advanced by one of the leading authorities on organizational culture. Hofstede (2001) cites research that shows the persistent influence of national cultures on consumer behaviour. This questions the validity of marketing theories and practices, including advertising, that stress a standardization strategy. Services, for example, are less likely to be globalized than goods because they are personalized toward the customer: 'What motivates people to buy and use certain products is largely a matter of culture' (Hofstede, 2001: 449).

But even specialized international marketing texts, whilst according prominence to culture, are unclear about the 'ethnic group' concept and reticent in addressing ethnicity. Usunier (1996) is an exception, addressing ethnic consumption, assimilation and ethnic identity. The assimilation model is questionable because it assumes a linear assimilation process that is doubtful in an environment that allows free choice and has low structural constraints (Pires and Stanton, 2000). Usunier effectively destroys the implicit association of ethnic groups with nationality, pointing to examples of ethnic groups overriding the nation and the existence of transnational ethnic segments. The Kurds and Basques are examples.

International marketing is often distinguished from global marketing. International marketing often focuses on environmental and cultural differences between countries, leading to the adaptation of both communication and products to different country environments. In contrast, global marketing, rather than emphasizing differences, seeks to find the similarities between countries. Driven by the desire to generate economies of scale and scope, a single strategy is applied across countries and the different subcultures they may contain. It is driven not only by perceived cost advantages, but also by a belief in the increasing convergence of environmental and customer requirements. Standardization is modified if, given the costs of adaptation, markets still appear sufficiently attractive, but this is unlikely to extend to subcultures within a country.

Multicultural marketing

Apart from textbooks, a rapidly growing body of literature addressing 'multicultural marketing' has recently emerged. 'Multiculturalism' derives from recognition that societies are culturally diverse or multicultural (Joppke and Lukes, 1999: 3), a concept that goes beyond ethnic diversity. Rationales offered for a growing marketing focus are relatively uniform. Nwankwo et al. (1998) argue that multiculturalism has become a 'central discourse', as marketers struggle to cope with increasing diversity of markets. This is attributable to 'the unabating mobility of populations across national frontiers'.

Similarly, Wilkinson and Cheng (1997) assert that Australia is becoming more multicultural through overseas migration. At its widest, multicultural marketing is an acknowledgement of the cultural diversity that exists within advanced economies and the opportunities for dividing by subcultures, not necessarily ethnicity, in order to communicate better with a target group.

For many years international multicultural marketing conferences have been held addressing issues of marketing to different subcultures. No dominant view of multicultural marketing has emerged other than recognition of cultural diversity among consumers, both domestically and internationally, and that marketing must take into account such differences. How it should take those differences into account varies in interpretation from minor communication adjustments (translation of a flyer into the preferred language of the ethnic group) to a voluntary altering of product specifications to meet the needs of a group better.

Ethnic marketing

We will address the identification of ethnic minority consumers later. The heart of a viable ethnic marketing approach is the targeting of such consumers if there are affirmative answers to three questions:

1. Are the consumption needs and preferences of the consumers making up a minority ethnic group different from those of either other minority ethnic groups or of the majority of mainstream consumers?

2. Are the information sources and communication channels used by ethnic minority consumers different from those of either other consumers of distinct minority ethnicity or mainstream consumers?

3. If yes, is it likely that these differences can be targeted by businesses in a way that increases the value of the business?

Cui (1997) argues that an ethnic marketing strategy should be applied when ethnic minority consumers have 'unique needs that cannot be fulfilled by the products designed for majority consumers and when they can not be reached through traditional channels'. In targeting groups of consumers with a particular offer it is rare that every individual consumer will find the offer exactly to his or her particular preference. Strategically, ethnic marketing seeks to tailor an offer that consumers identified by their ethnicity will perceive as superior to the offer directed to majority consumers or to other minority consumers with distinct ethnicities. In that sense, ethnic marketing may involve the targeting of ethnic minority consumer groups with relatively few members; it also approximates at that level to what has been described as micro-marketing, that is, target marketing in which companies tailor their marketing programmes to the needs and wants of a narrowly defined segment

(Kotler, 1997). Because micro-marketing can be undertaken using a range of segmentation variables and the size of minority ethnic consumer groups varies immensely, ethnic marketing is more specific than micro-marketing.

1.4 The resilience of ethnic minority groups

Effective ethnic marketing depends on the identification of consumer groups based on a common ethnicity of the members in each group, who are likely to respond in the same way to a targeted offer. The scope of ethnic marketing depends on effectively identifying minority ethnic groups likely to respond in the same way to that targeted offer. Hence, ethnicity itself is a necessary but not sufficient condition to warrant an ethnic marketing strategy. Ethnicity has three defining characteristics:

1. perception by others that the group is different (unique);
2. perception by those in the group that they are different from others, that is, that the group is unique; and,
3. those defined as being in the same group, with the same identity, share activities based on their perceived similarity, whether this similarity is real or imagined.

Figure 1.1 depicts the three defining characteristics, illustrating the potential mutual reinforcement between the characteristics. Perception by others that the group is different strengthens the perception by those in the group

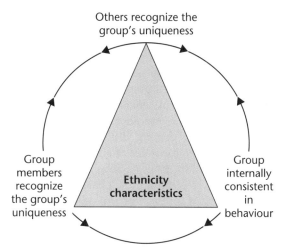

Figure 1.1 Ethnicity-defining characteristics

of their own uniqueness, that extends to consumer behaviour by individual group affiliates. Evidence of such behaviour provides further support to group uniqueness as perceived by others.

Ethnicity is therefore about awareness, identity, belonging, culture, external difference and internal similarity. A multi-ethnic society is a collection of different ethnic groups; usually a much larger majority or mainstream 'national' ethnic group, alongside a number of smaller (hence minority) ethnic groups. The self-identity of some ethnic groups might be based on a mother society outside the host society, while some ethnic groups might be disadvantaged in relation to other groups in the same society (Yinger, 1976). The degree of distinctiveness from the host culture and economic prosperity of an ethnic group may vary, providing potential grounds for targeting using different marketing strategies.

Yet there are some eminent authors who see ethnicity as ephemeral within advanced economies. Hofstede (2001) argues for the predominance of national cultures in the long term. The argument is that the first generation of migrants faces an acculturation process that involves cultural clashes, the second generation acquires conflicting mental programmes, while the third generation is mostly absorbed into the host country population, assuming host country values, being mainly distinguished by their names and maybe their religious and family traditions (p. 430). Whether this shifting process towards integration occurs quickly or slowly depends as much on the majority as the migrants themselves. Segmentation based on a shifting and unstable cohort of consumers is untenable. Within a national culture, developing strategies with a focus on ethnic groups would become redundant.

Berry and Sam (1997) reject the view that ethnic minorities inevitably become part of the mainstream. They argue that this does not always occur, resulting in continuous cultural diversity regardless of migration inflows. This continuous cultural diversity is described as a process of acculturation with the society becoming culturally plural – people of many cultural backgrounds living together in a diverse society forming a multicultural society.

All individuals within such a society acculturate. Hence acculturation, as used by Berry and Sam, is a neutral term, encompassing a process of interaction and adjustment. 'Acculturation comprehends those phenomena which result when groups of individuals having different cultures come into continuous first-hand contact with subsequent changes in the original culture patterns of either or both groups' (p. 293). Change may take place in one or both groups, but in practice there is often more change in one group than another. In addition, the process of interaction and adjustment is not unilateral. Integration is a two-way process and the ability to integrate does not rest with newcomers alone, as illustrated in Exhibit 1.1. Acculturation may follow several alternative paths, including assimilation or integration as possible outcomes.

> **EXHIBIT 1.1: Integrating the foreigners who call Germany home**
>
> With its seven million legal resident foreigners or 9 per cent of the total population, Germany has quietly developed into a nation of immigrants. More than a quarter of the people living in Frankfurt, for example, are foreign nationals, and there are plenty of districts throughout the country which are referred to – fondly or not – as 'little Istanbul', reflecting the country's single biggest immigration community.
>
> 'I mostly always feel German, I feel totally at home here', said John, an Australian with no previous connection to Germany who has lived here for around 11 years. The experience of his German-born-and-raised partner Jasmin, whose parents came from Turkey, is different, however. 'I feel German, but would never call myself such. I'm not thought of as being German here', she says, describing the paradox lived out by many children of immigrants in this country.
>
> Jasmin's experience of Germany is far from unique. Most second-generation immigrants like Jasmin already appear perfectly integrated. They were born here, speak the language flawlessly and often work for traditional companies like Lufthansa and Siemens. Most hold German passports. Yet, less than a fifth of all second-generation immigrants consider themselves German, a recent study carried out by Frankfurt's department of multicultural affairs revealed. 'It was drummed into me from an early age that I wasn't German', Jasmin explains. 'Not from my family, but from other Germans.'
>
> Experts point out that since integration is a two-way process, the ability to integrate does not rest with newcomers alone. It requires an equal degree of commitment and will to succeed on both sides.
>
> *Source*: Extracted and adapted from Heidi Sylvester (2002), 9 August, *F.A.Z. Weekly*: 4.

Globalization strengthens ethnicity

Ethnicity was expected to disappear as a social force during the twentieth century (Bentley, 1981; Hutchinson and Smith, 1996). The global process by which industrialization, urbanization and mass communications have been transforming society was supposed to end the social and political importance of ethnicity and consequently its economic relevance. Instead, 'globalisation has precipitated identity construction on an unprecedented scale' that has reinvigorated ethnicity (Cornell and Hartmann, 1998: 250). While there are alternative scenarios on the future of ethnic groups (Stratton and Ang, 1998), a major implication of the contradiction created through globalization is that strong ethnic identities are locally constructed, arising from the situations groups and individuals deal with every day. This local construction casts doubt on the usefulness of targeting transnational ethnic segments, as called for by Usunier (1996), as well as the unqualified transferring of a domestic marketing strategy (marketing to Koreans in Korea) to a wider international context (the Korean ethnic group residing in Japan), or of using a ethnic marketing strategy (marketing to the French ethnic group residing in Brazil) for cross-cultural marketing purposes (Brazilian organizations marketing to the French people in France).

An ethnic group can be seen as a social construct with its boundaries constructed either through ascription by the dominant group and/or by self-ascription (Vasta, 1993; Langer, 1998). Barth (1969) advocates ascription as the basis of recognition because it defines exclusiveness and thus the continuity of the ethnic group regardless of boundary changes. Dichotomizing members and outsiders establishes socially relevant factors as the basis for membership. In Australia, ethnic group membership arises from ascription both by self and by others, including government (Langer, 1998; Stratton and Ang, 1998), which has encouraged and helped construct ethnic groups (Langer, 1998: 170–5), a policy which Stratton and Ang (1998: 156) refer to as 'inclusive particularism'.

The contradictory effect of globalization on ethnicity is variously explained (Castles *et al.*, 1992; Hutchinson and Smith, 1996; Cornell and Hartmann, 1998; Langer, 1998). Using Australia as an example, Vasta (1993) explains that 'ethnicity operates as a process through which migrants live their minority cultures in relation to the dominant economic, socio-cultural and political relations of Australian society' (p. 218). This requires subsequent generations to give continuity to ethnic communities. Langer (1998) argues that a formalization of ethnic communities occurs under a government's multiculturalism policy. In liberal democracies, governments' attention to differences may be no more than 'the development of a climate that encourages, although reluctantly, increased respect for group empowerment' (Grant, 1999: 1).

In summary, while ethnicity was expected to disappear as social force during the twentieth century due to global processes, globalization has reinvigorated ethnicity, resulting in locally constructed strong ethnic identities. The persistence of these ethnic identities is a symptom of the continuous cultural diversity, which Berry and Sam (1997) acknowledge to be independent of migration inflows. Hence it matters to consider further the role of migration in creating ethnic diversity.

The role of migration

The role of migration in creating ethnic diversity differs from country to country. Inward migration to many European countries has slowed as restrictions on permanent migration have tightened. Other advanced countries such as Canada, Australia and the USA continue to be large net importers of people, although at reduced rates. In Australia, using country of birth and excluding the UK, Ireland and New Zealand because of their potential cultural proximity, 'overseas born' rose rapidly from 2.1 per cent in 1947 to 14.8 per cent in 1981 and to 15.1 per cent by 1998 (ABS, 2000: 95). In the USA, tighter immigration restrictions were imposed in 1990. Between 1989 and 1991 immigration reached a new post-1945 peak due to the United States of America: Immigration Reform and Control Act [IRCA] (1986), which allowed certain classes of aliens to seek permanent residency. New arrivals increased far less. Due to the IRCA the rate of immigration per 1000 of US population was 7.2 in 1991 but had fallen to 3.5 in 1993. In the UK, the ethnic minority population is increasing faster than the rest of the population. Its link to post-war immigration from former colonies is a weakening influence.

Castles and Miller (1993) outline a four-step model that captures the migratory process of the post-1945 period. While it applies to many advanced economies, it recognizes that global restructuring since the 1970s has engendered new migratory patterns. Temporary economic-driven labour migration (stage 1) leads to prolonged stay, the development of social networks based on kinship or common origin, and the need for mutual help (stage 2). In stage 3, family reunion, consciousness of long-term settlement and increasing orientation towards the host country give rise to the emergence of ethnic communities. Stage 4 marks permanent settlement, which either leads to secure legal status and citizenship or to exclusion and the formation of permanent ethnic minorities. Ethnic minority groups can grow and survive both through self-ascription and definition by others outside the group. Tightened restrictions on permanent immigration suggest that population movements are unlikely to sustain the growth of ethnic groups but, as seen around the world in many countries, ethnic groups survive and may even increase in importance (e.g. after migration from India ceased, the Fijian Indian ethnic group continued to grow in importance).

If liberal democratic governments are neutral with respect to multicultural policy (for example, do not attempt to prevent the establishment of ethnically based schools and ethnically based communication networks), even if immigration is tightly controlled it is highly unlikely ethnic groups will decline in importance. Their importance may well increase as a result of increasing economic and cultural globalizing tendencies leading to a search for community identity. Technological change, improving communications and the growing integration of markets encourages the pursuit of difference, whether in terms of individual lifestyles, group cultural identity, or assertion of national uniqueness (Castles et al., 1992). This view echoes Melucci (1989) who reasons that ethnicity is a response to the increasing complexity of society. Complex societies are unable to provide forms of membership and identification to meet individual needs for self-realization, communicative interaction and recognition. Ethnic identity offers channels of solidarity and identification. Ethnicity need not be related to open discrimination, but a response to a need for collective identity that assumes greater importance in complex societies (p. 89). Similarly, Hutchinson and Smith (1996: 9–14) see ethnicity as socially constructed. They argue that, while globalization has tended to reduce ethnicity, recent advances in electronic communications and information technology provide sub-national ethnic groups with cultural networks that can sustain interaction in the face of depersonalizing bureaucratic structures.

Ethnic identity is not dependent on continuing immigration and neither does it necessarily disappear with the successive generations. Asked how strong their sense of belonging was to their ethnic or cultural group, more than half of Canadians participating in a large ethnic diversity survey responded that they had a strong sense of belonging to their ethnic group. This varied between groups (highest for the Filipinos) and between generations. While 57 per cent of the first generation reported a strong sense of belonging, 47 per cent of the second generation also reported similarly, and this rose to 48 per cent for the third generation, suggesting a plateau effect rather than a linear assimilation (Statistics Canada, 2003). In Germany, less than a fifth of all second-generation immigrants consider themselves German.

1.5 Marketing opportunities

Cultural diversity within many advanced countries is growing and many advanced countries are now trying to measure the cultural diversity of their populations. Statistical classification of ethnic minorities varies immensely between countries. Some countries (Australia and New Zealand) have recently developed sophisticated ethnic group classification systems that are only in the process of being implemented (ABS, 2000). The USA uses a more racially based, aggregated system. The challenge for marketers is to dig beneath these statistical definitions, to reach persons who self-identify with a particular ethnic group and behave as consumers in a homogeneous manner. Broad-based statistical classifications provide a starting point. Table 1.1 shows how classifications vary between some advanced countries and the differences in the sizes of minority populations in these countries.

As a snapshot, the table shows widely different treatment of ethnic groups. Populations have been aggregated (Hispanic or White), hiding the distinctiveness of ethnic groups based on Yinger's (1976) dimensions. In each country cultural diversity has increased significantly and the dominant population group has declined in relative importance over the last forty years. This is a trend expected to continue, with changes also occurring in the relative strength of particular minority groups. For example, in Australia, the dominant Anglo-Celtic group is expected to decline to 66 per cent of the population while Asian ethnic groups increase to 13 per cent by 2030. In the USA similar

Table 1.1   Dominant and minority population groups, selected advanced countries

Percentage distribution of total population*

New Zealand (2001)	Australia (1999)	Canada (2002)	United Kingdom (2001)	France (2000)	USA (2000)
73.8 European	69.9 Anglo-Celtic	21 Anglo-Celtic	92.1 White	92.0 France	71.9 White
13.5 Maori	18.3 Other European	19 Non-French, Other European	4.4 Asian	4.0 Arab/North African	12.1 Black, not-Hispanic
6.1 Asian	9.6 Asian	13 Non-European	2.0 Black	2.0 German	11.6 Hispanic origin
6.0 Pacific Islander	1.5 Aboriginal and Torres Strait Islander	10 French origin	1.1 Mixed	1.0 Breton	3.7 Asian/ Pacific Islander
0.6 Other	0.7 Other	15 Canadian only or mix of French, British and Canadian	0.4 Other	1.0 Catalan	0.7 American Indian, Eskimo, Aleut
		22 Other mixed heritage + Unknown			

Sources: Statistics New Zealand (2001); ABS (2002); Statistics Canada (2003); France (2003); United Kingdom (2003); United States Census Bureau (2003).
* Canadian distribution is for persons 15 years or older.

projections show the white mainstream declining to 62 per cent, with the Hispanic and Asian origin groups continuing to increase significantly to 18 per cent and 7 per cent by 2025. Given this forecast growth in cultural diversity and the need for marketers to reach potential customers better than their competitors, standardized marketing approaches that ignore cultural differences that exist within national economies are often likely to be less effective in reaching ethnic groups with a strong sense of identity.

1.6   The path ahead

Chapter 2 establishes the theoretical framework that grounds ethnic marketing, that is, the efficient targeting of individual ethnic groups. This framework is provided by STP (segmentation, targeting and positioning) analysis, subject to the basic need of internal segment homogeneity and heterogeneity across segments. Each of the criteria commonly identified in the marketing literature as necessary for effective targeting is then reviewed in general terms. The objective is to identify the major issues/challenges that need to be considered when ethnic groups become the focus of analysis. These are then discussed in Chapters 3 to 7.

Ethnic groups consist of aggregates of ethnic consumers. This aggregation requires a clear identification of consumer ethnicity to ensure group homogeneity in a marketing environment. Are place of birth, nationality, or other similar indicators suitable for ethnicity? Chapter 3 addresses these issues.

The issues involved in aggregating ethnic groups are discussed in Chapter 4. To be important for marketing, such groups need to be identifiable, measurable, substantial, actionable and stable. Practical difficulties in the identification of consumers of a given ethnicity may combine with preconceptions about ethnic group minority status to question the importance of the group for marketing based on substantiality requirements. Chapter 4 explains why current substantiality tests are inadequate for assessing ethnic group substantiality, and considers the circumstances when the aggregation of ethnic groups may constitute an acceptable practice.

Chapter 5 develops a pragmatic and simple method for preliminary assessment of ethnic group substantiality and presents a framework for systematizing decision-making processes regarding the targeting of minority ethnic groups. Chapter 6 examines ethnic consumer behaviour, providing a framework that can assist in developing a better understanding of the buyer decision processes in which ethnic consumers are likely to engage. As in mainstream marketing, achieving sustainable competitive advantage is, therefore, very important for marketing to ethnic groups, requiring the use of effective STP analysis, combined with specific supplier skills including cultural awareness, sensitivity and responsiveness. Chapter 7 adds to the attractiveness of ethnic marketing by showing that ethnic consumer behaviour, as discussed in Chapter 6, is conducive to the generation of consumer loyalty.

Chapters 2 to 7 combine to establish the theoretical underpinnings of ethnic marketing and its potential attractiveness for marketers. This attractiveness justifies a relative proliferation of 'professional' ethnic marketing agencies within certain culturally diverse countries (e.g. Australia, Canada, the UK and the USA) and some attempt of large firms to vie episodically for the ethnic dollar.

Nevertheless, for most marketers ethnic marketing continues to be the exception rather than the rule. Some of this apathy may be explained by a variety of factors (such as limited understanding of ethnic markets, unattractive ROI estimates, unavailability of the necessary cultural skills, unsuccessful trials and fear of retaliation by mainstream consumers). The following chapters address a number of major issues and challenges that need to be overcome by practitioners of ethnic marketing.

Chapter 8 discusses a methodology for acquiring information necessary for decision-making in ethnic marketing and successfully reaching ethnic groups. Information about ethnic groups doesn't come cheaply. Even using basic indicators such as country of birth or nationality, it is often a very difficult task to establish ethnic group size because, amongst other reasons, many ethnic groups are not separately reported in official censuses. Chapter 9 provides a perspective on the product classifications where ethnic marketing is likely to be most successful. Services offer evaluation difficulties for all consumers. These difficulties are likely to be heightened for ethnic consumers, particularly those with communication difficulties. Chapter 9 reviews the characteristics that make services harder to evaluate than goods and explains why evaluation is likely to be more difficult for ethnic consumers. Continuing with supply issues, Chapter 10 examines human resource management (HRM) problems that providers targeting ethnic minority consumers need to address. This chapter explains that there are instances where firms elect to employ ethnic staff as a means to overcome these skills shortages. In other situations firms opt for cultural awareness training. In any case this training is unlikely to suffice, since the need for cultural responsiveness and successful interaction with ethnic consumers also depends on people and customer service skills. It is, therefore, apparent that not all people will have the necessary skills for supporting successful ethnic marketing, including communication skills. Chapter 11 explains the importance of developing a marketing communication strategy to reach ethnic consumers and also to retain them. The elements of the communication process are reviewed and linked to the range of difficulties that can arise in communicating across cultures, within a country.

Communication challenges, limited market knowledge and dependence on preferred suppliers leave ethnic consumers open to predatory and other types of unethical behaviour. Chapter 12 discusses issues of ethics and social responsibility that may impact upon ethnic marketing. Finally, Chapter 13 examines the likely challenges and opportunities that lie ahead for ethnic marketing. Globalization and electronic commerce are developing areas of current interest for marketers in general and ethnic marketing is no exception. This chapter reviews the main issues permeating the use of electronic commerce by ethnic marketing.

References

Australian Bureau of Statistics (ABS) (1996) *Census of Population and Housing, Ethnicity Thematic Profile Service*, http://www.abs.gov.au/Websitedbs/D3310108.NSF?Open Database (accessed 15 October 2003), Canberra: ABS.

Australian Bureau of Statistics (ABS) (2000) *Australian Standard Classification of Cultural and Ethnic Groups, Catalogue no. 1249*, Canberra: ABS.

Australian Bureau of Statistics (ABS) (2002) *Year Book of Australia 2002* (Population centenary article – 'A century of population change in Australia'), http://www.abs.gov.au/

Ausstats/abs@nsf/LookupOB82C2F2654C3693CA2569DEO (accessed 25 November 2003).

Baker, M. (1998) *Marketing*, 8th edn., London: Macmillan.

Barth, F. (1969) 'Ethnic groups and boundaries' (extract from *The Social Organization of Ethnic Groups and Boundaries*, Boston: Little, Brown) reprinted in J. Hutchinson and A. Smith (eds) *Ethnicity* (1996), Oxford: Oxford University Press.

Bentley, G. (1981) *Ethnicity and Nationality: A Bibliographic Guide*, Seattle, WA: University of Washington Press.

Berry, J. and Sam, D. (1997) 'Acculturation and adaptation', in John Berry, Ype Poortinga and J. Pandey (eds) *Handbook of Cross-cultural Psychology*, Vol. 3, 2nd edn., Boston, MA: Allyn and Bacon, pp. 291–326.

Castles, S. and Miller, M. (1993) *The Age of Migration*, Basingstoke: Macmillan.

Castles, S., Cope, B., Kalantzis, M. and Morrissey, M. (1992) 'Australia: multi-ethnic community without nationalism?' (extract from *Mistaken Identity*, Sydney: Pluto Press, pp. 139–48) reprinted in *Ethnicity* (1996) (eds John Hutchinson and Anthony Smith), Oxford: Oxford University Press.

Cornell, S. and Hartmann, D. (1998) *Ethnicity and Race*, London: Sage Publications.

Cui, G. (1997) 'Marketing strategies in a multi-ethnic environment', *Journal of Marketing Theory and Practice*, 5 (Winter): 122–34.

Cui, G. (2001) 'Marketing to ethnic minority consumers: a historical journey (1932–1997)', *Journal of Macromarketing*, 21(1): 23–31.

France (2003) General data, official site of France in the USA, http://www.library.uu.nl/wesp/populstat/Europe/franceeg.htm (accessed 25 November 2003).

Gonçalves, A., da Silva, E. and Seniuk, S. (1986) *The Portuguese Community in the Illawarra*, Regional Migrant Health Centre, State Health Publication No. (ILR) 86-071, Sydney.

Grant, C. (ed.) (1999) *Multicultural Research: A Reflective Engagement with Race, Class, Gender and Sexual Orientation*, London: Falmer Press.

Hofstede, G. (2001) *Culture's Consequences*, 2nd edn., Thousand Oaks, CA: Sage Publications.

Hutchinson, J. and Smith, A. (eds) (1996) *Ethnicity*, Oxford: Oxford University Press.

Joppke, C. and Lukes, S. (1999) 'Introduction: multicultural questions', in C. Joppke and S. Lukes (eds) *Multicultural Questions*, Oxford: Oxford University Press, pp. 1–24.

Kotler, P. (1997) *Marketing Management: Analysis, Planning, Implementation and Control*, 9th edn., New Jersey, NJ: Prentice-Hall.

Kotler, P., Armstrong, G., Brown, L. and Adam, S. (1998) *Marketing*, 4th edn., Sydney: Prentice-Hall.

Langer, B. (1998) 'Globalisation and the myth of ethnic community', in D. Bennett (ed.) *Multicultural States*, London: Routledge, pp. 163–77.

McColl-Kennedy, J. and Kiel, G. (2000) *Marketing: A Strategic Approach*, Sydney: Nelson.

Melucci, A. (1989) *Nomads of the present: Social Movements and Contemporary Needs in Contemporary Society*, J. Keane and P. Mier (eds), London: Hutchinson Radius.

Miller, K. and Layton, R. (2000) *Fundamentals of Marketing*, 4th edn., Sydney: McGraw-Hill.

Nwankwo, S., Aiyeku, J. and Ogbuchi, A. (1998) 'The marketing challenge of multi-culturalism: an exploratory study', *Journal of International Marketing and Exporting*, 3(1): 47–61.

Pires, G. and Stanton, J. (2000) 'Ethnicity and acculturation in a culturally diverse country: identifying ethnic market segments', *Journal of Multilingual and Multicultural Development*, 21(1): 42–57.

Statistics Canada (2003) *Ethnic Diversity Survey: Portrait of a Multicultural Society*, Statistics Canada, catalogue no. 89-593-XIE, Ottawa: Ministry of Industry.

Statistics New Zealand (2001) *2001 Census: Ethnic Groups*, Wellington, NZ: Statistics New Zealand.

Stratton, J. and Ang, I. (1998) 'Multicultural imagined communities', in D. Bennett (ed.) *Multicultural States*, London: Routledge, pp. 135–62.

United Kingdom, House of Lords Statement (1983), *Patterns of Prejudice*, vol. 17, issue 2.

United Kingdom (2003) *National Statistics Online*, http://www.statistics.gov.uk/cci/nugget.aop?id=273 (accessed 25 November 2003).

United States Census Bureau (2003) *Population Profile of the United States*, chapter 2, http://www.census.gov/population/pop-profile/1999/chp02.pdf (accessed 20 June 2004).

Usunier, J-C. (1996) *Marketing Across Cultures*, 2nd edn., Sydney: Prentice-Hall.

Vasta, E. (1993) 'Multiculturalism and ethnic identity: the relationship between racism and resistance', *Australia and New Zealand Journal of Sociology*, 29(2): 209–25.

Wilkinson, I. and Cheng, C. (1997) 'Multicultural marketing: synergy in diversity', *Proceedings*, Australia and New Zealand Marketing Educators' Conference, Melbourne, December, pp. 1404–14.

Yinger, J.M. (1976) 'Ethnicity in complex societies', in A. Lewis *et al.* (eds) *The Uses of Controversy in Sociology*, New York: Free Press.

From target marketing to ethnic marketing

2.1 Chapter objectives

This chapter establishes the theoretical framework that grounds ethnic marketing, that is, the efficient and effective targeting of individual ethnic groups. This framework is provided by STP (segmentation, targeting and positioning) analysis, subject to the basic need of internal segment homogeneity and heterogeneity across segments. Each of the five criteria commonly identified in the marketing literature as necessary for effective targeting – identifiability, measurability, accessibility, substantiality and stability – is then reviewed in general terms. The objective is to identify the major issues/challenges that need to be considered when ethnic groups become the focus of analysis. These are then discussed in Chapters 3 to 7.

Attending to consumers' needs and preferences is a major component of the marketing concept. It is also a necessary object of an organization's efforts as a whole, only moderated by organizational objectives and social responsibility. Competitive advantage ensues from customers' perception of the organization as the best provider of value, embodied in the value proposition of an augmented good or service offered to satisfy those needs and preferences. Perceived value is the difference between all benefits perceived by the customer as associated with that value proposition, less all the perceived costs incurred in gaining the benefits. Organizations may choose to adopt, or not to adopt the orientation provided by the marketing concept. But the value of their propositions is unavoidably determined by consumers' own perceptions of what is on offer.

2.2 The business case for mass marketing

If all consumers use the same criteria to evaluate an organization's offer and arrive at the same outcome, then the organization faces a homogeneous consumer group. Any differences between consumers (for example in age, gender or income) are not relevant for marketing purposes. In this case the organization should offer the same marketing mix to all customers.

The decision to use a mass marketing strategy is not a simple one. It requires the organization to study the consumer group's identity (that is, who the consumers are as a group) and to construct a dynamic profile for the group. This involves the gathering of enough detailed, reliable and relevant knowledge about the consumers in the group (for example, price elasticity of demand) to be able to ascertain if the group is homogeneous. Homogeneity presumes that the group members behave the same in their reactions to the marketing mix and in their assessment of the organization's value proposition.

The construction of the mass marketing mix should, therefore, be based on knowledge about the group evaluative criteria for their offer. Importantly, the organization should be able to discern, from the importance attached by the group to the various attributes or characteristics of their offer, which ones are determinant in their consumer decision-making behaviour before and after consumption. It is these determinant criteria that provide orientation for the development of the organization's value proposition, grounded in one marketing mix that allows for economies of scale to be realized through mass production, mass distribution, and mass communication.

This is the business case for undifferentiated or mass marketing, only moderated by the competitive environment and by the extent to which consumers' needs and wants are perceived as more or less important by the organization. These needs and wants may be deemed less important in situations of monopoly, and more important in highly competitive markets.

The drawback of mass marketing, particularly where the strategic decision is not based on careful profiling and evaluation as discussed above, is that consumers' needs and preferences may differ and the same offering is unlikely to be evaluated and valued identically by all consumers.

2.3 The business case for target marketing

The business case for target marketing is tied to the realization that different consumers have different needs and preferences, and it is rarely possible to satisfy all consumers by treating them alike. If one organization ignores differing customer needs and preferences, another may conceivably offer a more attractive value proposition to those consumers (potential customers) whose needs and preferences are not being met, the former organization losing those consumers.

Target marketing recognizes that consumers constitute a heterogeneous group, that is, that different consumers, or groups of consumers have diverse needs and preferences; hence an organization applying target marketing strategies does not attempt to please all consumers with the same value proposition.

Moreover, some consumer needs and preferences may be outside the capabilities of some organizations. Depending on the degree of consumer market heterogeneity and the intensity of the competitive environment, an organization needs to recognize its unique capabilities or competencies in meeting the diverse consumer needs and preferences. These capabilities include the skills and collective learning that enable the organization to coordinate processes and activities.

To make effective use of its assets the organization needs to focus on those consumers, or groups of consumers, whose needs and preferences are better aligned to their unique competencies. This requires the organization first to define their consumer market (both actual and potential) and to have a good deal of knowledge of the diversity in that consumer market. Second, the organization needs to be able to identify any and all groupings of consumers that share identical needs and preferences with respect to its offer. The identification of these groupings is commonly referred to as market segmentation.

2.4 Market segmentation process

The concept of market segmentation is recognized in the literature as 'one of the corner stones of marketing' (Evans, 1994; Storbacka, 1997), the foundation for all other marketing actions and, arguably, key to developing a sustainable competitive advantage based on differentiation, low cost, or a focus strategy (Aaker, 2001). Equally applicable to consumer and business markets, market segmentation is commonly defined as the process of partitioning markets into (identified) groups of potential customers that have similarities in characteristics or needs who are likely to exhibit similar purchase behaviour (Smith, 1956). Somewhat prescriptively, each market segment is said to be 'composed of a group of buyers who share common characteristics, needs, purchasing behaviour and consumption patterns' (Lovelock, Patterson and Walker, 2001: 162). There are, however, many alternative methods for segmenting consumer markets.

Table 2.1 lists potential segmentation criteria advanced in the marketing literature, distributed over various different bases for segmentation:

Table 2.1 Bases for segmentation in consumer markets

Base for segmentation	*Segmentation criteria*		
Demographic	■ Age ■ Gender ■ Height ■ Race ■ Weight	■ Occupation ■ Income ■ Education ■ Marital status ■ Family size ■ Family lifecycle	■ Ethnicity ■ Nationality ■ Religion ■ Social class ■ Generation (e.g. baby-boomers, Generation X)
Geographic	■ Region (e.g. continent, country, state, neighbourhood) ■ Area size (e.g. size of population) ■ Population density (e.g. urban, suburban or rural) ■ Climate (as per weather patterns common to certain geographic regions)		
Behavioural

Has the advantage of using variables that are closely related to the offer | 1. *Motivational* – Based on variables that relate to why customers make purchases: occasions (e.g. holidays, major sporting tournaments), benefits sought, most valued attributes | 2. *Descriptive* – Based on actual and measurable customer behaviour towards offers: usage rate, usage pattern, brand loyalty, readiness to buy, user status (e.g. potential, 1st time, regular), time pressures | |
| Psychographics

Groups consumers according to lifestyle | ■ Activities (e.g. desire for relaxation) ■ Interests ■ Opinions ■ Ideology | ■ Attitudes (e.g. risk aversion) ■ Values ■ Personality type ■ Lifestyle | |
| Predictive

Seeks to understand what variables distinguish 'the best customer' | 1. Identifies one or several dependent variables that are key indicators of good customers (e.g. usage rate, profitability, retention rate) 2. Identifies which predictive variables are drivers for the dependent variables (e.g. past purchase patterns, lifestyle variables) 3. Groups consumers into segments with similar values of the predictive variables but different values across groups | | |
| VALS and PRIZM clusters | Assist in predicting consumers' purchasing power, motivation, self-orientation, and resources. | | |

demographic, geographic, behavioural, psychographics, predictive and VALS and PRIZM clusters.

Because selecting the most useful segment-defining variables is rarely obvious, using segmentation criteria that combine variables from different bases may avoid missing some useful way to segment the market (Aaker, 2001). That use may also be justified by scientific reasons, because segments are perceived to have multifaceted profiles, or it may be a reflection of what limited information is available to an organization.

While the use of a hybrid base for consumer market segmentation is, arguably, the most common in practice (Thorson, 1989), it is vital to understand that useful consumer segments will seldom develop from segmentation processes that use the wrong criteria.

2.5 Benefits, criticisms and limitations

In terms of benefits, Smith (1956) advances the classic price discrimination model as a major theoretical rationale for applying segmentation. Accordingly, faced with heterogeneous markets, an organization following a market segmentation strategy can usually increase expected profitability (Wind, 1978; Storbacka, 1997). Alternatively, segmentation may be useful in achieving an efficient allocation of resources because it helps to direct the appropriate amounts of promotional attention and money to the most potentially profitable segments (Yankelovich, 1964). Also, as a competitive tool, it helps in matching the organization's core competencies with market needs (Brierty *et al.*, 1998).

Grounded on environmental analysis and internal analysis, the potential benefits from market segmentation analysis and strategy are invaluable for organizations. The following are strategic activities of organizations that may benefit from market segmentation analysis and strategy:

1. the design of market-oriented cost-efficient goods and services;
2. the development and implementation of effective and cost-efficient communications, including media selection;
3. the development and implementation of effective and cost-efficient tactics and promotional strategies;
4. assessment of market position and, in combination with competitor analysis, assessment of how the organization and its value proposition are perceived by actual and potential consumers relative to those of competitors;
5. strategic fine-tuning of the marketing effort.

While the general potential benefits from market segmentation remain mostly unchallenged in the relevant marketing literature, market segmentation is recognized as far from straightforward for most marketing managers and many academics (Dibb and Simkin, 1996). A sample of criticisms from the literature is provided below:

- Questioning the reliability of selected bases for segmentation, Yankelovich (1964) posits that 'the key requirement of segmentation analysis is that the marketing director should never assume in advance that any one method of segmentation is the best' (p. 84). See also Evans (1994) for a critique of a variety of segmentation methods.

- Wind (1978) emphasizes segment validity – whether a particular segment actually exists in the market and its size and behaviour are accurately predicted – and cost considerations. These stem from the realization that 'higher research reliability may involve somewhat higher costs. Explicit cost tradeoffs therefore should be made which lead to a selection of research designs based on the intended purpose, the expected information, and the costs involved' (p. 328).

- Young, Ott and Feigin (1978) argue that 'market segmentation studies have been disappointing because the segments derived . . . have not been actionable from a marketing standpoint'. Specifically, segmentation is not useful when the market is so small that marketing to some portion of it is not profitable, when heavy users make up such a large proportion of the sales volume that they are the only relevant target, and when the brand is the dominant brand in the market (p. 405).

- Dibb and Simkin (1996) argue that the strategic changes required by market segmentation may be difficult to apply in real business situations, so 'practitioners must reconcile potential segmentation benefits with the realities of a well-entrenched company structure, distribution system and sales force'. Ultimately, 'the market segmentation evaluation is only worth incorporating into revised marketing strategies if there are clear financial, competitive and market benefits . . . seen to outweigh the practical and financial costs associated with implementing the change' (p. 3).

- ' "Markets" are fragmenting rapidly and we are moving towards a time when the only relevant segment is the individual customer' (Storbacka, 1997: 479). Segmentation here is based on relationship revenue and relationship cost (p. 482).

Finally, looking at limitations, market segmentation is generally perceived as a valuable marketing tool to help marketers understand consumer needs, preferences and evaluation criteria. More precisely, it clarifies how needs, preferences and criteria vary from consumer group to consumer group in a given market. But market segmentation is not suitable for all purposes linking consumers with products. Arguably, 'when segmentation is used to solve product definition problems, the results are often suspect' (Brechin, 2002).[1] Market segmentation is useful for forecasting market acceptance for a given product, but not as a guide for defining *a priori* what the product should be (such as features, navigation, interactions and visual design) in order to achieve that acceptance.

2.6 Market segmentation strategy

Dibb and Simkin (1996) provide a comprehensive perspective of market segmentation strategy, proposing that market segmentation also aims to select which segments to target, to determine how to position products to appeal to target segments, and to develop marketing programmes which convey the desired brand positioning (p. xv). Along similar lines Weinstein (1997) identifies STP marketing as a three-step process involving segmentation, targeting and positioning.

While there is a large literature which focuses on the criteria that can be used for segmenting a market, far less attention appears to have been paid to the accompanying requirements for what Kotler *et al.* (1998) term effective segmentation. Some of these requirements are noted in the criticisms outlined above and discussed below.

Effective market segmentation

Market segmentation involves the identification and profiling of relevant, valid and actionable, homogeneous market segments. In responding to the marketing mix targeted to them, each market segment needs to be homogeneous in itself (that is, all consumers in the group must respond in the same way), as well as heterogeneous relative to all other market segments (that is, no consumer outside the designated segment will respond in the same way). Effective market segmentation, however, is likely to be organization-specific. It requires verifying that the proposed segments exist and are useful for marketing purposes, as well as testing the various segments for consistency with the organization's own objectives and resources, prior to target market selection.

To be effective, any proposed segmentation needs to pass tests for measurability, accessibility, stability and substantiality (Thomas, 1980). These four tests are summarily described in Table 2.2.

Apparent differences in the number and types of tests proposed by other authors are more illusory than real. Baker (1996) includes uniqueness as an extra condition to express the need of the segment to respond uniquely to the efforts directed at it. This contrasts with Donthu and Cherian (1994) and Kotler *et al.* (1998), who omit stability and uniqueness but include actionability, 'the degree to which effective programs can be designed for attracting

Table 2.2 Tests for marketing segmentation effectiveness

Measurability	Consumers making up the segment need to be identifiable by marketers
Accessibility	Marketers must be able to reach the consumers making up the segment and attend to their needs, preferences and evaluation criteria
Stability	Consumer behaviour by the segment must be predictable over time
Substantiality	The segment must be sufficiently *profitable* to repay the effort of the organization

and serving the segments', a term that effectively encompasses both the omitted qualities. Variously described as requirements or preconditions for establishing the viability of a segment, each of these tests is reviewed below.

Baker (1996) cites Engel, Fiorillo and Cayley (1972) to argue that the concept of segmentation rests on three propositions:

1. that consumers are different (the market is heterogeneous);
2. that segments of consumers can be isolated within an overall market (there is intrasegmental homogeneity); and,
3. that the differences are related to differences in consumer demand (different segments have unique consumer behaviours).

It is apparent that, without the ability to identify and measure the segmenting variables, there is no informed basis for the segmenting decision. Similarly, if a business cannot obtain data about a potential segment and/or it is unable to target its promotional and distribution efforts towards it, then the segment cannot be accessed and the effectiveness of a segmentation strategy is clearly undermined. In addition, a segment needs to be homogeneous within the heterogeneous market, hence unique. That is, if a segment does not respond differently from other segments, then segmenting is a waste of resources. Furthermore, if the segmenting variables are highly unstable so that predictability is extremely poor, the cost-effectiveness of a segmentation strategy is also questionable.

All of the tests just discussed rest on a positive identification of particular phenomena. Before the decision to select a particular segment is progressed it is necessary to establish whether the proposed segment is measurable, accessible and actionable (valid if we use Wind's terminology), hence unique and stable. This is an endeavour that may be achievable with more or less difficulty. However, the best of market research will be unable to establish whether the potential market is substantial. That will depend on the assumptions underlying both market and cost forecasts and, in particular, on the objectives a firm is seeking to achieve through its segmentation strategy.

Measurability, accessibility and actionability are necessary conditions that can be approached positively. The test of substance is essentially an exhortation to evaluate the value of the segmenting opportunity and therefore should be applied so as to be consistent with achieving the organization's objectives. These may, or may not, focus on viability or profitability (Stanton and Pires, 1999).

Wood (1991) suggests five ways to value a segmenting opportunity without addressing profitability: sales potential, fit with the organization's existing resources, the cost of segmenting, competition and growth. Such an approach at least acknowledges strategic considerations in the decision to segment. Since the matter of segment substantiality is central to the decision to target or not to target ethnic minority consumer groups, as argued later in this book, it is important to address the substantiality test in greater depth. The literature review that follows illustrates widely different, and often very loose, views of the substance test.

The meaning and role of substantiality

Common interpretations of substantiality focus on profitability or viability of the segment market size in terms of numbers, and market potential. It is evident that there is lack of clarity associated with the concept.

Wind and Carroll (1972) express the test of substance indirectly: segmentation is only appropriate if profits from such a strategy outweigh the costs of focusing on that segment or of following different segments. As profits are a residual the literal meaning of the test is lost, other than for the useful view that the segmentation decision should be seen in the context of all other alternatives and their costs. Wind (1978) later provided a simpler rule without worrying about the evaluation of alternatives: the cost of segmentation should be far less than the benefits.

Thomas (1980) again focused only on the relevant segment and its size, measured in terms of both revenues and profits it was likely to generate. However, Cravens (1997) dispenses with profits: segmentation must be attractive in terms of revenues generated and costs incurred. The 'objective' is a 'favourable' revenue and cost combination.

For McColl-Kennedy and Kiel (2000), successful segmentation requires that a target market be large enough to be a potential profit maker for the firm. This is linked to physical size, an approach also subscribed by Su Lim, Zalloco and Ghingold (1997), because the numbers might not make the additional effort worthwhile.

Also linked to McColl-Kennedy and Kiel's view is the concept of market potential: the maximum amount of a product that could be sold by all firms in a market during a given period, with a maximum level of industry marketing activity and under an assumed set of environmental conditions. McDonald and Dunbar (1995) interpret substance as having sufficient potential size to justify time and effort involved in planning. Finally, Kotler *et al.* (1998) define substance as the degree to which the segments are large or profitable enough. Clearly, there is imprecision and confusion in what the

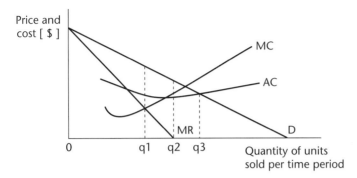

D   Demand
MR Marginal revenue
AC Average cost
MC Marginal cost

Assumptions:
- a market segment has been identified
- measurability, accessibility and actionability tests have been met
- best possible forecasts for the firm of the segment's demand and costs of supply have been made

0–q3   Substance equated with achieving maximum unit volume with zero profits
0–q1   Substance measured at maximum profit possible
0–q2   Substance measured at maximum sales revenue from the segment

Figure 2.1   Alternatives for firms' assessment of segment substantiality

substantiality test implies. Only the earliest writers suggest the need to apply the test beyond the potential segment under focus, that is, in a process of selection from a range of alternative segments. Widely used texts tend to treat the segmentation decision in isolation rather than as a part of a strategic plan. The implications of this partial approach and looseness in terminology can be appraised in Figure 2.1.

Figure 2.1 is drawn for an organization based on assumptions that a market segment has been identified, that the tests of measurability, accessibility and actionability have been met, and that best possible forecasts for the organization of the segment's demand and costs of supplying that segment have been made. Using the various and static interpretations of the requirement that a segment must have substance, then the following alternatives hold:

Given the forecast demand schedule (D) and associated marginal revenue curve (MR), projected average unit costs are (AC) and the associated marginal cost curve is (MC). If substance is equated with simply achieving an unspecified level of profitability, this can occur up to a segment size of q3, where price equals average unit costs and profits are, therefore, zero. This is an upper constraint on the segment while the usual emphasis of the substantiality test appears to imply a minimum size limit on the determination of profitability.

Alternatively, if substantiality requires the organization to earn a particular profit level, say the maximum possible, then q1, corresponding to the point where (MC = MR), becomes the minimum and maximum segment size. However, if the aim is maximum sales revenue from the segment, then the minimum and maximum size is q2, where marginal revenue is zero. Finally, if the aim is simply to cover costs, this can allude to either the marginal or the average cost of supplying the segment, with the covering of marginal costs, implying a more stringent test on the segment's substance. In any case organizational objectives need to be taken into account.[2]

It is apparent that the concept of substantiality is open to several possible interpretations, often focusing on viability or profitability. These are shown to be just some of a variety of possible purposes, ultimately determined by business objectives. The test of substance is essentially an exhortation to evaluate the value of the segmenting opportunity and needs to be consistent with achieving these objectives. While a test of value to the business prior to making a decision about segmentation is necessary, substantiality, which appears to address this test, is restrictive, imprecise, partial in its focus and, therefore, inadequate.

2.7   Effective target market selection

The market segmentation process may ultimately identify one or more market segments. If only one market segment is identified and profiled, and its targeting by the organization is assessed as consistent with organizational capabilities and objectives, the earlier discussed mass marketing situation applies. It should be noted that this process of arriving at the decision that one unique marketing mix is sufficient for the market in question is quite distinct from a similar outcome resulting from unresearched assumptions that (1) the market is homogeneous, (2) any eventual differences are of no importance or (3) the market will have enough critical mass to justify its targeting by the organization. If the outcome in the first case may be a rotund failure of the marketing effort, cases (2) and (3) clearly question the effective use of the organization's resources, potentially leading to marketing failure.

If more than one market segment is identified and profiled, each segment may vary in their willingness and ability to pay for, and to use the goods and services on offer. Accordingly, each segment needs to be assessed (in terms of its needs, preferences and evaluation criteria before and after consumption) as consistent with the organization's capabilities and objectives. To the extent that resource constraints or competitive pressures may require that only the 'best' segments be targeted, the organization needs to evaluate the value (contribution) of each segmenting opportunity relative to objectives.[3]

Effective target market selection depends on effective segmentation of the potential market. The various segments are profiled, assessed for consistency with organizational competencies, and evaluated for their contribution to organizational objectives and associated cost implications. Since segment profiling distinguishes between important and determinant evaluative criteria, organizations are able to make more informed decisions about which segments to target and how to target them (that is, how to position their offers to appeal to target segments, a process that involves the development and implementation of better marketing programmes). Clearly, effective targeting implies not only the choice of the more relevant strategic marketing tools, but their fine-tuning to each segment (such as setting the right price, rather than pricing above or below what the average consumer is willing to pay) in order to maximize outcomes.

Limitations on the STP process

It is apparent that the process of segmenting the market, selecting target segments and developing positioning strategies is time-consuming, complex and probably imperfect. Segmenting based on imperfect information and limited organizational sense-making capabilities may eventually lead, for example, to incorrect profiling of segments, inaccurate appraisal of the competitive environment and inability to reliably identify organizational outcomes for comparison with set objectives.

Popular explanations advanced by organizations in settling for limited information decision-making include:

1. Information gathering, even from secondary sources, is often expensive and time-consuming, resulting in limited information gathering from the market.

2. Although the inherent limitations from the limited information may be reduced by market experience (organizational learning) over time, markets are dynamic and the organizational knowledge available for decision-making is likely to remain imperfect.

3. The marginal cost of information collection, analysis and dissemination may be perceived to exceed associated incremental benefits.

4. Organizational outcomes and other evaluative criteria may be difficult to assess.

One possible scenario resulting from these limitations may be that there is a critical level of available market information (incorporating organizational knowledge and new information gathering) after which diminishing returns are perceived by the organization to apply (point (3) above). Hence no additional information is gathered, notwithstanding a possible loss of STP effectiveness.

Possibly compounding those limitations is the neglect of some less economically attractive market segments revealed by the segmentation process.

This neglect may be moderated by strategic motivations, such as the aim of deterring potential entrants from entering the market. Segments that would be otherwise disregarded may be targeted.

In contrast, since common interpretations of substantiality focus on profitability or viability of the segment market size in terms of numbers, good marketing opportunities may be foregone on account of inappropriate inferences about segment size, if segments so defined are neglected. As argued earlier, segment substantiality may be difficult to establish precisely.

Similar to the critical level of available market information, the difficulty of precisely establishing segment substantiality may justify that segment selection be assessed based on meeting minimum substantiality requirements (for example, the estimated cost of targeting the segment plus some margin of profit). That is, the decision to target a particular segment, or indeed to overlook market heterogeneity and use mass marketing, may be based on some inference about segment critical mass, related to segment size, whereby the target segment(s) is/are perceived to be large enough to meet some desirable criteria.

The discussion above suggests that there may be practical limitations impinging on the STP process. What is lacking is an understanding of the implications of those limitations.

Earlier, we argued that to make effective use of its assets an organization needs to focus on groups of consumers whose needs and preferences are better aligned to the organization's unique competencies. Any other focus will have a negative impact on consumers and be conducive to a misallocation of resources. For example, the following events may occur if an organization overlooks market heterogeneity that actually exists, instead using mass marketing:

1. A fraction of the communications budget is likely to be wasted on uninterested consumers.
2. To the extent that taking into account market heterogeneity corresponds to more effective serving of the market, mass marketing results in a loss of sales.
3. Mass marketing blinds the organization to market growth opportunities.
4. Misallocation of resources, loss of sales and missed growth opportunities may result in a weaker competitive position.

From the customer perspective, those whose needs, preferences and evaluative criteria are disregarded will perceive lesser value in the organization's proposition. In a competitive environment there is an incentive for consumers to switch demand to the organization that meets their requirements more closely. This may be an avenue available to ethnic minority consumers. As argued in Chapter 1, while ethnicity may be a relevant characteristic of the population being marketed to, ethnicity-based market segmentation is often placed in the too-hard basket. It matters to understand the implications of this.

2.8 Linking market segmentation to ethnic marketing

Many advanced countries recognize the ethnic diversity of their populations and proclaim their status as multicultural societies. Issues related to the ethnic uniqueness of population groups are subject to research in many disciplines, from anthropology, sociology and psychology, to healthcare, politics and management. In marketing, the dominant tendency in the literature is to equate ethnic marketing with segmentation and targeting based on some concept of ethnicity (Laroche, Kim and Clarke, 1997; Cui, 1998). However, attention to ethnicity issues in culturally diverse countries has been afforded minimal importance compared with cross-cultural research.

The relative lack of interest in the implications of ethnic diversity for marketing may be due to marketer scepticism. This may be supported by a low level of importance being given to the analysis of coherent consumer groupings and correspondingly inadequate or implausible consumer profiles (Firat and Shultz II, 1997). Perhaps the relative lack of interest can also be explained by a lack of understanding of the process and dynamics of minority ethnic group formation, as discussed in Chapter 1.

More specifically, the lack of interest can be explained on several grounds. In some cases ethnic diversity is taken to refer to consumers' original ethnic background, assumed to decline in importance in a process of assimilation to the dominant host culture. Ethnicity is, therefore, of no consequence. In other cases, any uniqueness in individuals of different ethnicities is perceived as unimportant because knowledge diffusion, technological progress and wide availability have a globalizing effect on people's needs and wants. Hence, the prescription is to concentrate on what is the same across ethnic groups rather than to focus on their uniqueness, even because global supply is needed to meet a global demand. A third perspective emphasizes the uniqueness and defends domestic market fragmentation to account for minority ethnic groups (of varying size and strength of communication and information networks) that adapt, but do not assimilate to, the dominant group in the country. Hence, because minority ethnic groups exhibit unique characteristics that reflect on members' behaviour as consumers, they must be important for marketers. This importance, however, is questioned by the common presumption that minority ethnic groups in countries such as Australia, Canada, the UK and the USA are too small for their uniqueness, if it exists, to be useful.

It is apparent that the marketing implications associated with the uniqueness of minority ethnic groups and their members are not well understood. Ethnicity, broadly defined as the condition of belonging to a particular ethnic group, becomes important for marketing when market segmentation yields segments that are conspicuous for distinctive needs, preferences and evaluative criteria before and after consumption, as reflected in subsequent distinctive consumption behaviour. This distinctive consumption behaviour converts into opportunities for organizations, which may or may not be accepted, but cannot be ignored.

The development of the European Community illustrates the risks of marketers ignoring differences. In considering the post-1992 development of a single-market Europe, Moss and Vinten (2001) support the view that there are real obstacles to a pan-European market because of 'the deep cultural differences' (Johnson and Moran, 1992). 'Although the similarities between the business cultures in Europe are legion, so are the differences' (Randlesome, 1990). Although there can be a universal pan-European approach, national cultural considerations will need to be taken into account.

Using ethnicity for segmenting markets

Heterogeneity is sometimes raised as a problem within an ethnic group. Miller and Layton (2000: 205) explicitly acknowledge ethnicity-based segmentation within national boundaries as useful for the segmentation of some products and an interesting challenge in terms of understanding a group's behaviour and motivations because of potential intra-group heterogeneity. Heterogeneity in terms of age, income, education and class is inevitable in any ethnic group, and these differences may qualify how ethnicity is used for particular segmentation purposes. Langer (1998) observes class differences within the small Salvadorean community in Australia, differences in the degree of ascription to the community, as well as the creation of a 'hybrid culture' that is neither 'Salvadorean' nor mainstream 'Australian'. For segmentation purposes, these intra-group differences may need to be addressed. The overall frame of reference provided by the ethnic community in terms of members' awareness of their interdependence, an acceptance of a shared set of beliefs that helps regulate their mutual conduct, and the network of support and communications often in place in such groups, provides the means.

More recently, Chudry and Pallister (2002) carried out a study of the importance of ethnicity as a segmentation criterion focused on the case of Pakistani consumers' attitude towards direct mail compared with the indigenous population in the UK. The Pakistani community in the UK is the second largest ethnic group at nearly half a million people. The study found that attitudes varied considerably between the two population groupings, grounding the categorical conclusion that ethnic groups are a viable segmentation opportunity. This contrasts with the findings of another cross-cultural study, carried out at about the same time and also in the UK, investigating 'culture' as a viable variable for market segmentation. Lindridge and Dibb (2003) found a significant difference in the impact of a range of cultural values upon the buying behaviour of British Indians and British Caucasians with respect to brown goods. Their conclusion, however, is that the amount of similarity between the two sample groups suggests ethnicity should not be used as a segmentation variable.

Clearly, there is considerable complexity in using ethnicity as a segmentation variable that effectively identifies and permits the targeting of ethnic minority groups distinct from the majority, mainstream population. Coupled with higher marketing costs in using the micro-marketing road (Cui and Choudhury, 1998), this complexity may explain methodological inconsistencies and contradictory findings (Parker, 1999). For example, Usunier (1996) addresses the matter of assimilation of ethnic minorities into the mainstream, together with issues related to ethnic identity and ethnic consumption. A rapid or even predictable assimilation process would undermine the case for segmenting by ethnic group, but the assimilation model is questionable (Pires and Stanton, 2000).

2.9 The business case for ethnic marketing

Similar to any other group of consumers, segmenting and targeting an ethnic group requires a firm to assess whether that group meets the different tests for effective segmentation and represents a viable opportunity. Both the transaction and opportunity costs of designing specific marketing strategies need to be evaluated against the resulting expected benefits, taking into account the competitive environment and the firm's objectives. This requires a clear profile of the ethnic group, its networks of communication, location, concentration and demographic make-up. Two potential pitfalls to be avoided are:

1. to devise distinct strategies for different ethnic groups when their consumption behaviour regarding the firm's goods and services is homogeneous; and,

2. to aggregate two or more ethnic groups in the same segment when their consumption behaviour is heterogeneous.

The first potential pitfall leads to unnecessary costs; the second is even more dangerous because the firm's resources are allocated to ill-conceived marketing campaigns, while failure may not be traced back to the group aggregation.

Ethnic marketing recognizes that all consumers in a market may be distributed into internally homogeneous groups through ethnicity-based segmentation. Each resulting ethnic group is made up of consumers who have common needs, preferences and evaluation criteria before and after consumption, hence an organization applying ethnic marketing strategies does not attempt to please the various ethnic groups with the same value proposition.

Subject to recognizing their own unique capabilities or competencies in meeting diverse consumer needs and preferences, an organization concentrates its efforts on the group(s) that value their proposition the most. Other opportunities may be considered and rejected, but cannot be ignored. Similarly, if one organisation ignores the unique consumer needs, preferences and evaluation criteria specific to its chosen target, another may conceivably offer a more attractive value proposition to those consumers (potential customers) whose needs and preferences are not being met, the former organization losing those consumers.

To the extent that ethnicity conditions consumer behaviour it 'needs to be considered before demographic criteria, because it helps to establish whether marketers can use such demographics across ethnic boundaries' (Pires and Stanton, 1998: 279). The use of ethnicity for market segmentation clearly requires ethnic-group boundaries to be determined before any consideration about their marketing value. This questions the common marketing practice of targeting ethnic group aggregates.

Notes

1. Elaine Brechin was a practising senior designer with Cooper: Interaction Design, when she was writing on the inadequacies of market segmentation for product definition purposes in 2002. This followed work by Kim Goodwin, a director of design with the same company in 2001, on the perfecting of *'personas'*. These are user models made out of fictional, representative user archetypes based on the behaviours, attitudes and goals of widely different demographic groups who may share commonalities regarding the product. There is no necessarily direct correlation between market segments and personas, since consumers yielding the most revenue may not be the best design target. Each product is designed based on one or a small set of personas, sufficient to illustrate key goals and behaviour patterns. One possible implication from using personas together with market segmentation is that products may be developed to appeal to various segments. Hence personas may be very useful for informing a positioning strategy.
2. Stanton and Pires (1999) present a model that illustrates that profits generated by a particular segment (whether it has sufficient substance) may be subservient to the strategic advantage gained from segmenting. An increase in producer surplus is the necessary condition, not profitability. A test of value to the business is required but substantiality is both imprecise and restricted in its focus. The issue is not simply a matter of profits but whether there is strategic advantage in segmenting, that is, on the long-term impact on the organization's competitive position. An increase in producer surplus is a more general measure that allows the business to evaluate a specific segmentation decision in relation to its strategic objectives.
3. Yield management, involving the generation of asset revenue-generating efficiency indices for assessing segment yields, may be useful for this purpose, particularly where the provision of services is concerned.

References

Aaker, D. (2001) *Strategic Market Management*, New York: Wiley.

Baker, M. (1996) *Marketing*, 6th edn., London: Macmillan.

Brechin, E. (2002) 'Reconciling market segments and personas', *Cooper: Interaction Design*, Newsletter February–March, http://www.cooper.com (accessed 1 July 2004).

Brierty, E. G., Eckles, R. W. and Reeder, R. R. (1998) *Business Marketing*, 3rd edn., New Jersey, NJ: Prentice-Hall.

Chudry, F. and Pallister, J. (2002) 'The importance of ethnicity as a segmentation criterion: the case of the Pakistani consumers' attitude towards direct mail compared with the indigenous population', *Journal of Consumer Behaviour*, 2(2): 125–38.

Cravens, D. (1997) *Strategic Marketing*, 5th edn., Chicago, IL: Irwin.

Cui, G. (1998) 'Ethical issues in ethnic segmentation and target marketing', in J. Chebat and A. Oumlil (eds) *Proceedings*, Multicultural Marketing Conference, Montreal, Canada, September, pp. 87–91.

Cui, G. and Choudhury, P. (1998) 'Effective strategies for ethnic segmentation and marketing', in J. Chebat and A. Oumlil (eds) *Proceedings*, Multicultural Marketing Conference, Montreal, Canada, September, pp. 354–61.

Dibb, S. and Simkin, L. (1996) *The Market Segmentation Workbook: Target Marketing for Marketing Managers*, London: International Thomson Press.

Donthu, N. and Cherian, J. (1994) 'Impact of strength of ethnic identification on Hispanic shopping behaviour', *Journal of Retailing*, 70(4): 383–93.

Engel, J., Fiorillo, H. and Cayley, M. (1972) *Marketing Segmentation*, New York: Holt Rinehart.

Evans, M. (1994) 'Domesday marketing? From an inaugural lecture', *Journal of Marketing Management*, 10: 409–31.

Firat, A. and Shultz II, C. (1997) 'From segmentation to fragmentation markets and marketing strategy in the postmodern era', *European Journal of Marketing*, 31(3/4): 183–207.

Goodwin, K. (2001) 'Perfecting your personas', Cooper: Interaction Design, Newsletter July–August, http://www.cooper.com (Accessed 20 December 2003).

Johnson, M. and Moran, R. (1992) *Robert T. Moran's Guide to Doing Business in Europe*, London: Butterworth-Heinemann.

Kotler, P., Armstrong, G., Brown, L. and Adam, S. (1998) *Marketing*, 4th edn., Sydney: Prentice-Hall.

Langer, B. (1998) 'Globalisation and the myth of ethnic community', in D. Bennett (ed.) *Multicultural States*, London: Routledge, pp. 163–177.

Laroche, M., Kim, C. and Clarke, M. (1997) 'The effects of ethnicity factors on consumer deal interests: an empirical study of French–English–Canadians', *Journal of Marketing Theory and Practice*, 5(1): 100–11.

Lindridge, A. and Dibb, S. (2003) 'Is "culture" a justifiable variable for market segmentation? A cross-cultural example', *Journal of Consumer Behaviour*, 2(3): 269–87.

Lovelock, C., Patterson, P. and Walker, R. (2001) *Services Marketing: An Asia-Pacific Perspective*, Sydney: Prentice-Hall.

McColl-Kennedy, J. and Kiel, G. (2000) *Marketing: A Strategic Approach*, Sydney: Nelson.

McDonald, M. and Dunbar, I. (1995) *Market Segmentation*, London: Macmillan.

Miller, K. and Layton, R. (2000) *Fundamentals of Marketing*, 4th edn., Sydney: McGraw-Hill.

Moss, G. and Vinten, G. (2001) 'Choices and preferences: testing the effect of nationality', *Journal of Consumer Behaviour*, 1(2): 198–208.

Parker, B. (1999) 'The consumer behavior of Hispanic populations in the United States', *Journal of Segmentation in Marketing*, 3(2): 61–78.

Pires, G. and Stanton, J. (1998) 'The marketing relevance of cultural diversity: a framework for understanding ethnicity and acculturation', in J. Chebat and A. Oumlil (eds) *Proceedings*, Multicultural Marketing Conference, Montreal, Canada, September, pp. 279–92.

Pires, G. and Stanton, J. (2000) 'Ethnicity and acculturation in a culturally diverse country: identifying ethnic market segments', *Journal of Multilingual and Multicultural Development*, 21(1): 42–57.

Randlesome, C. (1990) *Business Cultures in Europe*, London: Heinemann.

Smith, W. (1956) 'Product differentiation and market segmentation as alternative marketing strategies', *Journal of Marketing*, 21 (July): 3–8.

Stanton, J. P. and Pires, G. M. (1999) 'The substantiality test: meaning and application in market segmentation', *Journal of Segmentation in Marketing*, 3(2): 105–15.

Storbacka, K. (1997) 'Segmentation based on customer profitability – retrospective analysis of retail bank customer bases', *Journal of Marketing Management*, 13: 479–92.

Su Lim, J., Zalloco, R. and Ghingold, M. (1997) 'Segmenting the Hispanic market based on ethnic origin and identity: an exploratory study', *Journal of Segmentation in Marketing*, 1(2): 17–39.

Thomas, M. (1980) 'Market segmentation', *Quarterly Review of Marketing*, 6(1): 27.

Thorson, E. (1989) 'Products, Positioning, and Market Segmentation', in E. Thorson (ed.) *Advertising Age: The Principles of Advertising at Work*, Lincolnwood, IL: NTC Business Books.

Usunier, J.-C. (1996) *Marketing across Cultures*, 2nd edn., Sydney: Prentice-Hall.

Weinstein, A. (1997) 'Strategic segmentation: a planning approach for marketers', *Journal of Segmentation in Marketing*, 1(2): 7–16.

Wind, Y. (1978) 'Issues and advances in segmentation research', *Journal of Marketing Research*, Vol. XV (August): 317–37.

Wind, Y. and Carroll, D. (1972) 'International market segmentation', *European Journal of Marketing*, 5(1).

Wood, M. (1991) 'Five steps to more effective business to business marketing', *Sales and Marketing Management*, 143 (April).

Yankelovich, D. (1964) 'New criteria for market segmentation', *Harvard Business Review*, 83–90.

Young, S., Ott, L. and Feigin, B. (1978) 'Some practical considerations in market segmentation', *Journal of Marketing Research*, XV (August): 405–12.

CHAPTER 3

Ethnic consumers and ethnic groups

3.1 Chapter objectives

Ethnic groups consist of aggregates of ethnic consumers. A clear identification of consumer ethnicity is required to ensure group homogeneity in a marketing environment. This is not always an easy task to accomplish, sometimes leading to the use of indicators such as place of birth, nationality, language or other similar variables that are likely to provide false estimates of group size. The identification of consumer ethnicity is a necessary part of using ethnicity as a segmentation variable. The elusiveness of the ethnicity concept and its application, and a poor understanding of the process and dynamics of minority ethnic group formation, all contribute to the relative lack of attention given by marketers to ethnicity as a segmentation variable.

In this chapter, alternative approaches to ethnicity and acculturation are examined. The interrelated concepts of ethnic origin, ethnic identity and ethnic intensity are placed within a three-dimensional framework with the purpose of providing a conceptual understanding of how these dimensions develop within the acculturation process. The framework can be used to delineate and aggregate ethnic groups (as discussed in Chapter 4), providing guidance for the segmentation decision.

3.2 Introduction

By now the reader will be aware that a comprehensive STP analysis is essential to the development of a marketing strategy. This need applies in all markets, for all products and for all consumer groups, including ethnic minority consumer groups.

Cultural sensitivity is often recognized as a key to international business, with emphasis not only on recognizing and accepting different cultures and their manifestations, but particularly on the willingness to understand the differences (Harich and LaBahn, 1998). When marketing across countries, the need for cultural differences to be taken into account is almost axiomatic and, accordingly, largely unchallenged.[1] Even organizations commonly considered as typical mass marketers of their goods and services, such as McDonald's and Coca-Cola, have recognized the need to adapt their global offerings in response to local cultural environments. This local adaptation of mass market (global) goods, or glocalization, is essentially an exercise in STP analysis. The change to the marketing mix is justified by the need to reformulate the organization's value proposition in order to match better potential customers' needs and preferences.

3.3 Basic requirements for identifying ethnic marketing segments

Recent research into product-country image effects has found that, contrary to common implicit assumptions that national markets are composed of homogeneous consumers, there are consumer subcultural differences in the evaluation of culturally affiliated countries and their products, not only within a national market (Canada) but also within a city (Montreal) (Laroche *et al.*, 2003). This finding should come as no surprise since, by the same rationale that justifies the need to account for cultural differences in marketing across countries, each minority ethnic group in a given country is potentially unique and relevant for marketing purposes. Why, then, the relative scarcity of reported examples of rigorous ethnicity-based segmentation, targeting and positioning?

Identifying segmentable ethnic markets within a culturally diverse country is challenged by two basic requirements:

- To establish a basis for identifying and comparing ethnic groups (Bond, 1988): coincidentally, identifying ethnic groups is a prerequisite for deciding whether an ethnic group is segmentable. Using ethnicity as a segmentation criterion is justifiable by its nature as an 'obviously relevant causal construct' for both seller–buyer and consumer behaviour (Hui *et al.*, 1992).

- To assess the relevance of the identified ethnic groups for marketing purposes: the use of ethnicity for marketing segmentation requires ethnic-group boundaries to be determined before any consideration about ethnic group marketing value can be made.

The potential marketing importance of ethnic groups has motivated the development of a genetically adjusted framework for ethnicity (Chan and Rossiter, 1996, 1997). An alternative line of thought is that ethnicity is characterized by acculturation and ethnic identity, with ethnic identity remaining mostly constant (Laroche, Kim and Clarke, 1997). Here, ethnic identity refers to the extent of a person's natural identification with an ethnic group – the degree to which original values are maintained. Acculturation refers to the degree these values are replaced or increased with host country's values: that is, a person's or cultural group's learning and adoption of the values and norms of another culture – the values, attitudes, traditions, language, religion, etc., inherent to each ethnic group.

Ethnicity

Consumer attitudes are influenced by cultural differences due to ethnicity (Laroche, Kim and Clarke, 1997), suggesting that the description of ethnicity as 'both an automatic characteristic of racial group membership and a process of group identification in which people use ethnic labels to define themselves and others' (Hui *et al.*, 1992: 466–73) may be too narrow.

The conceptual complexity of ethnicity is reflected in its multidimensionality, including the sense of common descent extending beyond kinship, political solidarity vis-à-vis other groups, common customs, language, religion, values, morality and etiquette (Weber, 1961; Deshpande, Hoyer and Donthu, 1986). It is, therefore, not surprising that extant research reflects looseness and a possible disagreement between analysts about the nature of ethnicity and, naturally, its relevance as a segmentation criterion.

The identification of ethnicity usually relies on one or more indicators. From an objectivist perspective, ethnic groups are identified by any one or more of surname, country of origin, paternal ancestry, language spoken at home or area of residence. From a subjectivist perspective, the ethnicity of a group is seen to reflect ascriptions made by people in that group about themselves (Barth, 1969). In this case ethnic groups result from self-identification (Faber, O'Guinn and McCarty, 1987). While the combination of the objective and subjective perspectives may reduce the liabilities inherent to each one (Handleman, 1977), there has been a call for studies about ethnicity to measure the intensity of ethnic identity, that is, the intensity of the affiliation with the ethnic group (Alba and Chamlin, 1983; Deshpande, Hoyer and Donthu, 1986).

Multi-item measures of consumer ethnicity include ethnic identification and religious affiliation (Hirschman, 1981), ethnic identification as part of an index of acculturation (Valencia, 1985), and the combination of language spoken at home and Hirschman's self-identification measures (Webster, 1997). Other perspectives on ethnicity have examined the effects of ethnicity on consumers' interest in sales 'deals' (Laroche, Kim and Clarke, 1997), and developing a genetically adjusted framework that can increase the explanatory power of ethnicity.

A genetically adjusted framework

The genetically adjusted framework proposes that an individual's ethnicity is determined by the combination of their biological and physical characteristics, actual and perceived personality traits, and cultural values and norms. Biological and physical characteristics thrive on 'strong evidence that the influence of physical appearance is manifest in personal interactions between individuals, as in seller–buyer behaviour'. Personality characteristics are explained in terms of the belief that 'groups of people with ethnic or geographic unity share important traits, not only perceptual but also actual across different ethnic groups', because people have personalities and, by aggregation, so do ethnic groups. As for cultural values and norms, the contention is that cultural values for most nations are highly coincident with ethnic values and deserve to be studied as such (Chan and Rossiter, 1996).

Following means–end theory,[2] ethnicity is thus presented as a causal construct of seller–buyer and consumer behaviours, since 'cultural values affect behaviour through norms, which are beliefs held by consensus of a group concerning the behaviour rules for individual members' (Engel, Blackwell and Miniard, 1993). No allowance is made for changes in cultural values resulting from interaction among ethnic groups.

Ethnic identity and acculturation

Laroche, Kim and Clarke (1997) agree that ethnicity is a powerful predictor of various consumer attitudes and behaviours. Ethnicity, however, is proposed to involve ethnic identity, complemented by socio-economic status (including educational level and occupational status) and cultural awareness or acculturative balance (encompassing language proficiency, preference and use, tradition, customs and cultural identification).

Ethnic identity is taken as a given, not affected by acculturation. It is used to refer to an individual's natural identification with an ethnic group and 'remains largely unchanged even after extended contacts with the majority group over the long period of time' (Laroche, Kim and Clarke, 1997: 102).[3] This is consistent with the treatment of ethnic identity as a 'de facto' characteristic only reflective of the extent of an individual's ethnic origin, such as language and country of birth (Hui *et al.*, 1992).

Acculturation is the degree of a person's or cultural group's learning and adoption of the values and norms of another cultural group, and is perceived as a diachronic process (Olmedo, 1979; Faber, O'Guinn and McCarty, 1987). Hence, if ethnic identity remains unchanged, ethnicity is determined by acculturation. However, the process by which ethnicity changes in response to acculturation remains unclear. Laroche, Kim and Clarke (1997), for example, argue that individuals may be simultaneously 'slightly ethnic' (as reflected in media language choice) and 'strongly ethnic'. This contrasts with the method used by Deshpande, Hoyer and Donthu (1986) to investigate Hispanicness. 'Strong ethnic identifiers' and 'weak ethnic identifiers' were determined by drawing upon ethnic group members' personal views about their own strength of ethnic identification. A strong ethnic identifier is understood, therefore, as a person who expresses a strong self-identification with an ethnic group.

The interim conclusion about ethnicity is that consumers are 'ethnic' by origin or birth. In this sense they are genetically determined and, by origin, belong to a specific 'ethnic group' (ethnicity). This group is understood as 'a socially or psychologically defined set of people who share a common culture or cultural background, often because of similarity of race, nationality, or religion' (Aboud and Skerry, 1984). Ethnic origin is thus acquired at birth and never changes, even when a consumer formally adopts a different nationality. It is independent of country or time of residence, or cultural behaviour. Without acculturating influences from other ethnic groups, ethnic origin can then be equated to ethnicity.

In contrast, ethnic identity, defined as the actual or perceived behavioural association with a given ethnic group, may be treated as an endogenous variable. It is variable between individuals and for the single individual over time, due to economic or political factors, family socialization, occupational integration or educational influences (Deshpande, Hoyer and Donthu, 1986). In the same way that group members' overall degree of cultural and behavioural cohesion determines the degree of tightness or looseness of an ethnic group (Pelto, 1968), an individual's 'degree of association with an ethnic group' determines ethnic identity. This perspective corresponds to the concepts of 'ethnic loyalty' (Padilla, 1979) or 'value acculturation' (Szapocznik *et al.*, 1979), reflecting 'the extent to which individuals affiliate with their original culture and adhere to its traditional values' (Olmedo, 1979: 1069–70).

Ethnic identity is perceived as one of three orthogonal (or only moderately correlated) dimensions of acculturation rather than as a dimension of ethnicity. This conceptual variation, however, is not considered useful for this analysis because there is no apparent reason to question ethnic identity (or identification) and intensity as potentially dependent on the degree of learning and adoption of a different culture, or acculturation, discussed below.

Acculturation

Traditional assimilation model

Cultural assimilation involves the adoption by a minority ethnic group of a host (dominant) culture's beliefs, attitudes, values and behaviours via a linear, progressive learning process or model. This 'traditional assimilation model' predicts that behavioural patterns will become more like those of the host culture and less like those of the culture of origin (Kim, 1979; Padilla, 1980; Berry, 1990; Roberts and Hart, 1997). The assumption is that individuals follow a linear path between the original home culture and the host culture. New values and behaviours are acquired additively through increased contact with the new culture and the influence of mass media (O'Guinn, Lee and Faber, 1986), presumably replacing at least some of the earlier acquired values and behaviours. Because acculturation is defined as an individual's learning of the traits of another culture, the greater the progression towards the attitudes and values of the host culture, the greater the degree of acculturation (Laroche, Kim and Clarke, 1997). This progression may imply a widening gap in relation to the values and behaviours acquired in the home country.

Criticisms of the traditional assimilation model

The traditional assimilation model is subject to criticism on both empirical and theoretical grounds. Contrary to prediction, a study of Mexican–American consumption patterns found that these did not fit neatly between the culture of origin and the host culture, being distinctly different from both groups (Wallendorf and Reilly, 1983; Faber, O'Guinn and McCarty, 1987). Other limitations include cases of over-acculturation to the host culture and hyper-identification with the culture of origin, as well as cultural interpenetration, involving the host culture and the acculturating group's mutual influence on each other's values and behaviours (Andreasen, 1990; Gentry, Jun and Tansuhaj, 1995). Also reported is the overlooking of alternatives to assimilation (Penaloza, 1994).

Alternatives to assimilation

Mendoza (1989) investigated the development and validation of an acculturation scale for Mexican–American individuals and identified two alternative approaches in the literature: a monocultural approach, concerned with the degree of immersion into an alternative culture (hence consistent with one-directional assimilation); and a multicultural one, concerned with the degree of immersion into alternative and native cultures (hence bidirectional, involving both acculturation and ethnicity).

Mendoza went on to develop a Cultural Life Style Inventory measure designed to assess the type and degree of acculturation. This incorporates six theoretical and methodological premises that recognize the acculturation process as multidimensional, dynamic, multicultural, involving multifaceted individuals, requiring measures sensitive to individual differences and involving four distinct patterns of acculturation. These patterns are:

1. cultural resistance, the attempt to ignore the new culture while maintaining the culture of origin;

2. cultural shift, the substitution of new cultural norms for native customs;

3. cultural incorporation, the adoption of some of the new culture while keeping some of the culture of origin; and

4. cultural transmutation, the alteration of original and new cultural practices to create a unique subcultural entity.

Berry (1990) largely endorses these patterns or modes of acculturation, albeit under alternative designations of:

1. separation;

2. assimilation; and

3. integration.

His preference for the term 'marginalization' over 'cultural transmutation' involves a conceptual difference. Marginalization applies when the individual feels rejection by the host culture but does not wish to keep the culture of origin.

While Berry and Mendoza see assimilation as a pattern of acculturation, the latter is also seen in the literature as a stage in the overall assimilation process, corresponding to 'cultural or behavioural assimilation' (Olmedo, 1979). Cultural assimilation is perceived to involve changes in the behavioural patterns of individuals with respect to language, food consumption and dress.

It may precede or occur concurrently with structural assimilation, involving entry into groups, clubs and other organizations of the dominant culture (Gordon, 1978). The overall assimilation process also allows for marital assimilation between an individual and a member of the dominant culture (Roberts and Hart, 1997).

The need to distinguish attitudinal from behavioural dimensions of acculturation provides the grounds for further criticism of the traditional model. Gentry, Jun and Tansuhaj (1995) show that attitudinal dimensions (such as cultural identification, pride, ethnic attitude, ethnicity, self-identification, spouse's ethnic identity and social interaction) tend to change more slowly than behavioural ones (measured by the ownership of durable goods and language preference). Attitudes must therefore be treated as relatively independent of behaviour. Overall, the acknowledgement of occurrences inconsistent with the simple assimilation model adds to the complexity in marketing to ethnic groups. The traditional model cannot accurately predict an individual's acculturation behaviour.

The consumer acculturation process is subject to many possible influences. A list developed by Gronhaug, Gilly and Penaloza (1993) includes cultural characteristics, structural elements, language and symbols, cultural values, the social (cultural) context, the influence of the roles and situations that occur in the social cultural context and some individual descriptive characteristics. Individual characteristics have been speculated to include mental health or status, availability of social support, deviance, alcoholism and drug use, political and social attitudes, risk of coronary heart disease and risk of suicide (Marin et al., 1989). It is apparent that observations of individual behaviour are complex.

Ethnic groups and acculturation

In addition to weaknesses in predicting all instances of individual acculturation behaviour, the traditional assimilation model appears even less effective when the analysis focuses on ethnic groups. Ethnic groups may persist within host countries over time but there is no theoretical explanation for either their persistence or demise, or differing rates of change.

The shift in research orientation since 'Franz Boas (1896) inferred that a process of change occurs in cultures in contact because such cultures tend to become more like each other' (Seelye and Wasilewski, 1996: 78–80) may have been too narrow. Analysis has largely been limited in scope – usually involving a (two-country) bicultural space – and biased because, dealing with group behaviour, it ignored the variations found in the behaviour of the individuals who made up the group. In addition the analysis has been limited in number and, perhaps, by the actual circumstances.

There are few studies that discuss ethnic group acculturation. Olmedo (1979) identifies two main difficulties with ethnic-group acculturation:

1. an elusive definition of culture; and

2. interdisciplinary research, encompassing anthropology, sociology, psychology and psychiatry, only loosely able to be consolidated by behavioural science.

Olmedo argues that 'psychologists and psychiatrists tend to view acculturation in terms of intrapsychic mechanisms' (pp. 1062–3), dealing with changes in the perceptions, attitudes and cognition of the individual. In contrast, anthropologists and sociologists view acculturation as interpsychic, a group process. Olmedo then endorses the conclusion of an earlier study, that 'it is axiomatic that acculturation may be treated as either an individual phenomenon, a group phenomenon, or both . . .' (Teske and Nelson, 1974: 352).

It is apparent that, while the acculturation process is influential in defining ethnicity, the process by which ethnicity changes in response to acculturation remains unclear. This process needs to be understood in order to identify ethnic-group boundaries. In the next section we develop a three-dimensional operationalization of ethnicity. The purpose is to show that ethnic group boundaries can be identified by establishing a correspondence between ethnic groups and unique sets of intensities of measurable cultural values.

3.4   A three-dimensional construct of ethnicity

Figure 3.1 depicts ethnicity as a three-dimensional construct resulting from the interaction of ethnic origin, ethnic identity and ethnic intensity.

Ethnic origin is an individual's natural identification with the original ethnic group, that into which the individual is born. Ethnic origin is simply a fact that occurred in the past. It is immutable.

Ethnic identity is the individual's affiliation with a specific ethnic group and requires recognition by that group. It is multidimensional because it may involve simultaneous identification with different non-competing groups (as

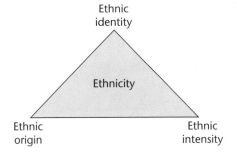

Figure 3.1 Components of ethnicity

in Portuguese, Caucasian, Christian, descendant of the Celts and Iberians). Like national identity, ethnic identity is mutable for individuals, in that it may reflect changes in individuals' preferences at different times depending on the circumstances.[4] Individual preference or self-identification, however, requires endorsement by the group and typical behaviour reflecting shared values, shared liabilities and social conformance. Changes in ethnic identity at a group level require collective adherence and may involve a prolonged, perhaps enduring transformation of the environment. To the extent that affiliation with a specific group reflects a choice or preference between competing groups, ethnic identity may be perceived as an endogenous variable.

Ethnic intensity is the variable degree of association with an ethnic group, reflecting the intensity associated with coincidental cultural values. It is an endogenous reciprocal variable in that it both reflects and can influence the degree of eventual learning and adoption of the values of other groups. While ethnic intensity applies to both individuals and the group, changes in the latter are likely to be slower as they require behavioural changes reflecting changes in the values held by individuals.

This three-dimensional construct of ethnicity is grounded in the argument that all societies exhibit cultures based on their common descent, language, customs, traditions and institutions. The behavioural pattern of an ethnic group expresses the shared values and beliefs within that group. Thus, different cultures will display different patterns of behaviour (Wallendorf and Reilly, 1983).

Figure 3.2 illustrates the process through which ethnic group identity and ethnic group intensity are generated. The figure shows the partial overlapping of rectangles. Each rectangle represents the set of values of an individual within a given ethnic group. An ethnic group is represented by the set of all individual rectangles. For simplicity only three such rectangles are shown, for individuals A, B, and C, but the exercise can be extended to all individuals

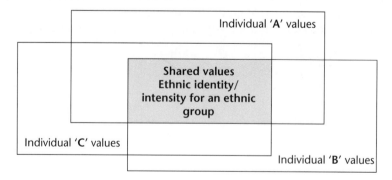

Figure 3.2 Generation of an ethnic group's identity/intensity through shared values
Source: Figure draws from a framework used by Hawkins *et al.* (1994) to discuss shared values in the context of organizational buying behaviour.

in the group population. The rectangles are of the same size to illustrate the presence of all values in each set. The shapes are of no consequence for this analysis.

Ethnic intensity for the group is represented as the area resulting from the overlapping of individuals A, B and C's values. The greater the overlap, the greater the group's ethnic intensity. To the extent that greater ethnic intensity implies a stronger maintenance of ethnic-group values by individual affiliates, ethnic identity is also likely to be stronger (reflecting a sense of belonging, or bond, between individuals and the group). Ethnic intensity and identity therefore determine ethnic group strength. Individuals may have stronger or weaker ethnic identities and this will affect group strength. Group strength also depends on the proportion of shared intensities in the individual's overall values, a conceptualization that is similar to Valencia's (1985) index to measure strength of Hispanic identity and Webster's (1991) weak and strong Hispanic identifiers. In addition, group strength reflects the individual characteristics noted in the section discussing alternatives to assimilation. Hence, an English-speaking individual, born and living in Australia, may have no ethnic identity at all with the Australian ethnic group, if there is no overlap between the intensities of their values and those of the group. From a marketing perspective it appears reasonable to expect that, provided general segmentation requisites are met, ethnic-group relevance is a direct function of group strength.

3.5 Ethnicity and the acculturation process (a two-country environment)

Without permanent population movements ethnicity is geographically specific. This location will generally be broadly coincident with national borders. In such a case ethnic origin coincides with ethnic identity (and nationality), and ethnic intensity is given by the horizontal summation of the inhabitants' variable degree of association with their original ethnic group.

Allowing ethnic-group affiliates to settle in another country involves direct contact between at least two groups with different cultures (ethnicities) and is likely to result in subsequent changes in the original behaviour patterns of either or both groups (Redfield et al., 1936). Acculturation, defined as the degree of an individual's or ethnic group's learning and adoption of another group's values, may involve radical changes in ethnic intensity, eventually resulting in ethnic identity changes. Ethnic identity must now be perceived as an endogenous reciprocal variable in that it both reflects and can influence the degree of learning and adoption of the values of other groups.

The greater the coincidence of the intensities of shared values between the acculturating parts when the process starts, the easier and faster the acculturation is likely to be (Wong-Rieger and Quintana, 1987). This outcome should be reinforced by greater ethnic-group strength because, if acculturation is occurring, the immigrant group will move as a whole towards the host group. In this scenario, an immigrant group with strong collective values would acculturate faster towards a host group with collective values than a group coming from an individualistic society.

Perfect acculturation implies a change in ethnic-group identity through total adoption of the values of another group. Over time, this is consistent with both the rationale of the traditional model, and Olmedo's (1979) explanation that acculturation is a direct function of the exposure to the dominant host culture (time since settlement for individuals and generational distance for the ethnic group). However, the assumption that later generations are more acculturated is weakened by the consistent finding that not all acculturation dimensions are strongly related to generation or length of residence. Furthermore, perfect acculturation, at least at the group level, contrasts with contemporary evidence of the separate and continued coexistence of ethnic groups in host countries.

The acculturation process is not a cultural transition between two static cultures. Cultural transition may, in some instances, generate synergistic behaviour within the group that strengthens the group bond, counteracts acculturation and increases marketing relevance. An ethnic group may be acculturating to a culture itself in mutation, and cultural changes in the home country may create an effective cultural separation with the emigrant ethnic group over time. Hofstede (1991) argues against this in defending the reliability of his cultural dimensions (Hofstede, 1980; Hofstede and Bond, 1984). The argument is that, excepting 'superficial manifestations, such as in dress, consumer products, television, movies and sport . . . the deeper underlying values, which determine the meaning people give to these activities and practice, are not likely to change in the foreseeable future' (p. 81). However, the view that 'traits may change as a result of the changes in macroenvironments such as economic, social and demographic trends' (Laroche, Kim and Clarke, 1997: 102) recognizes ethnicity as a dynamic and adaptable concept and that cultural changes may occur in the home country over time (Gentry, Jun and Tansuhaj, 1995).

Changes in the country of origin can be argued to widen the cultural gap created by the acculturation of the emigrant ethnic group and create differences in the home culture embodied by new arrivals to the settler group. The result is that, given time, the settler group will have their culture modified by the acculturation process, somewhere between two dynamic cultures, possibly evolving in various directions. Paradoxically, when interpenetration, over-acculturation and hyperidentification are allowed, there may be forces in operation that perpetuate the settler group as a separate entity and hinder assimilation.

Immigrants tend to bond primarily to people like themselves (Weingrod, 1965) because 'acculturating people are frequently under high levels of stress, including lowered mental health status (especially confusion, anxiety and depression), feelings of marginality and alienation, heightened psychosomatic symptoms, and identity confusion' (Berry and Annis, 1974). Where an expatriate ethnic group with 'similar' identity already exists in the new environment, even if the similarity is only in label and language, involvement with that group may reduce uncertainty for the new arrival. This may be specially so when ethnic institutions (clubs, press, shops, schools, neighbourhood health and legal services, religious services, childcare services, employment opportunities, etc.) are already in place. In 'acculturating' to the expatriate ethnic group (rather than to the host group), individuals attain an ethnic affiliation that additionally provides them with a network of communication and a frame of reference, based on shared values. The result is an overall pattern of consumption behaviour likely to be significantly different from that of the host and other groups (Laroche, Kim and Clarke, 1997), a matter discussed further in Chapter 6.

3.6 Allowing for cultural diversity (a multi-country world)

While a culturally diverse society may benefit economically from that diversity,[5] different unwritten rules of social conduct may result in friction or costs due to communication problems and inefficiencies caused by the lack of fit between the cultures. Acculturation effects across all the ethnic groups existing within a country need to be taken into account in assessing ethnic group marketing relevance.

Figure 3.3 represents the intensities in the sets of values of four separate ethnic groups, one of which is the host. These intensities are assumed to have

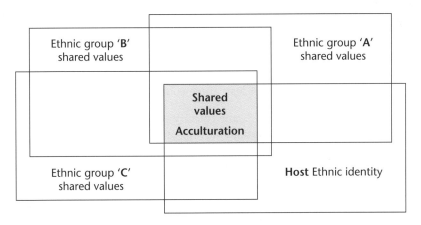

Figure 3.3 Identifying shared values across ethnic groups

been derived from the process of generation of ethnicity discussed earlier. Again, there are no particular reasons for the rectangular shape and the rectangles are equally dimensioned.

The process of acculturation works in reverse to that of the generation of ethnicity, as increases in the area of overlap correspond to greater acculturation. When acculturation is towards the dominant culture the result is lower marketing relevance, because of the decrease in the uniqueness of separate ethnic groups. The area of total overlap at the centre reflects some degree of homogeneity of market values. If the intensities of all values for all ethnic groups were to match exactly those of the host ethnic group the market would be homogeneous and no ethnic group alone would be marketing relevant. The difficulty in identifying marketing relevance increases if we account for acculturation and consumption patterns that may vary from group to group and from individual to individual, sometimes for the same person from one context to another. Conceivably, one ethnic group may acculturate to another, other than the host ethnic group. Exogamy (between subcultural groups) may facilitate this subcultural acculturation, whereas it may contribute to assimilation when involving the host culture.

Summing up, individuals and groups have distinct ethnicities (sets of intensities of cultural values and norms) that condition consumer behaviour in terms of specific needs and attitudes, as well as preferences and evaluation criteria before and after consumption. The dynamic processes that generate ethnicity and acculturation suggest the possibility of changing boundaries for ethnic groups over time, explained by changes in cultural values. Because cultural values shape both seller and buyer behaviour such changes influence segmentation and targeting decisions. In addition, identification of similarities and differences between consumer groups (the degree of homogeneity), and of changes occurring over time (stability), are important elements in making a segmentation decision. All of these are marketing concerns. Since the frame of reference that guides group consumption patterns varies with the intensity of shared values, an ethnic group may be expected to differ significantly from other groups.

Overall, the prior analysis suggests that the traditional linear assimilation model should be rejected on at least three counts:

1. Cultural changes in the home country may create an effective cultural separation with the emigrant (minority) ethnic group over time. Hence, acculturation to a new culture may cause a change from earlier acquired behaviour and values that were shared with consumers in the home country.

2. There may be forces in operation that perpetuate the minority ethnic group as a separate cultural entity, with its own characteristic consumption behaviour. Therefore, assimilation into the dominant host

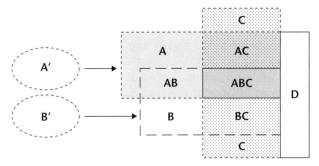

Figure 3.4 The acculturation process in a culturally diverse country
Explanation: Assume two possible home or source countries (**A'** and **B'**), one host country (**C**) and two minority ethnic groups (**A** and **B**), residing in the host country. (**A**) is the expatriate group of (**A'**). (**B**) is the expatriate group of (**B'**). Depending on the degree of ethnic intensity of new arrivals, they may adjust to the dominant host culture (**C**), to a minority ethnic group (**A, B, AB, AC, BC** or **ABC**) and some may over-acculturate (**D**). The broken lines reflect the possibility that the sets of values in each area change over time, towards (cross-acculturation) or apart from each other. Other possible identification outcomes or instances of hyperidentification with the home countries are not shown for simplicity. Each area represents a potentially unique and homogeneous segment.

country culture is not the necessary outcome of the acculturation process.

3. In a culturally diverse environment, a minority ethnic group is in contact with a variety of others, besides the dominant host group. Each group may be expected to reflect different acculturation stages and their contact may result in cross-acculturation. Hence, the behaviours and values of both the host culture and of minority ethnic groups also may be changing in different directions and to varying degrees.

Commencing from the premise that cultural differences between individuals and ethnic groups can be identified by sets of values of varying intensities, the process of acculturation suggests the possibility of changing ethnic group boundaries over time, explained by changes in cultural values. Figure 3.4 depicts a range of acculturation outcomes that may result from the settlement of new arrivals in an advanced, culturally diverse country. Depending on personal and environmental circumstances a new arrival will acculturate into one of a variety of different ethnic groups or to the dominant host culture. It follows that descriptors such as country of origin, birthplace or nationality are likely to be poor measures of the size of an ethnic group and poor indicators of its potential for segmentation.

A minority ethnic group may maintain its identity because new arrivals perceive greater value from acculturating to an ethnic group that is closer to their culture of origin than to the dominant host culture. Arguably, adjusting to a culture in close proximity to one's own can reduce stress (Mendenhall and Oddou, 1985) arising from psychological uncertainty engendered by a new learning situation (Black, Mendenhall and Oddou, 1991). Learning is facilitated if an experienced person can guide a neophyte in the new environment (Mendenhall and Oddou, 1985), but such a relationship is more likely if there is cultural proximity. Thus, acculturating towards an ethnic group closer to their own culture of origin can provide the new arrival with a network of communications and a frame of reference for behaviour within the host country that fosters a relationship with the group. How the relationship may evolve and strengthen can be examined from the perspective of how expatriates learn and adjust, guided by social learning theory (SLT).

3.7 Acculturation and the expatriate adjustment process

Social learning theory (SLT) starts from the premise that the learning and behaviour of individuals are based on their observations and subsequent imitation of other people's modelled behaviour. Adjusting to a new culture is likened to a learning process. The learning of acceptable behaviours and the adjustment process for a migrant choosing to move to another country may have an analogue in the movement of an expatriate worker to another country, often for a relatively long period of time. The pattern of incentives and motivation operating on expatriates influences their attention to host country behaviours, retention in the observers' memory and their ability to reproduce these behaviours (Bandura, 1977).

The satisfaction level of an expatriate with a host country appears to be initially high, then to fall before rising again, giving the description of the 'U curve' (Torbiorn, 1982; Black and Mendenhall, 1990). Driving these changes are an initial novelty and then the pressures to adjust and learn enough of the host culture to function effectively, regardless of the cultural distance between home and host countries. Usunier (1998) uses changes in oral pleasure deprivation as an explanatory variable for this pattern of change. Figure 3.5 depicts the U curve framework, also called the 'culture shock cycle'.

Following extensive empirical work initiated by Lysgaard (1955), the U curve framework is a description of a process rather than a theory explaining what might cause transition from one phase to the next. It is used to describe the cross-cultural adjustment process of expatriate employees or sojourners within a host culture. The U curve relates the time path of an expatriate's adjustment to a host country's culture. It involves a honeymoon stage, followed by culture shock and a process of improvement or adjustment to the host culture, culminating in a mastery stage, characterized by small incremental increases in the expatriate's ability to function effectively. The degree of adjustment is measured not by conformity to the host country culture but in terms of variables such as comfort or satisfaction with the new

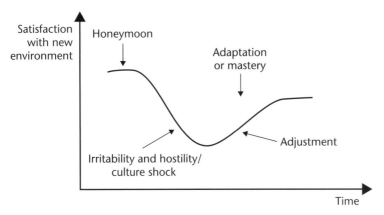

Figure 3.5 The U curve framework (also the 'culture shock cycle')
Rather than following host country behaviours, having a better knowledge of how to function effectively within the host country is what increases satisfaction.

environment, attitudes, degree of contact with host nationals, or difficulties with aspects of the new environment.

The different stages suggest that there is a transition in cultural understanding and perceived quality of living standards when shifting from a home to a host country environment. Cross-cultural adjustment places the expatriate in a situation where many past behaviours and associated consequences may no longer be appropriate and new sources of modelled behaviour are different from the past. Initially, cultural adjustment difficulties may be over-ridden by a cultural infatuation caused by the newness of the environment. A honeymoon stage initially prevails because there may be a short-term failure to recognize negative outcomes and/or ignorance of the appropriate feedback cues. Time is required for negative outcomes and reinforcement to become sufficient for the person to recognize and act on these negative elements. Inappropriate actions that potentially lead to personal discomfort are likely to ensue and, to the extent that the host culture is generally dissimilar to the home culture, inappropriate behaviours may be substantial, leading to culture shock. That is, culture shock sets in when coping with the new environment on a daily basis becomes necessary because the newly arrived individual begins to recognize some degree of unpreparedness for dealing effectively with the environment.

The onset of culture shock can be caused by negative feedback to individuals who exhibit a high ratio of inappropriate behaviours relative to appropriate behaviours learned, coupled with a low utilization of modelled and observed behaviours appropriate to the new culture. Individuals may know they are exhibiting inappropriate behaviours but not know what corrective action to take. Lack of available models in relation to specific situations may initially increase the ratio of negative consequences to the learning of new appropriate behaviours, providing an incentive for the expatriate's adjust-ment to the new environment. Accordingly, the adjustment stage occurs because repeated exposure to the new environment and models in the host culture increases the repeated availability of modelled behaviours. Familiarity of the models, their attractiveness and perceived similarity, in turn increases attention and retention. An increased ability to reproduce appropriate beha-viours causes the expatriate both to feel and to be more adept and adjusted in the host culture. Adjustment is, therefore, marked by an increasing degree of satisfaction in being able to cope with the cultural norms of the host country, as well as a diminishing need for additional cultural learning and adaptation. This is reflected in the mastery stage, when the expatriate perceives his or her own competence in negotiating the new environment. Increasing satisfaction may have nothing to do with following host country behaviours but, rather, having a better knowledge of how to function effect-ively within the host country. Hence, there is no implication of assimilation to the dominant host culture. Familiarity with the host country may result in more realistic expectations of that culture and people, rather than any desire or need to follow that culture (Usunier, 1998).

Finally, there is no reason to expect the length of time to be strongly asso-ciated with the degree of cultural adjustment. The process may depend on the degree of cultural distance between home and host cultures, and on the expatriate's previously acquired acculturation skills, such as acquired lan-guage skills and knowledge of the political and religious system (Mendenhall and Oddou, 1985; Black, Mendenhall and Oddou, 1991).

3.8 Relevance to minority ethnic groups

SLT provides an explanation of an expatriate's cross-cultural adjustment path towards reaching a self-perceived, satisfactory degree of behaviour efficiency in a host country. The socialization process offers an analogy that can be used to explain why a new arrival from one ethnic background may value more highly adjustment to, and interaction with, a minority ethnic group, as com-pared with the dominant host group. Uncertainty is reduced and value is cre-ated through reduction of the impact of culture shock and facilitation of the individual's adjustment process to the new environment. SLT suggests that the motivation to *adjust* to the new culture is not the same as the motivation to *change* to the new culture. Satisfaction with living in the new environment is the main element.

In progressing from expatriates to the marketing relevance of ethnic groups in a culturally diverse country, the issue is whether the adjustment of new arrivals occurs in relation to the dominant host culture or the culture of a minority group. When an ethnic group is relatively small and geographically fragmented, it may not be accessible to a new arrival. Hence, an arrival could be expected to use the dominant host culture models and behaviours. However, when an ethnic culture is established, identifiable and readily accessible, this can provide the models and behaviours sought by a similar arrival. The greater the differences between the ethnic identity of the host culture and the individual's ethnic identity, the lower will be the individual's motivation to use host country models of behaviour during the adjustment phase and the longer it will take to adjust fully to the host culture (Black and Mendenhall, 1990). By definition, both expatriates and voluntary migrants have an option of selecting their preferred behaviours either by returning 'home', learning from the behaviours of the dominant host culture or, if an identifiable resident ethnic group exists, learning from that group's behaviour.

Therefore, whether migrant or expatriate, a new arrival is engaged in an adjustment process of observing and learning new behaviours, regardless of the models used. An expatriate who is able to find parallel substitutes for his or her interests and activities in the host country, culinary adaptability and willingness and ability to communicate is more likely to be successful in adjusting to a new culture (Mendenhall and Oddou, 1985). Similarly, Usunier's (1998) explanation of the U curve rests on changing levels of oral pleasure deficiency, including language and culinary elements. Extending the analogy to migrants arriving in a host country with different minority cultures, oral pleasure deficiency will be lessened by learning the behaviours of the group with the closest ethnic identity. Consistent with the argument that similar others trust, and are more trusted, compared to dissimilar others (Dwyer, Schurr and Oh, 1987), learning the behaviours of similar others reduces uncertainty and the perceived risk of following inappropriate behaviours.

In addition to the initial exhilaration arising from the novelty of the experience, the honeymoon phase for a migrant may be extended by possible family reunion and because oral pleasure related to minority group habits will be discovered. There may be oral deficiencies when compared against the home culture but these are likely to be perceived as much more intense in relation to the host dominant culture. As a result of acculturation to a minority ethnic group, negative outcomes may not increase sufficiently to move adjustment to the culture shock stage, even if net oral pleasure deficiency may arise from the individual's eventual failure to be satisfied with group-based oral pleasures. In the same way that the group adjusts over time to be able to operate within a culturally diverse society, so the arrival must learn new and appropriate behaviours and will experience the social repercussions of the group from a failure to do so.

Adjustment occurs as the individual acquires the behaviours of the group. As argued earlier, increasing satisfaction may have nothing to do with following host country behaviours but rather having a better knowledge of how to function effectively in the host country, augmented by comfort and satisfaction with the new environment. Ethnic marketing may also contribute to this comfort and satisfaction, through the development of value propositions and communications targeting minority ethnic groups with which ethnic minority consumers may identify. Air Canada, for example, sought to appeal to Chinese Canadian consumers through advertisements that combined the Chinese language with the use of a maple leaf embroidery symbol. The objective was to combine Air Canada's symbol of the maple leaf with security attributes valued by the targeted population. As explained by Wong (1997), this combination succeeded in bringing together Air Canada's Chinese name (Maple Leaf Airlines) and the esteemed art of Chinese embroidery.

Overall, acculturation to the minority ethnic group provides an arrival with more familiar models of how to behave, as a resident and consumer, in an acceptable and effective manner in the new country. Because the process of learning and adjustment is dynamic a member needs to interact continually within the group to benefit from this relationship. That is, the link with the minority ethnic group persists in the long run.

Oral pleasure deficiency is unrelated to the duration of stay (Usunier, 1998). It may persist but on average it is likely to be outweighed by positive oral pleasure drawn from life in the host country. Contextual factors such as cultural and linguistic proximity of home and host country are important in determining the adjustment process. The capacity of individuals to manage their transition between complex cultural codes determines the outcome of their experience. Ultimately, their management of this transition is the force that perpetuates the minority ethnic group as a separate cultural entity and explains its continuation, strength and cohesiveness.

3.9 Conclusion

Identification of ethnic groups within a culturally diverse nation is important because ethnicity helps to explain both seller–buyer and consumer behaviour. Identification of similarities and differences between groups, and how these change over time, is important in making a segmentation decision.

The three-dimensional framework developed in this chapter illustrates how ethnic group boundaries can be defined, and some of the dynamics that may cause changing ethnic boundaries over time, as well as the interrelationship between ethnicity and the acculturation process in culturally diverse countries. An evaluation of the marketing relevance of ethnic groups requires an analysis that is dynamic and involves assessment of ethnic identity and ethnic intensity, variables themselves influenced by acculturation. The rationale for the framework is that cultural differences between individuals and ethnic groups can be identified by sets of values of varying intensities. Hence, the processes of ethnicity generation and acculturation can be explained by changes in shared cultural values. This is a useful approach because cultural values can be effective predictors of consumer behaviour (Manyiwa and Crawford, 2002), therefore relevant for marketers.

An ethnic group may maintain its identity because acculturating individuals may perceive greater value in acculturating to an ethnic group closer to their own ethnic identity than to the dominant host culture. This provides an individual with a network of communications and a frame of reference that determines consumer behaviour and fosters an ethnic bond. This bond determines consumer behaviour that may lead to relationships conducive to consumer loyalty, clearly marketing relevant.

The acculturation process is potentially more dynamic for individuals than for ethnic groups. In addition, acculturation and consumption patterns may vary from group to group and from individual to individual, sometimes for the same individual from one context to another. The identification of meaningful ethnic boundaries must acknowledge relationships among ethnic identity, intensity and strength and their crucial role in predicting behaviour. It is the latter that provides a basis for delineating ethnic boundaries.

Finally, the process of minority ethnic group formation produces stable groups with internal homogeneity, characterized by their relative heterogeneity to other consumer groups. This questions the common practice of aggregating minority ethnic groups for marketing purposes.

Notes

1. A recent study by Pressey and Selassie (2003) questions whether cultural differences are overrated. The study found *'little evidence to support the popular idea that culture exerts a significant influence on international business relationships'* (p. 354). Arguably, cross-national relationships are more influenced by communications/language barriers, geographic distance, economic factors, industry barriers, time differences, technology barriers, legal differences and infrastructure barriers. See also Ralston (1993) and Markoczy (2000) for further criticism of the importance of cultural differences in international business.
2. See Gutman (1982) and (1997) for an explanation of means–end theory.
3. See also Schaninger, Bourgeois and Buss, 1985; Kim, Laroche and Lee, 1990; Lim, Zalloco and Ghingold, 1997).
4. See Seelye and Wasilewski (1996) for further insight into ethnic identities.
5. See Stanton, Aislabie and Lee (1992), and Stanton and Lee (1995) for a discussion of the potential economic benefits for countries driven by cultural diversity.

References

Aboud, F. and Skerry, S. (1984) 'The development of ethnic attitudes: a critical review', *Journal of Cross-Cultural Psychology*, 15(1): 3–34.

Alba, R. and Chamlin, M. (1983) 'Ethnic identification among whites', *American Sociological Review*, 48 (April): 240–7.

Andreasen, A. (1990) 'Cultural interpenetration: a critical research issue for the 1990s', in M. Goldberg, G. Gorn, and R. Pollay (eds) *Advances in Consumer Research*, 17, Provo, UT: Association for Consumer Research, pp. 847–9.

Bandura, A. (1977) *Social Learning Theory*, Englewood Cliffs, NJ: Prentice-Hall.

Barth, F. (1969) 'Ethnic groups and boundaries' (extract from *The Social Organization of Ethnic Groups and Boundaries*, Boston: Little, Brown) reprinted in J. Hutchinson and A. Smith (eds) *Ethnicity* (1996), Oxford: Oxford University Press.

Berry, J. (1990) 'Psychology of acculturation, in cross-cultural perspectives', in J. J. Berman (ed.) *Proceedings*, Nebraska Symposium on Motivation, pp. 201–34.

Berry, J. and Annis, R. (1974) 'Ecology, cultural and psychological differentiation', *International Journal of Psychology*, 5(4): 173–93.

Black, J. and Mendenhall, M. (1990) 'The U-Curve adjustment hypothesis revisited: a review and theoretical framework', *Journal of International Business Studies* (second quarter): 225–46.

Black, J., Mendenhall, M. and Oddou, G. (1991) 'Toward a comprehensive model of international adjustment: an integration of multiple theoretical perspectives', *Academy of Management Review*, 14(2): 291–317.

Boas, F. (1896) 'The growth of Indian mythologies: a study based upon the growth of the mythologies of the North Pacific coast', *Journal of American Folklore*, 9: 1–11.

Bond, M. (1988) 'Finding universal dimensions of individual variation in multicultural studies of values: the Rokeach and Chinese value surveys', *Journal of Personality and Social Psychology*, 55(6): 1009–15.

Chan, A. and Rossiter, J. (1996) 'Ethnicity in business and consumer behaviour', *Working Paper 9*, Nepean: Department of Marketing, University of Western Sydney.

Chan, A. and Rossiter, J. (1997) 'Understanding the causal relationship between values and consumer behaviour', *Working Paper 5*, Nepean: Department of Marketing, University of Western Sydney.

Deshpande, R., Hoyer, W. and Donthu, N. (1986) 'The intensity of ethnic affiliation: a study of the sociology of Hispanic consumption', *Journal of Consumer Research*, 13: 214–20.

Dwyer, F., Schurr, P. and Oh, S. (1987) 'Developing buyer–seller relationships', *Journal of Marketing*, 51(2): 11–27.

Engel, J., Blackwell, R. and Miniard, P. (1993) *Consumer Behaviour*, Fort Worth, TX: Dryden Press.

Faber, R., O'Guinn, T. and McCarty, J. (1987) 'Ethnicity, acculturation, and the importance of product attributes', *Psychology and Marketing*, 4: 121–34.

Gentry, J., Jun, S. and Tansuhaj, P. (1995) 'Consumer acculturation processes and cultural conflict: how generalizable is a North American model for marketing globally?', *Journal of Business Research*, 32: 129–39.

Gordon, M. (1978) *Human Nature, Class, and Ethnicity*, New York: Oxford University Press.

Gronhaug, K., Gilly, M. and Penaloza, L. (1993) 'Barriers and incentives in consumer acculturation', *European Advances in Consumer Research*, 1: 278–86.

Gutman, J. (1982) 'A means–end chain model based on consumers' categorisation process', *Journal of Marketing*, 46 (Spring): 60–72.

Gutman, J. (1997) 'Means-end chain as goal hierarchies', *Psychology and Marketing*, 14(6): 543–60.

Handleman, D. (1977) 'The organization of ethnicity', *Ethnic Groups*, 1: 187–200.

Harich, K. and LaBahn, D. (1998) 'A focus on consumer perceptions of salesperson role performance including cultural sensitivity', *Journal of Business Research*, 42: 87–101.

Hawkins, D., Neal, C., Quester, P. and Best, R. (1994) *Consumer Behaviour: Implications for Marketing Strategy*, Sydney: Irwin.

Hirschman, E. (1981) 'American Jewish ethnicity: its relationship to some selected aspects of consumer behavior', *Journal of Marketing*, 45: 102–10.

Hofstede, G. (1980) *Culture's Consequences: International Differences in Work-Related Values*, Beverly Hills, CA: Sage Publications.

Hofstede, G. (1991) *Cultures and Organizations: Software of the Mind*, London: McGraw-Hill.

Hofstede, G. and Bond, M. (1984) 'Hofstede's culture dimensions: an independent validation using Rokeach's value survey', *Journal of Cross-Cultural Psychology*, 15(4): 417–33.

Hui, M., Joy, A., Kim, M. and Laroche, M. (1992) 'Acculturation as a Determinant of Consumer Behaviour: Conceptual and Methodological Issues', in R. Belk *et al.* (eds) *Proceedings*, Winter Educators' Conference, Chicago, IL: AMA, pp. 466–73.

Kim, Y. (1979) 'Toward an interactive theory of communication–acculturation', in D. Nimmo (ed.) *Communication Yearbook 3*, New Brunswick, NJ: Transaction Books.

Kim, C., Laroche, M. and Lee, B. (1990) 'A taxonomy of French and English Canadians based on communication patterns', *Canadian Journal of Administrative Sciences*, 7(2): 1–11.

Laroche, M., Kim, C. and Clarke, M. (1997) 'The effects of ethnicity factors on consumer deal interests: an empirical study of French–English–Canadians', *Journal of Marketing Theory and Practice*, 5(1): 100–11.

Laroche, M., Papadopoulos, N., Heslop, L. and Bergeron, J. (2003) 'Effects of subcultural differences on country and product evaluations', *Journal of Consumer Behaviour*, 2(3): 232–48.

Lim, J., Zalloco, R. and Ghingold, M. (1997) 'Segmenting the Hispanic market based on ethnic origin and identity: an exploratory study', *Journal of Segmentation in Marketing*, 1(2): 17–39.

Lysgaard, S. (1955) 'Adjustment in a foreign society: Norwegian Fullbright grantees visiting the United States', *International Social Science Bulletin*, 7: 45–51.

Manyiwa, S. and Crawford, I. (2002) 'Determining linkages between consumer choices in a social context and the consumer's values: a means-end approach', *Journal of Consumer Behaviour*, 2(1): 54–71.

Marin, G., Marin, B., Sabogal, R., Sabogal, F. and Stable, E. (1989) 'The role of acculturation in the attitudes, norms, and expectancies of Hispanic smokers', *Journal of Cross-Cultural Psychology*, 20(4): 399–415.

Markoczy, L. (2000) 'National culture and strategic change in belief formation', *Journal of International Business Studies*, 31(3): 427–42.

Mendenhall, M. and Oddou, G. (1985) 'The dimensions of expatriate acculturation: a review', *Academy of Management Review*, 10(1): 39–47.

Mendoza, R. (1989) 'An empirical scale to measure type and degree of acculturation in Mexican–American adolescents and adults', *Journal of Cross-Cultural Psychology*, 20(4): 372–85.

O'Guinn, T., Lee, W. and Faber, R. (1986) 'Acculturation: the impact of divergent paths on buyer behaviour', in R. Lutz (ed.) *Advances in Consumer Research*, 13 Provo, UT: Association for Consumer Research, pp. 579–83.

Olmedo, E. (1979) 'Acculturation: a psychometric perspective', *American Psychologist*, 34: 1061–70.

Padilla, A. (1979) 'The role of cultural awareness and ethnic loyalty in acculturation', in A. Padilla (ed.) *Acculturation: Theory, Models, and Some New Findings*, Boulder, CO: Westview Press.

Padilla, A. (1980) *Acculturation: Theory, Models, and Some New Findings*, Boulder, CO: Westview Press.

Pelto, P. (1968) 'Difference between "tight" and "loose" societies', *Transactions*, 5: 37–40.

Penaloza, L. (1994) 'Atravesando fronteras/border crossings: a critical ethnographic exploration of the consumer acculturation of Mexican immigrants', *Journal of Consumer Research*, 21(1): 32–54.

Pressey, A. and Selassie, H. (2003) 'Are cultural differences overrated? Examining the influence of national culture on international buyer–seller relationships', *Journal of Consumer Behaviour*, 2(4): 354–66.

Ralston, D. (1993) 'Differences in managerial values: a study of US, Hong Kong and PRC managers', *Journal of International Business Studies*, 24(2): 249–75.

Redfield, R., Linton, R. and Herskovits, M. (1936) 'Memorandum on the study of acculturation', *American Anthropology*, 38(2): 149–52.

Roberts, S. and Hart, H. (1997) 'A comparison of cultural value orientations as reflected by advertisements directed at the general US Market, the US Hispanic market and the Mexican market', *Journal of Marketing Theory and Practice*, Winter: 91–9.

Schaninger, C., Bourgeois, J. and Buss, C. (1985) 'French–English Canadian subcultural consumption differences', *Journal of Marketing*, 49: 82–92.

Seelye, H. and Wasilewski, J. (1996) *Between Cultures: Developing Self-Identity in a World of Diversity*, Lincolnwood, IL: NTC Publishing Group.

Stanton, P., Aislabie, C. and Lee, J. (1992) 'The economics of a multicultural Australia: a literature review', *Journal of Multilingual and Multicultural Development*, 13(5): 407–21.

Stanton, P. J. and Lee, J. (1995) 'Australian cultural diversity and export growth', *Journal of Multilingual and Multicultural Development*, 16(6): 497–512.

Szapocznik, J., Scopetta, M., Kurtines, W. and Arnalde, M. (1979) 'Theory and measurement of acculturation', *Inter-American Journal of Psychology*, 12: 113–30.

Teske, R. and Nelson, B. (1974) 'Acculturation and assimilation: a clarification', *American Ethnologist*, 1: 351–67.

Torbiorn, I. (1982) *Living Abroad*, New York: John Wiley and Sons.

Usunier, J. (1998) 'Oral pleasure and expatriate satisfaction: an empirical approach', *International Business Review*, 7: 89–110.

Valencia, H. (1985) 'Developing an index to measure Hispanicness', in E. Hirschman and M. Holbrook (eds) *Advances in Consumer Research*, 12, Provo, UT: Association for Consumer Research, pp. 118–21.

Wallendorf, M. and Reilly, M. (1983) 'Ethnic migration, assimilation and consumption', *Journal of Consumer Research*, 10: 292–302.

Weber, M. (1961) 'Ethnic groups', in T. Parsons *et al.* (eds) *Theory of Society*, New York: Free Press, pp. 301–9. Translated by Ferdinand Kolegar, from Max Weber (1947) 'Entstehung ethnishchen Gemeinsamkeitsglaubens, Sprach und Kultgemeinschaft' in *Wirtschaft und Gesellschaft*, Tuebingen: J. C. B. Mahr, pp. 234–40.

Webster, C. (1991) 'Attitudes towards marketing practices: the effects of ethnic identification', *Journal of Applied Business Research*, 7(2): 107–16.

Webster, C. (1997) 'Resource theory in a cultural context: linkages between ethnic identity, gender roles and purchase behavior', *Journal of Marketing Theory and Practice*, Winter, 1–5.

Weingrod, A. (1965) *Israel: Group Relations in a New Society*, New York: Praeger.

Wong, K. (1997) 'The symbolic power of security', *Marketing*, 102 (8 September): 24.

Wong-Rieger, D. and Quintana, D. (1987) 'Comparative acculturation of Southeast Asian and Hispanic immigrants and sojourners', *Journal of Cross-Cultural Psychology*, 18(3): 345–62.

Australian standard classification of cultural and ethnic groups

Australian Bureau of Statistics*

The Australian Standard Classification of Cultural and Ethnic Groups (ASCCEG) is the Australian statistical standard for classifying data relating to the ethnic and cultural composition of the Australian population. ASCCEG is a classification of cultural and ethnic groups based on the geographic area in which a group originated or developed and the similarity of cultural and ethnic groups in terms of social and cultural characteristics. ASCCEG is intended for use in the collection, aggregation and dissemination of data relating to the cultural diversity of the Australian Population. For example, the classification should be used when collecting, classifying and presenting data related to personal characteristics such as ethnic identity, ancestry and cultural identity.

The Australian Bureau of Statistics (ABS) has developed ASCCEG to satisfy wide community interest in the ethnic and cultural composition of the Australian population and the characteristics of particular migrant community groups. The classification is intended to provide a standard to meet a growing statistical, administrative and service delivery need for data relating to these interests. It is envisaged that ASCCEG will assist in meeting the need for consistent methods for the collection and classification of ethnicity, ancestry and cultural diversity data in statistical, administrative and service delivery settings. A particularly important aspect of its adoption will be to improve the comparability and compatibility of data on ethnicity from these diverse sources.

It should be noted that the measurement of the ethnic and cultural diversity of the Australian population, and the degree to which Australians retain their

* ABS Catalogue no. 1249.0, ISBN 0 642 54287 2

ethnic and cultural identity, is primarily based on the use of a number of statistical variables related to a person's origins, including: country of birth, country of birth of mother/father, language variables such as main language other than English spoken at home, religious affiliation, proficiency in spoken English, and year of arrival in Australia. These variables are associated with other classifications such as the Standard Australian Classification of Countries (SACC), the Australian Standard Classification of Languages (ASCL) and the Australian Standard Classification of Religious Groups (ASCRG).

Information on ethnic identity, ancestry and cultural identity (collected and classified using ASCCEG) can be used in conjunction with these variables to provide a self-assessed measure of ethnicity and cultural background. A major advantage of such information is that it is able to measure an association with ethnic or cultural groups which does not equate directly to country of birth, language or religion and cannot be readily identified using these variables.

ASCCEG was developed by means of extensive research of Australian and overseas literature in the field of interest, use of principles and techniques relating to the development of statistical classifications, and analysis of existing data relating to the cultural and ethnic profile of Australia (primarily data from the 1996 Census of Population and Housing). This work was supported by information and advice from academics and other experts, by consulting organizations that are significant users or providers of cultural diversity data, and by consultation with ethnic and community groups interested in the topic.

The number of members of particular cultural and ethnic groups in Australia was treated as a significant factor in developing the hierarchical structure of the classification to ensure that the current ethnic profile of Australia is appropriately reflected. As a result, there is a narrower identification of some cultures and peoples compared to others. Cultural and ethnic groups for which available data indicate small numbers in Australia are not separately identified in the classification structure but are included in appropriate residual categories (see reserved codes for residual categories).

The ABS has produced ASCCEG in line with its commitment to provide leadership in the development and promotion of statistical data standards. The ABS will use ASCCEG in its own statistical work, including classifying responses to the question on Ancestry in the 2001 Census of Population and Housing, and will actively promote its use by other government agencies, private organizations, community groups, and individuals collecting, analysing or using information relating to cultural and ethnic groups.

The identification of cultural and ethnic groups in the classification, and the way in which they are grouped, does not imply the expression of any opinion on the part of the ABS concerning the recognition of any group by governments, organizations or individuals, or the status accorded them. Nor does it imply the expression of an opinion concerning the relative merit or importance of particular cultural and ethnic groups or the people who belong to them.

C1.1 Definition of the concept

ASCCEG is designed to be used for the classification of information relating to a number of topics such as ancestry, ethnic identity, and cultural diversity. Although these topics have elements of difference, it is considered that the fundamental concept common to them all, and thus underpinning the classification, is *ethnicity*.

It is difficult to define ethnicity in a way that is both useful and generally acceptable and it is not the function of this document to attempt an extensive definition of the concept. However, because the words 'ethnicity' and 'ethnic' are associated with many different meanings it is useful to provide some definitional material. *The Macquarie Dictionary* (3rd edn., 1997) provides the following meanings:

1. Relating to or peculiar to a population, especially to a speech group.

2. Loosely also to a race.

3. Relating to the origin, classification, characteristics, etc., of such groups of or relating to members of the community who are migrants or descendants of migrants and whose native language is not English.

4. Recognizable as coming from an identifiable culture.

For the purposes of ASCCEG it is sufficient, and not controversial, to say that the term 'ethnicity' refers to the shared identity or similarity of a group of people on the basis of one or more factors, including the following which were enunciated in a report entitled *The Measurement of Ethnicity in the Australian Census of Population and Housing*, Report to the Australian Statistician by the 1986 Population Census Ethnicity Committee (ABS Cat. no. 2172.0). This report was prepared under the Chairmanship of the late Professor W. D. Borrie, CBE, and is referred to henceforth as the Borrie Report.

The Ethnicity Committee considered that the most enlightening attempt to define an ethnic group is that contained in a United Kingdom Law Lords statement reported in *Patterns of Prejudice*, Vol. 17, No. 2, 1983. The Law Lords noted that the key factor is that the group regards itself, and is regarded by others, as a distinct community by virtue of certain characteristics, not all of which have to be present in the case of each ethnic group. The distinguishing characteristics which may be involved include:

- a long shared history, the memory of which is kept alive;
- a cultural tradition, including family and social customs, sometimes religiously based;
- a common geographic origin;
- a common language (but not necessarily limited to that group);

- a common literature (written or oral);
- a common religion;
- being a minority (often with a sense of being oppressed); and
- being racially conspicuous.

Since the publication of the Borrie Report in April 1984, the multicultural nature of Australian society has further developed, resulting in a more sophisticated and enlightened approach to cultural diversity. Nevertheless, the approach to the definition of ethnicity in the Borrie Report is still relevant and serves the purposes of ASCCEG well.

The approach of defining ethnic or cultural groups in terms of one or more relevant characteristics allows the notion of ethnicity to be viewed in terms of one of two broad sub-concepts. The Borrie Report describes these as a self-perceived group identification approach and an approach that is more historically determined. In ASCCEG, ethnicity is based on the self-perceived group identification approach for a number of reasons.

Self-perceived group identification measures the extent to which individuals associate with particular cultural or ethnic groups. A measure of active association produces data which is more useful in terms of policy and service delivery needs. An historically determined approach would produce data which relates individuals to groups with which they no longer have a particular affinity and with which they may have little social, cultural or economic similarity.

The method used to collect information on ethnicity or ancestry in the ABS and other organizations is self-perception based on a self-assessed response to a direct question. No attempt is made to determine historically the origins of individuals. It is important for the concept underpinning the classification and the categories of the classification to be in harmony with this approach.

The use of self-perception results in the need to include a number of categories in the classification that equate to national cultural identities. In particular, the self-perceived group identification approach allows the response 'Australian' and thus allows for the category 'Australian' in the classification. It also allows the meaningful classification of many other nationally oriented responses in statistical and administrative collections that would otherwise be unusable. A number of users indicated that the usefulness of the classification would be impaired if it did not allow for the concept of an 'Australian' ethnicity.

Considering ethnicity as a multidimensional concept based on a number of distinguishing characteristics using a self-perception approach allows for a practical and useful classification attuned to generally accepted notions of what constitutes ethnicity and cultural identity. This approach supports the collection and use of data in statistical, administrative and service delivery settings.

DISCUSSION QUESTIONS

1. Which of the alternative approaches to classifying ethnic groups would you prefer to use for marketing purposes? Give your reasons.

2. What are the problems likely to be encountered in using statistically based classifications as a basis for identifying market segments?

3. Why would knowledge of ethnic groups be useful to governments in their services provision?

4. Discuss how this classification could possibly be used to aggregate groups to create larger segments.

CHAPTER 4

Ethnic market segmentation and aggregates of ethnic groups

4.1   Chapter objectives

Ethnic groups consist of aggregates of ethnic consumers. To be important for marketing such groups need to be identifiable, accessible, measurable, stable and substantial. Practical difficulties in the identification of consumers of a given ethnicity may combine with preconceptions about ethnic group minority status and substantiality requirements to question the importance of the group for marketing purposes. This has been advanced in the marketing literature as a justification for the aggregation of ethnic groups sharing some attribute or set of attributes, such as language, country of origin and race.

This chapter discusses the consequences for effective ethnic marketing from using aggregates of ethnic groups and considers the circumstances when aggregation may constitute an acceptable practice. The tenet is that ethnic group homogeneity needs to be established on behavioural grounds.

4.2 Introduction

Very few individuals in isolation are ever likely to be targeted in a consumer market. This is because of segment substantiality, one of the requirements for effective market segmentation. For any given firm, substantiality is a contingent dimension that may depend on a variety of factors, including the firm's objectives, strategic planning, competitive environment and stage of the life cycle (Stanton and Pires, 1999). In any case, market segmentation is likely to involve some notional level of critical mass that, in consumer markets, is unlikely to be met by any one individual. Indeed an individual becomes important, if at all, only when associated with other similar individuals, creating an identifiable, measurable, stable and actionable group that is homogeneous within itself and heterogeneous in relation to other groups. This same reasoning may be applied to ethnic minority consumers.

4.3 Ethnic groups as references for ethnic consumers

In Chapter 3 we saw how individual ethnic consumers are in the foreground of ethnic group formation, being key figures in the process of generating ethnic group identity and intensity through their shared values. It is important to understand that individual consumers are unlikely to be significant in isolation from an ethnic group. For marketers entertaining ethnic marketing objectives, individual ethnic consumers are important as members of the ethnic group with which they identify. Individual ethnic group members, however, must exhibit needs and preferences *mostly* coincidental with those of the ethnic group, as well as similar evaluative criteria before and after consumption. It is this requirement that ensures that the ethnic group is internally homogeneous in consumption behaviour, and that marketers can predict that behaviour. The question is: why do individual minority ethnic group members act in such a predictable way?

Similar others

Experienced marathon runners are likely to be perceived as good sources of information regarding marathon running by most individuals with a desire to undertake that particular sporting activity. They are likely to be perceived as credible sources of information because they have been there, done that. However, if the aspiring marathon runner is also one-legged, information from an experienced, even if much less successful, marathon runner who has a similar disability will be particularly valuable and credible, compared with information sourced from the current Olympic marathon winner. This is because the disabled runner is more likely to have experienced the same type of specific difficulties that await the prospective runner. The Olympic champion lacks the context that brings the candidate and the experienced disabled runner closer together. This is why newly arrived, inexperienced ethnic minority consumers are likely to source consumption information from more experienced similar others (fellow ethnic minority consumers, not necessarily but preferably from the same ethnic group, who are perceived to be knowledgeable about the marketplace),[1] rather than from mainstream consumers.

Similar others (in terms of values, attitudes, etc.) trust, and are more trusted, compared to dissimilar others (Dwyer, Schurr and Oh, 1987). This is because similar others may have experienced the same consumption situation whilst subject to similar handicaps. As a result, faced with the need to manage the transition between complex cultural codes, the new arrival may perceive similar others as more sympathetic towards the handicaps and more likely to have experienced similar needs and preferences, as well as to have achieved successful consumption solutions based on similar evaluative criteria.

Because information from similar others is more credible, minority ethnic group members exchange information and experiences with other members of the same minority group, and group consumer behaviour is a reference for that of the members. Figure 4.1 depicts a two-way exchange of information between ethnic minority consumers and their minority ethnic groups of affiliation.

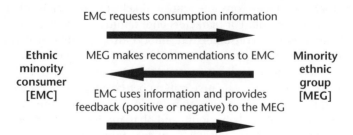

Figure 4.1 How information flows between ethnic minority consumers and minority ethnic groups

Ultimately, a recommendation from similar others is likely to be adopted because it is perceived to be more credible and reduces perceived risk. Adoption results in positive or negative experiences which feed back to the group reinforcing or weakening group preference. This reiterates the conclusion, in Chapter 3, that it is the consistent way in which new arrivals manage the transition from one country to another that perpetuates the minority ethnic group as a separate cultural entity, and explains its relevance for marketing purposes.

4.4 Reasons for aggregating minority ethnic groups

The gathering and interaction of several cultures, embodied in a variety of ethnic groups, within a national territory – or cultural diversity – has been recognized and extensively acknowledged in many countries, including Australia, Canada, France, Germany, Great Britain, India, Korea, Malaysia, New Zealand, Portugal, Romania, Russia, South Africa, Spain and the United States (Solomon, 1996; Leibold and Hugo-Burrows, 1997; Roberts and Hart, 1997; Pires and Stanton, 1998; Laroche *et al.*, 2003). Some marketers, however, appear to distinguish between domestic and international cross-cultural marketing by aggregating distinct ethnic groups in the first case and defending cultural uniqueness in the second. For example, Stanton, Miller and Layton (1994) argue that, domestically, attention tends to focus on some aggregate of resident ethnic communities, 'a large market made up of many smaller segments' (p. 126), often grounded on language similarity. In contrast, Wang (1997) argues that international marketers are challenged by cross-national differences to be culture-sensitive. It is, therefore, not surprising that ethnic marketing (that is, marketing to individual ethnic groups) within many of those countries is endorsed in principle although, in practice, marketers' attention tends to focus on aggregates of resident ethnic communities, often grounded on language similarity.

To illustrate, the development of new opportunities to deliver specialized products to racial and ethnic groups (such as African–Americans, Latinos and Asian–Americans) has been acknowledged for the United States (Solomon, 1996; Roberts and Hart, 1997). While 'Latinos' is, allegedly, a title preferred to 'Hispanics' by some Americans of Spanish-speaking background (Rossman, 1994, p. 46), 'Hispanics' is a term defined by the US Department of Commerce to include all people of Spanish ancestry, regardless of country of origin (Montgomery, 1994). This aggregates persons originating from at least 14 countries (Sukhdial *et al.*, 1993; Nicholls, Roslow and Dublish, 1997), as shown in Table 4.1. It is apparent that there are statistically significant differences among Hispanic subgroups that do not support the lumping of Hispanics together into a single minority group (Deshpande, Hoyer and Donthu, 1986; Menendez and Yow, 1989; Laskey and Seaton, 1990). Hence, 'unavoidable distinctions need to be made between different cultural groups,

Table 4.1 The Hispanic group in the United States

Hispanic demographics

The 2000 Census measured the population of the United States at 281.4 million, 11 per cent of whom (approximately 31 million) were foreign born. Of the foreign born almost 17 million (52 per cent) were of Hispanic origin [US Department of Commerce, *Census 2000, Brief: The Foreign-Born Population: 2000*, US Census Bureau, issued December 2003].

Overall the Hispanic community in the United States was estimated at 42.6 million people as of 2002, double its size in 1990. It is expected to grow by more than 1.7 million a year, or 5000 people a day. [According to reports by the Hispanic Association on Corporate Responsibility (HACR), *2002 Hispanics Today*, http://www.hacr.org/statistics.html and US Census Bureau, *Current Population Survey*, March 2002, Ethnic and Hispanic Statistics Branch, Population Division.]

While the entire population is classified as 'Hispanic', there are major ethnic subdivisions within the population. Hispanics comprise people originating in at least 17 countries, namely Mexico (approximately 60 per cent of the population), Puerto Rico, Cuba and Dominican Republic, including Spaniards (those reported as 'Spanish'), Central America (Costa Rica, Panama, Honduras, Nicaragua, Guatemala, El Salvador and other) and South America (Chile, Argentina, Peru, Ecuador, Colombia, Uruguay and other).

Hispanics are the largest and youngest minority group in the United States. At $630 billion (in 2002), the community's purchasing power represents the ninth largest economy of the world.

held together by a common language, religion and customs' (McCaughey, 1991, p. 9).

Clearly, rather than ethnic groups, African–Americans, Latinos or Hispanics and Asian–Americans are aggregations of different ethnic groups, so that the sense of the use of the 'ethnic' label in this context is elusive. The same argument applies in Australia and Canada, for example, to aggregations of ethnic groups apparently based on continent of origin, as in the case of the Asian community. In Australia, this community includes people originating from countries such as Vietnam, China, the Philippines, Malaysia, Hong Kong, Indonesia, Korea, Japan, Singapore and, in each case, their Australian-born descendants. In Canada, the cultural diversity of the Chinese was emphasized by Wong (1997), noting the large number of subgroups. Arguably, even if all the ethnic groups in mainland China were lumped together, there would still be the Hong Kong Chinese, the Taiwanese, the Southeast Asian Overseas Chinese, and many others, including 'a large representation of South African-born Chinese living in Vancouver' (p. 24).

The usefulness of focusing on narrowly defined minority ethnic groups may be disputed, in a general sense, along the lines of anti-segmentation arguments (as discussed in Chapter 2). After all, it is apparent that the composition of a minority ethnic group is likely to be similar to that of the mainstream population. Hence, there will be males and females, young or old, more or less educated, with larger or smaller disposable incomes, possibly with variable religious convictions. This implication that narrowly defined minority ethnic groups are not homogeneous in themselves may be perceived as good enough a reason to render ethnic group segmentation ineffective. However, there is no indication that this internal heterogeneity leads to any necessary similarity relative to consumers with distinct ethnicities identified by the same indicators. That is, gender, age, education, wealth and religion have not been shown to act as homogenizing factors across ethnic groups. In fact, it is argued that ethnicity conditions consumer behaviour and 'needs to be considered before demographic criteria, such as age or income, because it helps to establish whether marketers can use such demographics across ethnic boundaries' (Pires and Stanton, 1998).

Marketers' reliance on aggregates of ethnic groups, as opposed to narrowly defined minority ethnic groups, can be variously explained based on perceptions of:

- group smallness;
- increased marketing costs;
- an alleged shift from segmentation based on differences between ethnic groups to the formation of customer communities based on consumer similarities;
- group instability;
- social retaliation;
- homogeneous behaviour dictated by perceived advantage.

Each of these is discussed below in some detail.

Group smallness

Perceptions that many minority ethnic groups are too small to be considered for targeting purposes may result, for example, from their omission in the official statistics of a country's population. Since minority ethnic groups with the larger memberships are reported, omission is taken to indicate excessive smallness or lack of importance of the omitted minority ethnic groups, as well as increased difficulty in learning about these groups' specifics for profiling purposes. Since each of these groups is presumed to be too small to be targeted on its own, focusing on commonalities (such as language similarity) for their aggregation may result in perceived group substantiality and consequent targeting.

Increased marketing costs

An alternative explanation posits that, in some cases, the appeal of treating each individual minority ethnic group as a segmentable market separate from the macro market raises the spectre of higher marketing costs in departing down the micro-marketing road (Cui and Choudhury, 1998). While this is a possibility, one should bear in mind that ethnic marketing recommends targeting of consumers through their ethnic group of affiliation. Marketing costs will be relatively low because group mechanisms mean that one value proposition will suffice, provided it relies on the right attributes. Because there will be more hits and fewer misses, the proposition is likely to be more successful in attracting individual consumers, with a more effective use of resources. Ultimately, assessment of costs may be better considered in relation to the expected results of the marketing investment.[2]

Customer communities

Another argument for group aggregation is that emphasis has shifted from segmentation based on differences between ethnic groups to the formation of customer communities based on similarities.[3] Accordingly, any differences between consumer groups on ethnicity grounds are allegedly outweighed by the similarities (Minor, 1992). Although it was not possible to find reliable sources that fully articulate this view, the subjacent philosophy may find its routes in three different perspectives or approaches:

- development of 'personas';
- critical mass marketing approach;
- knowledge management.

Each is elaborated below.

Development of personas

Following Brechin (2002), 'personas' are user models or profiles made out of fictional, representative user archetypes based on the characterization of behaviours, attitudes and goals of widely different demographic groups who may have shared commonalities regarding a given product for which a market definition is sought. Rather than aimed at some sort of 'average' consumer, a product is subsequently designed based on one or a small set of personas, sufficient to illustrate key goals and market behaviour patterns. There is no necessary direct correlation between personas and market segments. Indeed, one possible implication from using personas together with market segmentation is that products may be developed to appeal to various segments.

While it is not difficult to understand why this perspective must appeal to businesses, it is apparent that too many liberties are being taken with the use of the segment concept. Effective segments need to be unique and internally homogeneous, while heterogenous relative to all other segments. Homogeneity needs to be assessed relative to the responses to marketing stimulus, hence segments need to be considered in the context of a particular marketing mix (of which a product is an element). If a product appeals in the same way to 'two segments', then there is only one segment.

A less controversial perspective may be to consider that a product may appeal to different segments as long as distinct value propositions are designed to acknowledge the determinant evaluation criteria for each segment. Or, perhaps, as may be the case of current practices for aggregating ethnic groups, consumer groups identified by some apparently reliable indicator (such as language, surnames typical of a certain ethnic group, race, neighbourhood) are assessed by their ability to yield some critical mass of outcomes. Here, the key is not to define what determines each homogeneous segment, but rather to develop a value proposition that encapsulates individual conditions. Resources may be abused but, as long as marketing costs are controlled (namely against budget), the number of misses becomes much less important than achieving the required critical number of hits that allow achieving the desired objectives. While ethnic marketing proposes that marketing to ethnic minority consumers must be through their ethnic group of affiliation, the use of personas or ethnic group aggregates does not infer any group influence on individuals' consumption decisions.

Critical mass marketing approach

The critical mass marketing approach resembles the argument for 'personas' just discussed in that it considers that a given product has wide (not necessarily universal) appeal, such that the objective is to achieve a critical number of sales. Moreover, there may be a presumption that product appeal is strong enough to rule out any need for a focused marketing investment, hence avoiding the spectrum of high marketing costs referred to by Cui and Choudhury (1998).

Applied to minority ethnic groups, the view may be that it is the exclusion from the mainstream that matters, rather than the uniqueness of each consumer group. Any impact of the ethnic group on the minority ethnic consumer is overlooked. Attention is given to what is the same across ethnic groups (language similarity as a common example), such that non-mainstream ethnicity becomes a characteristic of the resulting group (an output) rather than a driver of group formation. It may not be a matter of marketers ignoring that ethnic differences influence individual consumption behaviour. Rather, aggregation may be a consequence of either the difficulty in identifying, accessing and assessing narrowly defined ethnicity-based consumer groups or a simple preconception that individual ethnic groups are not large enough to justify their targeting.

Knowledge management perspective

The knowledge management perspective is a relatively recent addition to the debate concerning the role of culture (loosely used interchangeably with ethnicity) as a possible deterrent of globalization. As explained by Holden,

> (in the) traditional writing on culture and management in the context of international business . . . culture is about fundamental differences, which hang like swords of Damocles over international companies, poised to undermine their negotiations and pervert their strategies.
>
> (2002, pp. xiii–xiv)

However, he argues,

> the evidence . . . suggests overwhelmingly that cross-cultural impacts on managers and organisations cannot be anticipated or meaningfully analysed solely by the application of cultural categories such as values, language differences, or Hofstedian mental programmes without an appreciation of the peculiarities – even the idiosyncrasies – of contextual embedding.
>
> (2002, p. 14)

That is, important cultural differences do exist across ethnic groups that explain why demand should not be treated as global, hence questioning global supply strategies. However, any ethnic group uniqueness (as commonly attributed for example to the Pakistani in the UK, the Sikh in New Zealand, the Thai in Australia, the Walloon in Belgium, the Arab in Spain, the Timorese in Portugal, the African in France or the Taiwanese in Hong Kong) cannot be presumed to reflect some stereotyped ideology of cultural difference and needs to be appraised in the context where it realizes itself. Hence, it is not about focusing on the differences.

The knowledge management perspective is interpreted here as having its focus on the development and implementation of solutions for the economic negotiation of potential limitations derived from ethnic differences in the context of the various environments where they impact. Rather than constrained by unique consumer needs, preferences and evaluative criteria, businesses decide on the relevance of those factors subject to their own capabilities and competencies, as well as to their internal and external environments. Minority ethnic group aggregation may be justifiable on these contextual grounds, recognizing that group effects do not operate.

Refocusing the discussion of the various explanations for marketers' reliance on aggregates of ethnic groups as opposed to narrowly defined minority ethnic groups, three possible explanations have been addressed: group smallness, increased marketing costs, and the formation of customer communities based on consumer similarities. Attention is now given to concerns regarding group instability and potential social retaliation.

Group instability

While minority ethnic groups have persisted in host countries, their reported sizes may fluctuate. For example, the Australian Bureau of Statistics (ABS) reports a significant change in the source countries of new settler arrivals in Australia since the mid-1990s compared to the late 1960s.

Table 4.2 reports the top six countries contributing new settlers in each of the five-year periods ending in 1970, 1980, 1990 and 2000. Figures for each country refer to the number of arrivals, the country's percentage contribution from total arrivals in the period, and the percentage change relative to the periods preceding and following. As reported, in the five years to June 1970 almost half (46 per cent) of settler arrivals (375 100) were born in the UK and Ireland. These two countries contributed only 12 per cent of settlers (48 000) in the period to June 2000, in a clear loss of importance as feeder countries.

Even more interesting, in the present context, is the case of Italy and Greece. In 2000 these countries were still highly ranked (respectively third largest and seventh largest) as main countries of birth of the Australian population. But the number of residents born in Italy has fallen consistently from 288 000 in 1971 to 241 700 in 2000. In the case of Greece the loss has been from 159 000 in 1971 to 141 200 in 2000. While the numbers are still quite large (by Australian standards), to the extent that the birthplace numbers can be used as an indicator of ethnic group substantiality, these groups have declined in both relative and absolute importance.

Overall, ethnic groups are dynamic entities that depend on many uncontrollable environmental factors. The state of the economy in the home and host countries is likely to influence population flows. Unstable economic conditions cause ethnic groups to be unstable (Svendsen, 1997). Because marketing programmes take time to achieve results, group instability may increase the perceived risk of targeting individual ethnic groups. Aggregation increases perceived substantiality, through larger numbers, and cushions the impact of instability in narrowly defined consumer groups.

Social retaliation

Historically, ethnic groups have been singled out on racial issues from time to time. As argued by Pollock *et al.* (1993) in the context of Canada, 'we are still at the stage where the very existence of a Chinese mall raises a red flag in some people's minds' (p. 17). As marketing to ethnic groups is likely to be conspicuous to the mainstream population, there is a risk of negative response or retaliation (Chan, 1995). Aggregation and marketing across groups may blur boundaries and reduce the visibility of a single ethnic group.

Table 4.2 Country of birth of settler arrivals in Australia

Country of Birth	5-year period ending . . .	Number of arrivals '000	Percentage of all arrivals over the period [%]	Change in percentage of settlers relative to	
				Previous period	Next period
UK + Ireland	1970	375.1	46.2		−77%
Yugoslavia		73.7	9.2		Not top 6
Italy		61.9	7.7		Not top 6
Greece		53.1	6.6		Not top 6
New Zealand		22.8	2.8		+75%
Germany		19.0	2.4		Not top 6
All other		198.5	25.1		−24%
All countries		804.1	100.0		−57%
UK	1980	86.2	25.0	−77%	+24%
New Zealand		39.8	11.6	+75%	+107%
Vietnam		30.6	8.9	New to top 6	+27%
Lebanon		18.4	5.3	New to top 6	Not top 6
South Africa		10.2	3.0	New to top 6	Not top 6
Malaysia		8.4	2.4	New to top 6	+217%
All other		151.1	43.8	−24%	+97%
All countries		344.7	100.0	−57%	+79%
UK	1990	107.0	17.4	+24%	−55%
New Zealand		82.5	13.4	+107%	−2.3%
Vietnam		38.9	6.3	+27%	Not top 6
Philippines		36.3	5.9	New to top 6	Not top 6
Hong Kong		27.5	4.5	New to top 6	Not top 6
Malaysia		26.6	4.3	+217%	Not top 6
All other		297.3	48.2	+97%	−30%
All countries		616.1	100.0	+79%	−29%
New Zealand	2000	80.6	18.4	−2.3%	
UK		48.1	11.0	−55%	
China		36.3	8.3	New to top 6	
Former Yugoslavia		28.3	6.5	New to top 6	
South Africa		21.4	4.9	New to top 6	
India		16.4	3.7	New to top 6	
All other		207.5	47.2	−30%	
All countries		438.6	100.0	−29%	

Sources: Adapted from ABS data available on request, Overseas Arrivals and Departures Collection; Department of Immigration and Multicultural Affairs, 'Australian immigration – consolidated statistics', in *Year Book Australia 2003*, Population International Migration, Table 5.29.

Homogeneous behaviour dictated by perceived advantage

Particularly in the USA, marketers often dismiss the need for ethnicity-based segmentation and targeting, as abundantly demonstrated in the continued and growing infatuation with the Hispanics. Santamaria (2003) recognizes that the term 'Hispanic' defies definition, and includes 'roughly two-dozen immigrant nationalities, a variety of blood-lines, . . . and regional dialects that are sometimes incomprehensible to native Spanish speakers from other countries'. He strongly argues that 'Hispanic commonality runs thinner than it appears in America', quoting the chief operations officer of Goya Foods, the Latin gourmet conglomerate, that 'the commonality is that all these people speak Spanish, read Spanish print media, and watch the same TV'. Santamaria then argues that as divided as Hispanic identity is on paper, in marketing, the single strand of language is enough for success, quoting Notre Dame professor Allert Brwon-Gort: 'In the American political system there is strength in numbers . . . and since we [Hispanics] are going to get lumped together anyway, we use this for advantage.' Santamaria argues that 'many Hispanics have accepted a simplified stereotype of themselves'.

Summary of aggregation explanations

The basic question of if and when to aggregate ethnic groups to create a larger segment is conceptually challenging. Ethnic marketing plants its roots in the homogeneity of consumer groups defined by a common ethnicity – that is, by the condition that consumers belong to a particular ethnic group, and, as such, behave similarly in response to marketing stimulus directed to the group. Most importantly, the greatest value of ethnic marketing is that this behaviour can be predicted. This is because there are group mechanisms that not only sustain the groups' continued existence in the host country with a distinct and dominant ethnicity, but also regulate how affiliated consumers consistently behave socially and as consumers.

Aggregation of ethnic consumer groups for marketing purposes may be both sensible and justifiable in some specific context, but there are neither group mechanisms nor benefits derived from group synergies in operation. Aggregation cannot result in an ethnic group and, strictly speaking, it is outside the realm of ethnic marketing. This will be, for example, the case of marketing strategies focusing on Asian-(American, Australian, British, etc.), Hispanics or Latinos, Afro-Americans, Blacks, Indo-Americans, or Francophones, unless they can be grouped according to their behaviour as ethnic group members.

4.5 A framework for assessing aggregates of ethnic groups

Market segmentation based on ethnicity may be carried too far or not far enough because of a failure to ascertain correctly the differences and overlaps among groups. This is because the use of ethnicity for market segmentation requires ethnic-group boundaries to be determined before any consideration about their marketing value can be made.

The emic-etic distinction

An aggregation of ethnic groups involves the amalgamation of distinct ethnicities. The emic-etic distinction maintains that, in cross-cultural research, the findings within a specific ethnic group (the emic context) may not be valid in the etic context of aggregates of ethnic groups (Olmedo, 1979). Therefore, it is important to establish whether the values, attitudes and behaviours that apply for individual ethnic groups also hold at the aggregated level.

In terms of ethnicity, individual ethnic groups are relevant for marketing because they can be effectively distinguished by distinct sets of intensities of values and norms that influence needs, preferences and evaluative criteria, hence conditioning group consumer behaviour. Since the frame of reference that guides ethnic group consumption patterns varies with their values, each ethnic group may be expected to differ significantly from other groups, although some ethnic groups may be more acculturated (with the host group or with other minority ethnic groups) than others. An emic analytical approach to ethnic marketing is therefore required because of its focus on either individual ethnic groups or the comparisons required between ethnic groups, prior to amalgamation. Conversely, an etic analytical approach that commences from an *unqualified* or not previously researched aggregate of ethnic groups is highly questionable.[4]

The framework

Recall the rationale used in Chapter 3 for generating an ethnic group's identity/intensity through shared values (Figure 3.2) and identifying shared values across ethnic groups (Figure 3.3). Analysis revealed that the frame of reference that guides minority ethnic group consumption patterns reflects the intensity of shared values of the group's affiliates. That is, the cultural values and norms endorsed at the aggregate level of the ethnic group may not match exactly the individual values and norms of group members, but the overlap is likely to be extensive.

Individually, the greater the match with a group's values and attitudes (its distinctive needs, preferences and evaluative criteria before and after consumption) the greater the individual's acculturation to the group. Hence, individual minority consumers can be expected to have variable degrees of association (to be more or less acculturated) with different ethnic groups. This also implies that ethnic groups are not impermeable closed boxes in constant collision with other ethnic groups. There must be some degree of interpenetration, at least between those ethnic groups that share individual minority consumers.

Group strength reflects the intensity of collective shared values and each ethnic group may be expected to differ significantly from other groups,

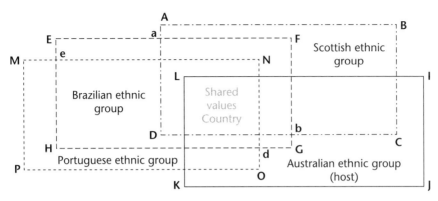

Explanation:
LIJK: host country mainstream (Australian) group
ABCD: Scottish ethnic group
EFGH: Brazilian ethnic group
MNOP: Portuguese ethnic group
All four groups have in common the 'shared values country'.
The Brazilian and Scottish groups have in common **aFbD**.
The Portuguese and Brazilian groups have in common **eNdH** (> **aFbD**).

Figure 4.2   Overlap of ethnic groups in a country

although some ethnic groups are more different than others. This was shown using Figure 3.3 as a possible scenario for four separate ethnic groups: three minority ethnic groups and the mainstream group. The intensities of the values of each separate ethnic group were mostly distinct from those of other groups although the area of overlap was variable in each case. For example, the overlap between group 'A' and group 'B' was much larger than that between group 'A' and group 'C', and so was the overlap with the host ethnic group. Figure 4.2 further illustrates the differences in overlap, and aggregation possibilities, that may occur between different ethnic groups.

Assume the Portuguese are recent arrivals to the host country, Brazilians long established. From social learning theory it is easier, and possibly also more pleasurable, for Portuguese consumers to acculturate to the Brazilian ethnic group. Eventually, EFGH = MNOP, in which case aggregation for seg-mentation purposes is a logical outcome. It is also likely that the Brazilian group may acculturate towards the Portuguese group, in which case EFGH moves to the left, ensuring greater overlap with MNOP. Again aggregation is supported, but with stronger force because there is now less in common between the pair of Brazilian and Portuguese consumers relative to the host and Scottish pair.

The 'melting pot' argument is that all four groups will converge to one over time but not coinciding with any one group. The 'assimilation' argument is that the Scottish, Brazilian and Portuguese groups will eventually overlap at

LIJK. The greater the overlap between ethnic groups, the lower the risk associated with aggregation of these groups. The same ethnicity-based marketing mix is likely to achieve very similar responses from consumers in the Brazilian and Portuguese groups. This should strengthen the need for ethnicity-based segmentation, whilst supporting selective aggregation of very similar ethnic groups.

It is also important that marketers adopt some pragmatic compromise that ensures marketing research of ethnic groups is practical. Indeed, 'one of the most difficult tasks for . . . marketers is assessing the cultural influences that affect their operations. In the actual marketplace there are always several factors working simultaneously, and it is extremely difficult to isolate any one factor' (Jeannet and Hennessey, 1995, p. 71). These factors include consumer demographics such as age, gender and income, as well as complexities associated with race and ethnicity. The difficulty is in the identification of behaviour explained by demographics and behaviour explained by ethnicity or culture. Casual observation reveals many situations where ethnic groups are aggregated based on single ethnic identification indicators, such as language, language spoken at home, country of birth, surname or geographical location, perhaps because this is a practical and convenient criterion.

4.6 Using single ethnic identification indicators for aggregating ethnic groups

Reliance on single ethnic identification indicators has been subject to criticism (Hui, Kim and Laroche, 1990). Table 4.3 demonstrates ambiguity in identifying ethnic groups by a single variable such as language or country of birth.

Table 4.3 Australian population by country of birth and language spoken at home (aged 5 and over), selected countries, 1996

Country of birth	Persons	Language spoken at home	Persons 5 yrs +	Change in persons
Italy	238 246	Italian	367 290	+129 044
Vietnam	151 053	Vietnamese	134 011	−17 042
Greece	126 520	Greek	259 019	+132 499
Germany	110 331	German	96 651	−13 680
Netherlands	87 998	Dutch	40 224	−47 774
Poland	65 113	Polish	61 023	−4 090
Malta	50 879	Maltese	44 674	−6 205
Indonesia	44 175	Indonesian	25 925	−18 250
Hungary	25 263	Hungarian	25 846	+583
Serbia	9 016	Serbian	35 392	+26 376

Source: ABS (1998).

The table draws on the results of the 1996 Australian Census to show distinct differences between the number of foreign-born persons and those speaking the dominant language of the country of birth. No consistent relationship exists across countries. Those speaking the parent language may be either more or fewer than the birthplace number, suggesting that neither birthplace nor language alone are useful indicators of ethnicity, and implying that acculturation may proceed at a different pace across ethnic groups. Together with the acknowledgment of minority indigenous cultures with their own languages, it is apparent that culture and language are not necessarily linked to a country of birth (Aislabie, Lee and Stanton, 1994, p. 18).

Clearly, reliance on a single ethnic identification indicator to determine consumer ethnicity – the condition of belonging to a particular ethnic group – is a questionable segmentation practice (Hui *et al.*, 1990). Hence, it is questionable whether ethnic group aggregations based on single demographic indicators can provide reliable consumer groups with predictable behaviour that marketers can use. Accordingly, there is a shift in marketing thought toward the use of multiple indicators, concentrating on cultural characteristics such as language, religion, family structures or community traditions and behaviour (Jupp, 1981; Hui *et al.*, 1990). Ultimately, pragmatism must be used with some discretion and the consequences clearly understood.

4.7 Chapter summary

Cultural diversity involves more than the sharing of a country by different ethnic groups with different cultures. Ethnicity and culture are characteristics of individual ethnic groups, that may change over time through acculturation, so ethnicity may weaken the case for the aggregation of ethnic groups for marketing segmentation purposes while acculturation may strengthen it (Pires, 1999).

Casual observation suggests that it may be acceptable to aggregate cultural or ethnic groups for some specific purposes. The question is 'what purposes?' and 'which groups?' The key issue is that, as noted earlier, some ethnic groups have more in common than others, for example, Brazilians and Portuguese groups in Australia. Hence, the greater the coincidence of values between ethnic groups, the lower the risk associated with ethnic group aggregation. From a different perspective, the greater the distance between the host ethnic group and other ethnic groups the greater the need for ethnic segmentation. This supports the view that, at least for discrete marketing purposes (like achieving critical mass and economies of scale), it may prove advantageous for marketers to aggregate some ethnic groups.

The final thought for marketers considering ethnic marketing must be that, to serve ethnic consumers, marketers must become familiar with their specific behaviours, attitudes, habits and preferences. As noted by Kaufman, when researching ethnic groups it is important to determine if ethnic subgroups from different foreign markets can be aggregated for the purposes of analysis . . . Subcultural groups have been found to demonstrate similar product preferences; as a result, retailers serve several ethnic groups in one enterprise.

(Kaufman, 1991, pp. 44–5)

Notes

1. This may be particularly so in relation to services and service providers. Information and recommendation (verbal or behavioural) from similar others may be used by newly arrived, inexperienced ethnic minority consumers to select their first providers in the new market, as well as to establish criteria for assessing service quality and provider credibility This is extensively discussed in Chapter 9, which deals with the marketing of services.
2. This matter is tied with misconceptions regarding group substantiality introduced in Chapter 2 and further discussed in Chapter 8, concerned with the calculation of the value of an ethnic group for marketing.
3. Allegedly, the assumption that a certain ethnic group corresponds to a certain set of needs may be over-simplistic and creates prejudice. A good process of identifying customer communities sees ethnicity as an output rather than an input. It is an attribute that will, together with others, define the customer community. A reviewer of the book proposal expressed these views, which were given extensive attention during the preparation of this book. Since the reviews were anonymous it is not possible to acknowledge the source. Our gratitude to the author is hereby expressed.
4. See Laroche, Kim and Clarke, 1997, for other references supporting group differentiation.

References

Australian Bureau of Statistics (ABS) (1998) *1996 Census of Population and Housing, Ethnicity Thematic Profile Service,* http://www.abs.gov.au/Websitedbs/D3310108.NSF? OpenDatabase (accessed 15 October 2003), Canberra, ABS.

Aislabie, C., Lee, J. and Stanton, J. P. (1994) *Australian Cultural Diversity and Export Growth,* Canberra: AGPS.

Brechin, E. (2002) 'Reconciling market segments and personas', *Cooper: Interaction Design,* Newsletter February–March, http://www.cooper.com (accessed 20 December 2003).

Chan, A. (1995) 'Multicultural marketing in Australia', in K. Grant and I. Walker (eds) *Proceedings,* World Marketing Congress, VII(I), Monash University, 2.71–2.76.

Cui, G. and Choudhury, P. (1998) 'Effective strategies for ethnic segmentation and marketing', in J. Chebat and A. Oumlil (eds) *Proceedings,* Multicultural Marketing Conference, Montreal, Canada, September, pp. 354–61.

Deshpande, R., Hoyer, W. and Donthu, N. (1986) 'The intensity of ethnic affiliation: a study of the sociology of Hispanic consumption', *Journal of Consumer Research,* 13: 214–20.

Dwyer, F., Schurr, P. and Oh, S. (1987) 'Developing buyer–seller relationships', *Journal of Marketing,* 51(2): 11–27.

Holden, N. (2002) *Cross-Cultural Management: A Knowledge Management Perspective,* London: Prentice-Hall.

Hui, M., Joy, A., Kim, M. and Laroche, M. (1990) 'Differences in lifestyles among four major subcultures in a bi-cultural environment', in *Proceedings*, 3rd Symposium on Cross-Cultural Consumer and Business Studies, University of Hawaii, December, pp. 139–50.

Jeannet, J. and Hennessey, H. (1995) *Global Marketing Strategies*, 3rd edn., Boston: Houghton Mifflin Company.

Jupp, J. (1991) 'One among many', in Goodman *et al.*, *Multicultural Australia: The Challenges of Change*, Melbourne: University of Melbourne.

Kaufman, C. (1991) 'Coupon use in ethnic markets: implications from a retail perspective', *Journal of Consumer Marketing*, 8(1): 41–51.

Laroche, M., Kim, C. and Clarke, M. (1997) 'The effects of ethnicity factors on consumer deal interests: an empirical study of French–English–Canadians', *Journal of Marketing Theory and Practice*, 5(1): 100–11.

Laroche, M., Papadopoulos, N., Heslop, L. and Bergeron, J. (2003) 'Effects of subcultural differences on country and product evaluations', *Journal of Consumer Behaviour*, 2(3): 232–48.

Laskey, H. and Seaton, F. (1990) 'The measurement of cultural and subcultural values', in *Proceedings*, 3rd Symposium on Cross-Cultural Consumer and Business Studies, University of Hawaii, December, pp. 313–24.

Leibold, M. and Hugo-Burrows, R. (1997) 'Broad marketing implications of recent trends in the multicultural South African market environment', *Journal of Marketing Theory and Practice*, 5(1): 67–76.

McCaughey, D. (1991) 'Australia is home', in Goodman *et al.*, *Multicultural Australia: The Challenges of Change*, Melbourne: University of Melbourne.

Menendez, T. and Yow, J. (1989) 'The Hispanic market: an overview of the major markets', *Marketing Research*, 1 (June): 11–15.

Minor, M. (1992) 'Comparing the Hispanic and non-Hispanic markets: how different are they?', *Journal of Services Marketing*, 6(2): 29–32.

Montgomery, P. (1994) *The Hispanic Population of the United States: March 1993*, US Bureau of the Census, Current Population Reports, Series P20-475, Washington, DC: US GPO.

Nichols, J., Roslow, S. and Dublish, S. (1997) 'Hispanic and non-Hispanic mall shoppers: segmentation by situational variables and purchase behaviours', *Journal of Segmentation in Marketing*, 1(1): 57–73.

Olmedo, E. (1979) 'Acculturation: a psychometric perspective', *American Psychologist*, 34: 1061–70.

Pires, G. D. (1999) 'Domestic cross-cultural marketing in Australia: a critique of the segmentation rationale', *Journal of Marketing Theory and Practice*, 7(4): 33–44.

Pires, G. D. and Stanton, J. P. (1998) 'The marketing relevance of cultural diversity: a framework for understanding ethnicity and acculturation', in J. Chebat and A. Oumlil (eds) *Proceedings, Multicultural Marketing Conference*, Montreal, September, pp. 279–92.

Pollock, J., Chiasson, G., Seto, M. and Bell, D. (1993) 'Special report on ethnic marketing', *Marketing*, 98 (19 July): 13–9.

Roberts, S. and Hart, H. (1997) 'A comparison of cultural value orientations as reflected by advertisements directed at the general US market, the US Hispanic market, and the Mexican market', *Journal of Marketing Theory and Practice*, Winter: 91–9.

Rossman, M. (1994) *Multicultural Marketing: Selling to a Diverse America*, New York: American Management Association.

Santamaria, N. C. (2003) 'Hispanic markets and marketing Hispanics', *Washington Times*, United Press International, 25 November. Accessed 3 June 2004, http://www.washtimes.com/upi-breaking/20031119-111317-5210r.htm

Solomon, M. (1996) *Consumer Behavior*, New Jersey, NJ: Prentice-Hall.

Stanton, J. P. and Pires, G. D. (1999) 'The substantiality test: meaning and application in market segmentation', *Journal of Segmentation in Marketing*, 3(2): 105–15.

Stanton, W., Miller, K. and Layton, R. (1994) *Fundamentals of Marketing*. 3rd Australian edn., Sydney: McGraw-Hill.

Sukhdial, A., Chakraborty, G., Arias-Bolzmann, L. and Amyx, D. (1993) 'Differences in values between Hispanic and Anglo-American consumers: what we know and what we need to know', in *Proceedings*, Fourth Symposium on Cross-Cultural Consumer and Business Studies, 15–18 Dec., Hawaii, pp. 33–7.

Svendsen, A. (1997) 'Building relationships with microcommunities', *Marketing News*, 9 Jun: 13.

Wang, C. (1997) 'Bases for international market segmentation', *Journal of Segmentation in Marketing*, 1(1): 5–21.

Wong, K. (1997) 'The symbolic power of security', *Marketing*, 102 (8 September): 24.

Stake your claim in the multicultural market

Rick Blume*

You know the numbers in the multicultural markets: 39 million Hispanics, 37 million African–Americans and 12 million Asian–Americans. The Census Bureau has documented these three groups as the fastest growing in the country, and soon they will make up close to 50 per cent of America's population – half of that of Hispanic descent. By 2007, with the general market's buying power projected to be in excess of $7 trillion, the multicultural market's buying power will be more than $2 trillion; Hispanics' spending power will rise to $927 billion, African–Americans' to $645 billion and Asian–Americans' to $454 billion.

It's no surprise that marketers are testing the waters of multicultural marketing. But what is a surprise is why hasn't everyone? In my opinion, three things are crystal clear:

- Marketers don't understand the overwhelming potential.
- Marketers fail to understand the urgency of establishing a dominant brand.
- Marketers have misconceptions about ethnic cultures.

C2.1 Cultural misconceptions

You would think marketers would find it very difficult to ignore the numbers when more than 30 per cent of the population currently is made up of these three ethnic markets. Especially the Hispanic and Asian–American sectors, where more than 50 per cent of their growth comes from immigration, ensuring a continuous fresh audience and creating an increased need for products and services.

---

* *Target Marketing*, October 2003, 26(10): 181

For those who don't know, Hispanics are very brand loyal. Despite the myth that Hispanics are a poor market, the reality is that education and income levels are rising rapidly with 14 per cent of Hispanics aged 18 to 34 earning annual incomes of more than $50,000. The penetration of credit cards is more than 50 per cent in the Hispanic sector, and increasing. The same holds true for African–Americans, where a record-high 17 per cent of adults ages 25 and older earn a bachelor's degree. And Asian–Americans are already at the top of the scale in income and education. The result: Hispanics, African–Americans and Asian–Americans are enjoying greater discretionary income than ever before.

Every marketer's ultimate goal is to dominate its market. Those marketers who establish this dominance in ethnic markets early on will be the winners. Brand recognition and loyalty score very high in these markets. Ethnic consumers appreciate being marketed to in their language of choice, or with culturally relevant offers in a meaningful way. Response rates are much higher than what companies typically receive in the overall marketplace. Many savvy direct marketers, such as Rodale Inc., Columbia House, BMG, The Reader's Digest Association, Covenant House, Salesian Missions and other Catholic fundraisers have known this for quite some time.

C2.2 Direct mail is welcome

One of the best ways to reach multicultural markets is through direct mail. These ethnic groups love to receive direct mail, especially Hispanic and Asian–American immigrants, because they receive so little marketing in their native language. And they will continue to prefer their native language long after they've learned English and assimilated in other ways. To these two groups, direct mail is typically new and exciting . . . something they didn't receive in their countries of origin to the same degree most Americans do in the United States.

Another reason direct mail is so successful with ethnic markets is because shopping at home is less intimidating than dealing with pushy sales people; or not receiving respect because of nationality, race or colour; or not being able to communicate effectively because of a language barrier.

Maybe the best reason direct mail works with first-generation ethnic markets is because the buying process is usually a family decision, and it's easiest to make such decisions when the prospect's family is all around the dining room table reading a mail piece.

C2.3 The ethnic list market is growing

Contrary to some popular beliefs, there are many multicultural lists available, both postal and e-mail, and their number is growing. While the count is considerably less than that of the general market (more than 25 000 general lists compared to fewer than 1000 ethnic lists), some of the biggest and well-known companies rent their ethnic names. Some of these lists on the market now (in addition to lists offered by the savvy direct marketers mentioned earlier) are from Editorial Televisa magazines, Family Digest magazine, Univision, Terra.com, Conde Nast/IPG magazines, Radio Unica, Bookspan's Mosaico, Midnight Velvet catalog and Essence magazine.

Some principles to keep in mind when renting ethnic lists:

■ Do your research. Rent lists that have been generated from responses of individuals of the particular ethnicity you are looking to reach. This may sound obvious, but there are many lists that make claims of being ethnic, but are not what they appear to be.

■ In the Hispanic market, use Spanish-language generated lists when mailing in Spanish, and use English-language surname lists when mailing in English. Both types seem to work for bilingual mailings. However, the greatest responses are achieved with Spanish-language lists.

■ In the multicultural market, TV-generated lists work well, albeit not as well as lists generated by direct mail.

■ Review your results geographically, as you may find differences in response rates due, in part, to where different nationalities have settled.

■ Proceed with a plan.

Now is the time to act, but more important, to act wisely. Do not take these markets for granted; there are many nuances. Ask specialists to help you develop ethnic marketing strategies, culturally relevant offers, and in-language copy and creative. Most of all, use a list specialist who has a thorough understanding of the ethnic markets, all the available lists/databases, and the differences between them. I don't have to tell you how important list selection is to the results of your mailing.

Direct marketers who are already marketing to one or more of these ethnic groups understand the need to get out there first. For those of you who are not, this is the time to start planting your seeds so you can reap the benefits in the near future and for years to come.

QUESTIONS

1. The multicultural market potential suggested by the author is exaggerated because these aggregates are not distinct markets. Do you agree or disagree?

2. Why would you expect brand recognition and loyalty to score high in these markets, compared with others?

3. If Hispanic and Asian–Americans start receiving a large increase in direct mail in their preferred language, would you expect the effectiveness of this sales medium to decrease or increase?

4. What are the likely problems from purchasing and using ethnic lists and how could you construct one suitable for your purposes?

Pepsi puts interests before ethnicity; aided by range of shops, marketer proves that passion comes first

Laurel Wentz*

Pepsi-Cola Co. is taking aim at the multicultural heart. Over a much longer period than most marketers – Pepsi did its first African–American ad in 1948 – the cola giant has evolved from the ethnic segmentation most companies still use, to looking at young ethnic consumers more as tribes bound by shared interests than ethnicity.

'Race is not the unifier', says Giuseppe D'Alessandro, Pepsi's director of multicultural marketing. 'The multicultural mind-set is more about your interests, like music, than whether you're African–American or Latino.' The Pepsi globe, he says, is 20 per cent Latino, 15 per cent African–American and 6 per cent Asian–American. Forty per cent of the Pepsi world is diverse, concentrated in major urban centers like New York, Los Angeles and Miami where youthful minorities are often the majorities. 'They see their reflection in the popular culture, almost to the point of exaggeration', Mr D'Alessandro says. 'We call it the multicultural heart.'

Pepsi's multicultural ads run all over. Pepsi-sponsored singers Beyonce Knowles and Shakira, for instance, aren't relegated to Black Entertainment Television and Univision, as they would have been just a few years ago.

* *Advertising Age*, 7 July 2003, 74(27): S24

C3.1   Selling the joy

Both performers star in ads that depict a world of imagination and passion as they sell 'the joy of Pepsi'.

In the dramatic mini-opera, *Pepsi's Carmen*, Spike DDB, New York, wrote new lyrics to the famous aria (to see the spot, go to AdAge.com QwikFind AA082i). In it, Zeke from Battle Creek loses his can of Pepsi as he stares in wonder around Times Square, and Beyonce as Carmen mobilizes a singing and dancing crowd to restore his drink, transforming tragedy into a joyous ending. The spot debuted on the Academy Awards telecast. 'We're very multicultural from day one', says Mr D'Alessandro. 'But that doesn't mean we don't do things that are more focused and relevant.'

One Shakira music spot has two versions, one sung in Spanish and one in English. And the Hispanic market was the first to be targeted for a joint promotion involving Pepsi and PepsiCo sibling Frito-Lay's Doritos. The promotion was titled *El Reventon de Sabor*, which loosely translates as a huge, flavourful party, and was heavily advertised on Spanish-language TV.

'Combining Pepsi and Doritos makes sense for all markets, but expression and product mix have to be different', Mr D'Alessandro says. Latinos love a fiesta, he says, while African–Americans are more mellow and cool, and the products had better be barbecue flavoured.

Pepsi has done a few products specifically for Latinos, like the launch of Gatorade's 'Xtremo' last year. The company has tested in Chicago *aguas frescas*, based on drinks Mexicans make at home by mixing juice with water and sugar, and is likely to roll them out in heavily Hispanic areas, though Mr D'Alessandro says a final decision has not been made. The bigger market lies in the appeal that certain drink brands have for different groups, like the Mountain Dew brand extensions Live Wire and Code Red that are popular in African–American households.

C3.2   Ad agencies get ideas going

Pepsi briefs its agencies, and Hispanic, multicultural and general-market shops all contribute ideas and compete. *Pepsi's Carmen* came from Spike DDB; Dieste Harmel & Partners, Dallas, did the first three Shakira spots; and BBDO Worldwide, New York, created a fourth one, *Tango*. All are part of Omnicom Group.

In *Tango*, a nerdy convenience store employee begins to dance to radio music with a life-size Shakira cut-out that comes to life. He tangos enthusiastically down the aisles of the store with her, a rose between his teeth as he gyrates to the beat.

Their enjoyment of the dance, and a Pepsi, ends abruptly when passers-by peer through the store window and see only a guy and a cardboard girl. Mr D'Alessandro says that in targeting youth it's hard to tell what percentage of Pepsi's ad budget is focused on any one group. Hispanic Business ranks Pepsi as the ninth biggest Hispanic advertiser, spending an estimated $35 million last year. In total, Pepsi spent $1.11 billion in measured and unmeasured media in 2002, according to *Advertising Age's* 2003 *Leading National Advertisers Report*.

Much of Pepsi's youth market are bicultural Hispanics. 'They consume a lot more English media than Spanish media, so we have to use English media more', says Mr D'Alessandro. '[English-speaking Hispanics] is obviously an area that is underrepresented. That can be hard for marketers to understand. They always thought Spanish was the main thing, when in reality it's not [about] the language.'

What does Mr. D'Alessandro, who is from the Dominican Republic, like to watch? 'I love [WB Networks'] *Sister, Sister*', he says. 'I watch it with my daughter. And the Garcia Brothers.'

QUESTIONS

1. Was Pepsi practising ethnic marketing in the first place?
2. What segmentation criterion is it now using?
3. Discuss alternative criteria for segmenting the soft-drink market.
4. Are soft drinks a strong candidate for using an ethnic marketing strategy?

CHAPTER 5

Assessing ethnic group substance for marketing purposes

5.1 Chapter objectives

Minority ethnic groups need to be assessed based on their strength or ethnic intensity, which is expressed through group behaviour and predictability. While this may establish their distinctiveness, are they worth targeting? Essential information for this assessment is unlikely to be readily available. When it has been made available, some critical marketing decisions will be required. This chapter develops a pragmatic and simple method for a preliminary assessment of ethnic group substantiality, and offers a framework for systematizing the decision-making process regarding the targeting of minority ethnic groups.

5.2 Introduction

Businesses contemplating ethnic marketing strategies need to assess the substantiality of narrowly defined minority ethnic groups. This assessment is difficult, probably biased by the assessor's preconceptions and a lack of guidelines that can be applied to all cases. In formulating guidelines this chapter explains the various influences bearing on the segmentation decision, starting with the concept of perceived net value. A framework for assessing substantiality is then explained followed by alternative methods of measurement.

Minority ethnic groups are potentially relevant for marketing because:

- members' consumption behaviour can be predicted, as a result of the group mechanisms and synergies, including community resources, that regulate how members consistently behave socially and as consumers; and

- the group encompasses relationships with its members that provide marketers with gateways for access to the members.

This suggests that minority ethnic groups need to be assessed based on their strength or ethnic intensity, reflecting the intensity of collective shared values and behaviours and expressed through predictable group behaviour. Assessing ethnic group substantiality involves the same analytical techniques (such as profitability analysis or the market-attractiveness/competitive-position matrix) used for market segmentation decisions involving other segments and other groups. Understanding about the group, its size and geodemographic characteristics (Goss, 1995), its lifestyle and how it behaves (Hassan and Kataris, 1991), its needs (particularly those that are not currently met in the market) and preferences, are among the common requirements. Such information is unlikely to be readily available in some convenient form, if at all, although it is essential to establish a group profile. Collecting this information, either directly or through consultancy services, can be an onerous, time-consuming and highly complex process.

Furthermore, crucial that this information is, it is not sufficient to ground sensible marketing decision-making. Each consumer group, such as a minority ethnic group, must be seen as a market opportunity in itself, and its opportunity cost calculated vis-a-vis other available market opportunities (Stanton and Pires, 1999), given that it is this that provides the context for the decision. It is not only about the consumer group. It is also about the strengths and weaknesses of the business, its capabilities and competencies and ultimately its objectives in the short and medium term. In addition to the internal environment, account must be taken of the external environment, both competitive and regulatory.

5.3 Perceived net value influences substantiality

Value creation is important for business because customers compare the perceived net value associated with each competing business proposition, and choose the highest value (Kijewski and Yoon, 1990; Kortge and Okonkwo, 1993). Competition based on customer's perceived value shifts business orientation towards the market. Hence, an adequate knowledge of what actual and potential customers consider important in determining their valuations, as well as competitors' value propositions, are essential requisites for a business to position itself as the best perceived provider of customer satisfaction. Given that competing businesses often offer the same core benefits, value creation requires the identification of *which* supplementary benefits provide competitive advantage, a task made especially difficult once variability across consumer segments such as minority ethnic groups is considered.[1]

The systematic development of effective marketing strategy encompasses conducting internal and external (environmental, market, customer and competitor) analysis, as preliminaries to formulating strategies for market segmentation, targeting and positioning. Each business can be seen as a unique entity with its own culture, own goals and own way of doing things. It is more or less resource rich, more or less risk averse. Its performance is likely to reflect particular strengths and weaknesses, core competencies, stage of the life cycle, orientation, nature of existing relationships with business partners, market power and such. Hence, it is appropriate to argue that the decision regarding which segments to target and in what way depends on the internal and external environments of the business (Hooley, Saunders and Piercy, 2004).

The elements of the process of choosing which segment to target are captured in Figure 5.1. As a compilation, the figure does not convey the flow and sequence of the interactions between the different types of analysis, or their interdependence. For example, the value proposition of the business (defined within internal analysis) is likely to be shaped or influenced by customers' needs, preferences and evaluative criteria (defined within customer analysis), as well as competing value propositions (defined within competitor analysis).

Another important gap of Figure 5.1 and of the marketing literature involves knowing what is best practice in defining feasible market segments. While segments need to be identifiable, measurable, actionable and stable, the decision about how to partition a potential market, that is to derive groups of consumers with those properties, ensues from analysis of that market. This tends to be business- and analyst-specific, dependent on marketers' market knowledge and experience.

Because ethnicity-based segmentation is not common practice, the likelihood is that this basis for segmentation will seldom be considered. This may be particularly so when individual groups are narrowly defined and possibly lumped in some 'other' classification in official statistics, compared with

Internal analysis

- Vision (where the business wants to be in the future), mission
- Stage of the life cycle
- Culture/orientation/commitment
- Resource availability (human, technical know-how, market experience, financial, assets . . .)
- Capabilities (what the business is really good at; including partnerships, networks, outsourcing)
- Gaps, constraints, barriers (entry/exit)
- Objectives (short/long term, profitability, growth)
- Value proposition

Environmental analysis

Which environmental elements may have some impact in the business? What is this impact? Consider technology, government, the economy, demographics, knowledge, culture, social concerns, externalities . . .

Market analysis

- Size (actual, potential)
- Potential basis for market segmentation
- Entry/exit barriers
- Cost structure
- Logistics and distribution
- Key success factors
- Expected growth/ profitability
- Power considerations
- Intensity of competition
- Quality of competition

BUSINESS DECISIONS ABOUT:
1. **SEGMENTATION CRITERIA**
2. **SEGMENT SELECTION FOR TARGETING**
3. **POSITIONING STRATEGY**

Customer analysis

- Profiles need to be developed in order to determine who are the actual/ potential customers/ customer groups
- What are their demographics, motivations, needs and preferences?
- Evaluative criteria before and after consumption?
- What is the degree of bargaining power? Empowerment?
- What is the degree of consumer empowerment?
- . . .

Competitor analysis

- Who is each competitor (actual, potential, direct/indirect)?
- Relative strengths/weaknesses
- Culture/orientation/commitment
- Barriers to entry/exit
- Objectives and strategies (current and past, short/long term, growth, profitability . . .)
- Image in the market and historical positioning
- Resource availability (human, technical know-how, market experience, financial, tangible and intangible assets . . .)
- Capabilities (what the competitor is perceived to be really good at)
- Cost structure
- Degree of differentiation
- Value proposition(s)

Figure 5.1 Influences on decision-making regarding segmentation, targeting and positioning

aggregations of groups based on single indicators such as language or country of origin, as discussed in Chapter 3.

Ethnicity-based segmentation may be perceived by marketers as dangerous and prone to social retaliation, or too difficult due to the lack of reliable and easily accessed information for segment profiling and consequent assessment. Yet, as argued by Walker *et al.* (2003), '. . . at the foundation of many marketing breakthroughs one often finds an insightful segmentation scheme that is sharply focused in a behavioural way' (p. 159), and it is primarily differences in behaviour between groups that ethnicity based-segmentation must address.

Prior to explaining how to assess ethnic segment substantiality, it is important to understand how marketers might profile minority groups in a practical way.

5.4 What to consider in profiling minority ethnic groups

Not many minority ethnic groups have been subject to rigorous profiling for marketing purposes and these profiles made widely available to researchers. As a consequence, the need to conduct primary research for creating ethnic group profiles may combine with possible scepticism associated with preconceptions about group size and substantiality to deter the profiling effort. Ultimately this may effectively hinder market segmentation based on ethnicity. In this section we argue that the decision to conduct group profiling may be made dependent on external signs of group substantiality, that is, the existence of easily identifiable indicators of group strength.

External signs of substantiality

For ethnic minority consumers newly arrived in a country, following similar others' behaviour has three important effects:

1. It provides relatively familiar and trusted models of how to behave in an acceptable and effective manner, as a resident and consumer in that country (Dwyer *et al.*, 1987).

2. It involves access to existing community resources. These include ethnic group-aligned institutions, such as clubs, newspapers, radio, television and communications networks, language assistance, shops, schools, health and legal services, religious services, childcare services, employment assistance, cultural undertakings, etc., and resources made available by governments in the host country, such as information on social issues using the ethnic language (e.g. non-smoking campaigns,

welfare entitlements), and home countries, such as funding of community associations.

3. It increases perceived value for the new arrival because, in addition to access to community resources and the benefits from appropriate behaviour, it reduces possible stress from unintended misbehaviour (Mendenhall and Oddou, 1985).

From the minority ethnic group perspective, the increase in the number of members with congruent behaviour reinforces the importance of the ethnic group for its members, for businesses targeting the group, and for governments and governmental organizations in the host and home countries. Ultimately, the gain in importance can be expected to contribute to the maintenance, refinement and possible expansion of community resources.

Many of the community resources are commonly listed in publicly available directories, like phone directories, conveniently listed in brochures available from consulates and, a sign of the new information economy, available through simple searches using the internet. Hence they are easily identifiable without much research effort.

External signs of substantiality reflect community resources

In 2000, preparatory work for a study of the Portuguese community in Sydney, Australia, involved in-depth interviews with gatekeepers to that community. These gatekeepers were identified using several sources, including the Portuguese Consulate, and other public entities linked to the community. It became apparent that several staff in the various institutions, including the Consulate, originated in Brazil. The 1996 Census of the population reported 3359 Brazil-born living in Australia, apparently closely involved with the Portuguese community. Additional to employment opportunities within the Portuguese community, lobbying of the Portuguese gatekeepers resulted in the inclusion of Brazilian contents in the radio and press in Portuguese. Notwithstanding, individuals of Brazilian origin that were contacted during a public and very well attended cultural event in Sydney expressed their hope that more Brazilians would make the trip to Australia, so that community numbers could at least justify their own radio station and community press, even if not sufficiently large to allow for a separate Brazilian community with its own resources. The cultural event celebrated 500 years of independence from Portugal.

Community resources are likely to be aligned to some mass of members, large enough to justify the investment on those resources. The study of the Portuguese community in Sydney found network incentives for Portuguese-speaking migrants to settle into the Portuguese community in Sydney. For example, community resources assist newly arrived ethnic minority consumers to adapt to the new environment and to establish and maintain socioeconomic ties within their community. This socialization process appears particularly important when a low level of English proficiency and low skills may reduce employment opportunities on arrival (Gonçalves Silva and Seniuk, 1986).

While the Portuguese community in Sydney is relatively small and remains invisible in most statistical reports, hence unlikely to awaken marketers attention,[2] its potential is reflected in community resources involving, for example, 14 health and social services to Portuguese-speaking people in early 2004, as shown in Table 5.1.

Table 5.1 Mainstream and community resources in health and social services for Portuguese-speaking people, 2004

Portuguese Welfare Centre, Camperdown	Information, referral, advocacy especially for new migrants. English classes, youth group, craft group, migration agency
Botany Migrant Resource Centre – Daceyville	Information, referral, advocacy for newly arrived migrants. English classes, home assistance for the aged living at home, migration agency
Anglicare Family Support Service, Marrickville	General welfare services, emergency assistance, home visits
Marrickville Community Health Centre	Assessment/referral to community-specific services. Health programmes according to the Portuguese-speaking community needs
Diabetes Centre, Camperdown	Clinical diagnosis, treatment, diabetes education and management
Children Services, Petersham Town Hall	Development of culturally appropriate children services programmes. Increased access to Commonwealth-funded children's services
Family Day Care – Marrickville	Family day care scheme. Children cared for in a home environment
'Os Unidos', Petersham	Social and senior citizen group for Portuguese-speakers
Health Care Interpreter Service, Camperdown	Portuguese-speaking interpreters for consultations in public hospitals, community health centres, etc.
Companheiros da Alegria, St Peters	Social and senior citizen group for people of Portuguese-speaking background
Home Visiting and Dementia Support Service, St Peters	Assistance/support by Portuguese-speaking field worker
Lucan Care At Home, Leichardt	Home assistance to the sick, aged and other people in need. Employs Portuguese-speaking workers
Parkland Nursing Home, Marrickville	Specially trained staff to meet the language and cultural needs of Portuguese-speaking residents
Sita Carter Day Centre, Marrickville	Transport, hot meals, appropriate cultural/recreational activities

Source: Extracted from a directory compiled by the Consulate-General of Portugal in Sydney. Accessed 1/24/2004 at http://www.consulportugal.server101.com/indice_de_profissionais.htm

Table 5.2 Businesses targeting the Portuguese community in Sydney, activity and number of providers, 1999, 2004

Type of activity	No.	Type of activity	No.
Accounting/Consultancy	3	General practitioners/Specialists (*)	7
Architecture/Engineering	1	Hairdressers	7
Bookshop	2	Jewellers/Watchmakers	2
Building contractors/Products	20	Masseurs/Physiotherapists/Nurses (*)	6
Car service and repairs	3	Medical specialists (*)	2
Cleaning	2	Pest control	2
Clothing and footwear	1	Psychologists (*)	5
Dental surgery/Prosthetist	2	Radio and press (*)	7
Driving schools	3	Real estate agencies	5
Electricity and electronics	4	Recreation, sport and leisure	1
Entertainment agencies	2	Restaurants, cafes, cake shops	44
Financial services (including representation of Portuguese banks)	5	Security systems	1
Food and beverages	8	Solicitors/lawyers (*)	8
Furniture, furnishings/Ceramics	4	Travel agents	5

Source: Full list with names and addresses produced by the Consulate-General of Portugal in Sydney (7 July 1999). Available at http://consulportugal.server101.com/directorio.htm
(*) Denotes updated in 2004 (http://www.portugueseorganisationsaustralia.com/....htm)

Notwithstanding the small size (estimated at approximately 27 000 people in 2000) this community is targeted by many commercial enterprises in a wide range of activities. A selected summary of these commercial enterprises by activity and number of providers is shown in Table 5.2.

Seven general practitioners, five psychologists and eight solicitors currently serve the Portuguese community in Sydney. In the area of communications there are currently two weekly Portuguese newspapers, five Portuguese language radio stations/programmes (including a programme in national SBS radio and a television channel received from Portugal (RTPI)). In culture and entertainment, there are two major recreation and sporting clubs, one ethnographic museum, a Portuguese Cultural Foundation, a Portuguese Youth Forum, several sports groups and seven folkloric groups. Portuguese is taught at nine community schools and four public schools. The community is served by two Catholic churches, one Pentecostal church, two Seventh-Day Adventist churches and one Assembly of God, each with a Portuguese priest or pastor.

Overall, this information can indicate:

- group members' congruent behaviour – necessary to justify the types of resources available and to enable behaviour predicability;
- potential gateways for reaching the group – points of access to the community communication network that can be used to reach the group members in a reliable manner;

Table 5.3 Decision table based on external signs of substantiality to indicate minority ethnic group potential substantiality

	Community resources	Portuguese community in Sydney	LOW < 2	MEDIUM 2–6	HIGH > 6
Congruent behaviour	Social clubs	2	X		
	Cultural/sports associations	10+			X
	Community and public schools	13			X
	Churches/Religious associations	5		X	
Group gateways	Ethnic radio	5		X	
	Ethnic press	2		X	
			LOW < 5	MEDIUM 5–10	HIGH > 10
	General practitioners	7		X	
	Solicitors/Lawyers	8		X	
	Accountants	3	X		
	Social services	14			X
	Total activities	69		2.1	

■ potential group substantiality – an indication of the size of the community judged by the proliferation of community resources.

Marketers seeking to evaluate minority ethnic groups can use a decision table based on external signs of substantiality to assess a group's substantiality potential, congruent behaviour and communications gateways (Table 5.3) prior to engaging in more in-depth research towards group profiling.

Analytical framework for assessing external signs of substantiality

Table 5.3 is a decision table that can be used to decide whether to pursue a segment profiling exercise. It is to be applied to different minority ethnic groups allowing a means for systematic comparison for potential group cohesion, access and substantiality using the same criteria across different groups. Applying a common analytical framework across segments is often better than allowing for managerial discretion (Walker *et al.*, 2003: 160). Table 5.3 is intended to illustrate a method that may be followed, rather than resulting from a deliberate situation analysis and environmental evaluation.

The left column lists 10 tactically selected external signs of substantiality criteria (or types of community resources). Four of these criteria (namely the number of occurrences of social clubs, cultural and sports associations, community and public schools, churches and religious associations) are deemed to involve associative characteristics, hence to indicate congruent behaviour. Two other criteria (namely the number of ethnic radio stations and newspapers) are deemed to indicate available communications gateways for marketers to access the group. Four other criteria (namely general practitioners, solicitors and/or lawyers, accountants and community organizations providing social services) are deemed to be both essential to an organized community with unique needs and preferences, and reflective of group mass.

Columns to the right show the number of actual occurrences for the Portuguese community in Sydney (from Tables 5.1 and 5.2), for each criterion. Finally, potential substantiality is given by the ratio of the aggregate of all observations (69) to the sum of the lowest possible scores in the medium range (that is $(4 \times 2) + (2 \times 2) + (4 \times 5) = 32$). The information in the table indicates a value of 2.1 (69/32) that can be interpreted to indicate a medium to low potential substantiality for the community, with relatively strong behaviour congruency and medium community gateways, but relatively low number of group members (to the extent that this can be indicated with any reliability by the number of professional practitioners) and some apparent reliance on social services. There would be good reasons to progress to the profiling stage of the STP analysis.[3]

Since ethnic groups must be analysed in the context of the internal and external environments of the interested business, the items in the left column may be replaced to reflect the specific strategic requirements of a business, and given weightings, reflecting their relative importance to the business.

In contrast with interpretations of segment substance anchored to some sufficient potential size to justify time and effort involved in planning (McDonald and Dunbar, 1995), the objective of this exercise is, first, to ascertain potential substantiality by considering several group dimensions, and second, to focus on the process of justifying further research effort in the profiling of the ethnic group, hence a step further away from the consequent segment selection decision.

Actual ethnic group consumer behaviour is likely to respond differently to different service products and to distinct value propositions. More comprehensive demographics and detail about needs and preferences, important and determinant evaluative criteria and, importantly, the group's contextual embedding need to be researched and thoroughly understood to help sensible marketing decision-making regarding the segmentation decision. This should ensure that the ethnic group meets the essential criteria for effective market segmentation – that the group is identifiable, measurable, actionable and stable – although substantiality considerations are more difficult to address. As discussed in Chapter 2, the test of substantiality is essentially an exhortation to evaluate the value of the segmenting opportunity for an organization and, therefore, should be applied so as to be consistent with achieving the organization's objectives. This is further discussed in the next section.

5.5   Ethnicity-based segmentation opportunities need to be assessed

Effective ethnic market segmentation yields segments that are conspicuous for distinctive needs, preferences and evaluative criteria before and after consumption, as reflected in subsequent distinctive consumption behaviour. We argued that this distinctive consumption behaviour converts into opportunities for organizations, which may or may not be accepted, but cannot be ignored. Because 'not all segments represent equally attractive opportunities for the firm' (Walker *et al.*, 2003: 160), it is important for businesses to evaluate the market value – substantiality – of different segments. Two alternative methods are briefly discussed below.

Market-attractiveness/competitive-position matrix

Borrowing from corporate models used for resource allocation across product markets, Walker *et al.* (2003) describe a very complex five-step process for choosing attractive market segments. Applied to segments that have already been identified and profiled (that is, for which a customer analysis has taken place), Step 1 involves the choice of criteria to assess *market attractiveness* (broadly the combination of environmental analysis and market analysis) and *competitive position* (competitive analysis) dimensions.

Step 2 involves assessing (by some unspecified method) each criterion for its relative importance in the overall assessment, and allocating weights to each criterion accordingly.

In Step 3, each segment (potential target market) is rated on each criterion on a scale from 0 to 10 (again by some unspecified method), using the segment profile. Multiplying the set weight and rating for each criterion, and adding the results for each dimension, produces totals for market attractiveness and competitive position. These are then plotted in a Market-attractiveness/ Competitive-position matrix.

Step 4 involves forecasting the future position of each market based on expected external environment trends. As explained by Walker *et al.*,

> the starting point is to consider possible shifts in customer needs and behavior, the entry or exit of competitors, and changes in their strategies. Managers also must address several broader issues, such as possible changes in product or process technology, shifts in economic climate, the impact of social or political trends, and shifts in the bargaining power or vertical integration of customers.
>
> (Walker *et al.*, 2003, p. 165)

This is only the beginning of the analysis in Step 4, which culminates with an assessment of segments as desirable targets. Desirability requires one dimension to be strongly positive and the other to be at least moderately positive.

Step 5 involves evaluating implications of possible future changes for business strategies and resource requirements.

Added to the apparent complexity of the five-step process for choosing attractive market segments, Walker *et al.* (2003) acknowledge that the desirability criteria that culminate in Step 4 may be ignored depending on:

- a manager's belief about trends in any of the dimensions;
- a segment being used strategically as a stepping-stone into a more attractive market in the future; or,
- the existence of shared costs.

Producer surplus

Because business objectives need to be taken into account in establishing whether a market segment is substantial, the concept needs to be redefined if it is to be used as a test for segment selection. This is enacted below by means of producer surplus analysis and adaptation of a model developed by Scherer (1979) to examine the desirability of introducing a new breakfast cereal into the American market.

Producer surplus is the difference between the price that a business would be willing to accept to supply a product (usually embodied in the marginal cost of supply) and the price the business actually receives for supplying that product (Perkins, 1994). Producer surplus provides an alternative measure of whether a market has sufficient 'substance'. Adapting the model used by Scherer (1979) allows for the examination of the economics of segmentation, and specifically of the relevance of segment substance in terms of the net change in producer surplus. The model illustrates that the issue is not simply a matter of profits generated by the particular segment (whether it has sufficient substance) but whether there is strategic advantage in segmenting, that is on the long-term impact on the business competitive position. An increase in producer surplus is the necessary condition, not profitability.

Figure 5.2 follows Scherer (1979) in adapting Hotelling's (1929) straight line duopoly model to characteristics space. The straight line segment between 0 and 1 depicts the consumer market for a particular product category, such as cereals or soft drinks, in a culturally diverse economy.

In a duopoly situation the market is segmented with location of the two products at the quartile points marked **A**, targeting mainstream consumers with relatively sweeter tastes, and **B**, targeting mainstream consumers with a preference for less sweetness. Consumers whose preferences are imperfectly satisfied by either **A** or **B** will have a loss of utility from consuming their less than ideal products. The more distant consumers' preferences lie from the attribute mix or value proposition of available products, the lower the quantity demanded of either product. This implies a decreasing producer surplus moving away from points **A** and **B**.

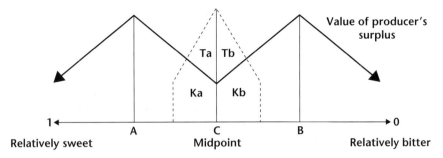

Assumptions:

\# All consumers have identical incomes and are evenly distributed over the consumer market space given by the straight line from 1 to 0.

\# The market is segmentable according to consumers' preference for sweetness in the product. Moving from the midpoint towards 1, consumers prefer an increasingly sweeter product. Moving from the midpoint towards 0, consumers prefer a decreasing degree of sweetness.

\# Products in the category are identical in all respects other than that they can vary in the degree of sweetness.

Figure 5.2 Assessing substance via producer's surplus

Realization that a given minority ethnic group has a preference for products that are neither sweet nor bitter is recognized as a market opportunity. However, further segmentation of the market by the introduction of brand C has several possible outcomes:

- It reduces the total surplus of brands **A** and **B**.

- If there is a single incumbent supplying both **A** and **B**, the decision to segment further generates an extra producer surplus of **Ta + Tb**.

- If the situation refers to a potential entrant, considering entry through the introduction of a brand at **C**, the gain will be perceived as including **Ka** and **Kb**.

As noted by Scherer, the costs of segmenting the market by the potential entrant will be compared against the generation of producer surplus with the introduction of brand **C**, that is the area **Ka + Kb**. For the incumbent, if it were to segment, the costs would need to be less than the net increase in producer surplus in order to meet the substantiality test.

Emphasis, nevertheless, need not be on covering segmentation costs. The issue may be whether there is a long-term impact on the competitive position of the business. Accordingly, the incumbent could choose to segment further, bearing short-term losses as an entry deterring strategy, for example. Hence, a focus on the net gain in producer surplus requires consideration of the marginal cost incurred in segmenting and supplying a further market, the impact on related segments, and the strategic objectives of the business. Ultimately, an increase in producer surplus is a more general measure than assessments of substantiality, and allows the business to evaluate a specific segmentation decision in relation to its strategic objectives.

From a managerial perspective, an assessment consistent with a firm's objectives has the potential to reduce the need for marketing practitioners to reconcile potential segmentation benefits with the business structure and competencies, a process that may ultimately result in ineffective and inefficient targeting. This, of course, requires business top management to participate in and contribute to the segmentation, targeting and positioning processes from the outset.

5.6 Chapter summary

This chapter has addressed the question of how to determine whether a minority ethnic group is worth targeting. Addressing that question required consideration of the types of internal and external analyses that need to be conducted to choose a segment and a positioning strategy. The profiling of an ethnic group is a key part of this determination. This must be integrated into a comparison of the potential substance of ethnic groups. An analytical framework for assessing substantiality was developed that can be applied across groups. Finally, the link between substantiality and the strategic object-ives of the business was discussed in terms of alternative measures.

Notes

1. Competition based on customer's perceived value has a two-tier consequence for business. First, it shifts business orientation towards the market. Specifically, adop-tion of the marketing concept directs efforts of a business as a whole to satisfaction of customers' needs, subject to business objectives and societal interest. Because the acquisition of new customers is believed to be more expensive than the retention of existing ones, business strategy focuses on good customers that can be targeted effect-ively. Second, this focus requires a firm to know its market and, more precisely, what actual and potential customers consider in their valuations, in order to position itself as the best provider of satisfaction to its customers, and to closely control and allocate resources.

2. 'Statistical invisibility' is an expression that denotes no separate reporting of the min-ority ethnic group in official statistical reports, linking to the lack of media exposure and consistent reporting on the realities, problems, activities and celebrations of the group. This contrasts with ethnic groups (and other lifestyle consumer group-ings), perhaps with larger memberships. The Portuguese ethnic group, for example, is reported as part of the 'other' in standard official statistical reports prepared by the ABS (1996; 2000). Non-reporting may be indicative, to marketing analysts, of lack of critical mass or substance. The demonstration of marketing relevance for that group indicates that other minority ethnic groups, particularly those separately reported in those statistical reports, justify marketers' attention (Pires, 2001).

3. Earlier we saw that Brazilian-born, Portuguese-speaking individuals, to access community resources for which they would probably lack critical mass, effectively use the Portuguese community in Sydney. If the Brazilian group opportunity was assessed independently, potential substantiality would be minimal and unlikely to justify comprehensive profiling. By acculturating to the Portuguese community they also contribute to that community's substance. This illustrates a case where aggregation of minority ethnic groups may be a sensible business strategy.

References

Australian Bureau of Statistics (ABS) (1996) *Census of Population and Housing, Ethnicity Thematic Profile Service*, Canberra: ABS.

Australian Bureau of Statistics (ABS) (2000) *2000 Year Book Australia*, Cat. 1301. 0, Canberra: AGPS.

Dwyer, F., Schurr, P. and Oh, S. (1987) 'Developing buyer–seller relationships', *Journal of Marketing*, 51 (2): 11–27.

Gonçalves, A., Silva, E. and Seniuk, S. (1986) *The Portuguese Community in the Illawarra*, State Health Publication No. (ILR) 86-071, Sydney: Regional Migrant Health Centre.

Goss, J. (1995) 'We know who you are and we know where you live: the instrumental rationality of geodemographics', *Economic Geography*, 71 (2): 171.

Hassan, S. and Kataris, L. (1991) 'Identification of global consumer segments: a behavioural framework', *Journal of International Consumer Marketing*, 3 (2): 16.

Hooley, G., Saunders, J. and Piercy, N. (2004) *Marketing Strategy and Competitive Positioning*, 3rd edn., London: Prentice-Hall.

Hotelling, H. (1929) 'Stability in competition', *Economic Journal*, 39 (March): 41–57.

Kijewski, V. and Yoon, E. (1990) 'Market-based pricing: beyond price–performance curves', *Industrial Marketing Management*, 19: 11–19.

Kortge, G. and Okonkwo, P. (1993) 'Perceived value approach to pricing', *Industrial Marketing Management*, 22: 133–40.

McDonald, M. and Dunbar, I. (1995) *Market Segmentation*, London: Macmillan, pp. 15–16.

Mendenhall, M. and Oddou, G. (1985) 'The dimensions of expatriate acculturation: a review', *Academy of Management Review*, 10 (1): 39–47.

Perkins, F. (1994) *Practical Cost Benefit Analysis*, Melbourne: MacMillan, p. 116.

Pires, G. (2001) 'The selection of service providers by ethnic minority consumers in a culturally diverse society', Unpublished Doctoral Thesis, University of Newcastle.

Scherer, F. (1979) 'The welfare economics of product variety: an application to the ready to eat cereals industry', *Journal of Industrial Economics*, 28 (2): 113–34.

Slater, S. (1996) 'The challenge of sustaining competitive advantage', *Industrial Marketing Management*, 25: 79–86.

Stanton, J. and Pires, G. (1999) 'The substantiality test: meaning and application in market segmentation', *Journal of Segmentation in Marketing*, 3 (2): 105–15.

Walker, O., Boyd Jr, H., Mullins, J. and Larréché, J. (2003) *Marketing Strategy: A Decision-Focused Approach*, New York: McGraw-Hill.

Wren, B., Souder, W. and Berkowitz, D. (2000) 'Market orientation and new product development in global industrial firms', *Industrial Marketing Management*, 29: 601–11.

CHAPTER 6

Understanding the decision processes of ethnic consumers

6.1 Chapter objectives

Consumer behaviour deals with the buying behaviour of consumers, either as households or individuals. Without trying to capture the scope of a consumer behaviour textbook, this chapter provides a framework that can assist in developing a better understanding of the buying decision processes that ethnic consumers are likely to engage, a necessary requirement if marketers are to target ethnic consumers effectively. While ethnic minority consumers' basic needs and wants are likely to be similar to mainstream consumers, that does not mean that offers cannot be tailored for a particular ethnic group that will be considerably more attractive to that group than to mainstream consumers or other ethnic groups.

The minority ethnic group, its networks and institutions, plays a major role in the decision processes of an ethnic consumer. The dependence of individual ethnic consumers on the group enables marketers to profile and predict ethnic consumer behaviour. Conversely, ethnic group behaviour necessarily reflects its members' behaviour. Using evoked sets and sequential choice theories of the decision-making process, this chapter explains that, while the individual consumer may choose products and suppliers based on ethnic group preferences and possible recommendation, dissatisfaction with these products and suppliers feeds back and influences group preferences. The implications are that marketers reach ethnic minority consumers through their group of affiliation and that effective targeting strategies need to recognize this.

There are several important consumer behaviour models that can assist marketers to understand better ethnic consumers' decision processes. The framework presented in this chapter integrates these models, highlighting critical activities undertaken by ethnic consumers (either as households or individuals) that lead to decisions concerning product and supplier selection, purchase and use. The framework brings out the importance of ethnic institutions and networks in the decision process. The overall focus of this chapter is on the process of supplier selection, where suppliers may range from offering highly tangible to highly intangible products, consequently raising a range of evaluation problems.

6.2 Why do ethnic minority consumers need to be treated differently?

Ethnic minority consumers' acquisition of market knowledge in a culturally diverse country, where suppliers' communications are generally directed toward mainstream consumers, may be constrained by limited access to sources of information that can help reduce the perceived risk of purchase and thus restrict choice, particularly in the context of intangible dominant products (*inter alia* services), high in credence qualities. This constraint challenges ethnic minority consumers in their selection of products and suppliers, as well as in consumption and evaluation.

Cognitive models of the decision-making process often model the selection of both products and suppliers using a 'traditional' flowchart of the decision process. The processes depicted in such models do not provide sufficient detail to explain differences between ethnic minority consumers and mainstream consumers. Ethnic minority consumers exchange information and experiences with similar others (other ethnic minority consumers) in their minority ethnic group of affiliation, so that group behaviour is a reference for the affiliates. This connection can lead to the maintenance of relationships between ethnic minority consumers and suppliers preferred by the group that are stronger than the relationship between mainstream consumers and their suppliers.

6.3 The process of supplier selection

Figure 6.1 depicts a cognitive process model of the consumer decision-making process that integrates several well-known models (Nicosia, 1966; Engel, Kollat and Blackwell, 1968; Howard and Sheth, 1969; Engel, Kollat and Miniard, 1986; Sheth, Newman and Gross, 1991).

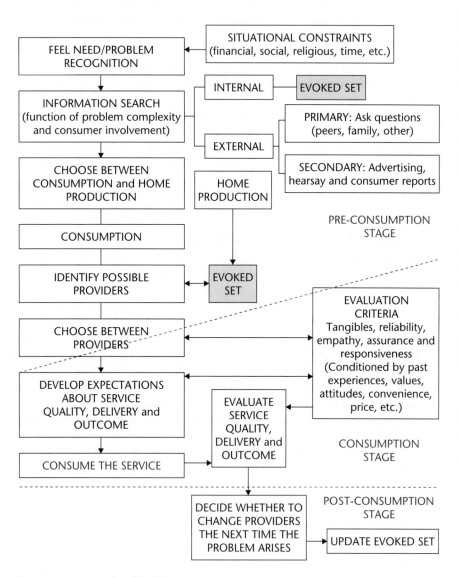

Figure 6.1 Integrated model of decision-making process

The process is depicted as a flowchart linking the various steps involved. The consumer passes through five phases (need recognition, information search, evaluation of alternatives, purchase decision, post-purchase behaviour) to reach a choice decision. Such a model does not specifically distinguish the applicability of the process in terms of choices about either goods, services, brands, retail and service outlets or service providers (Hawkins *et al.*, 1994; McGuire, 1999). Breaking the overall process into three stages, called pre-consumption, consumption and post-consumption, increases understanding of the decision processes, especially where there is a high service element (Fisk, 1981).

The *pre-consumption stage* of the decision process involves problem recognition, information search and selection of alternatives. All influence the evaluation that ensues. Information search and selection of alternatives involve a circular process of gathering and evaluating information using some undetermined criteria that culminates in a selection. Expectations are formed about the chosen provider, marking the transition to the *consumption stage*. Evaluation may follow, with purchase and consumption. Overall evaluation occurs in the *post-consumption stage* and takes all preceding evaluations into account. If the result is satisfaction the consumer experiences repurchase motivation that feeds back into the pre-consumption stage.

It is important that the different characteristics of products are taken into account. In contrast with search qualities associated with some physical or tangible characteristics of products (such as size, shape, colour or smell) that can be predetermined, examined and evaluated before purchasing takes place (Nelson, 1970), other products are more intangible, for instance service activities such as dentistry where the performance leads to the experience. Such intangible products may be high in credence qualities (Darby and Karni, 1973), and providers may provide utilitarian, temporal and spatial dimensions to their offerings, which can be augmented with social, emotional and other forms of value (Sheth, Newman and Gross, 1991). Searching for more tangible products may be easier than searching for highly intangible products, and selecting a supplier is increasingly difficult where products are credence-based. Supplier selection may occur before, after, or simultaneously with product selection and may be influenced by consumers' personal values, personality, lifestyle, family, reference groups, economic situation and level of object knowledge.

Even with adequate information on all the variables, and notwithstanding a wealth of research investigating particular aspects of the overall decision-making process (Fishbein, 1963; Ajzen and Fishbein, 1973; Sheth, 1974; Bettman, 1979; Shaw and Pirog III, 1997; Chan and Lau, 1998), the selection process depicted in this integrated model (Figure 6.1) does not provide sufficient detail to allow a prediction of a particular choice of brand or supplier. For this purpose, other studies have focused on a theory of consumer choice sets, perceived as outcomes of consumer decision-making processes

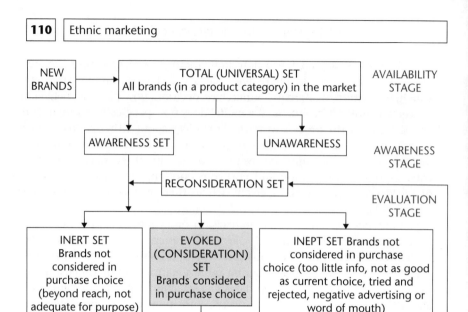

Figure 6.2 Integration of contributions to the sets model of sequential choice

(Narayana and Markin, 1975; Shocker *et al.*, 1991). Figure 6.2 combines the various contributions in this area into a model of sequential choice that shows the various sets of choice alternatives that enter into the decision process.

The model starts with a universal set that includes all possible choice items that might be considered by a consumer. These are then reduced to a set residing in a consumer's memory that comprises all the alternatives the consumer is aware of, even if some may not be recalled on any given occasion. In ways not specified in the literature this awareness set is updated over time by the addition of new items and, presumably, by the deletion of no longer available ones.

The awareness set contains lower hierarchy sets for each decision situation: an inert set (alternatives not recalled), an inept set (alternatives disregarded due to unsatisfactory past experience, negative or perceived as inferior in relation to current choices) and the alternatives actually considered by the consumer. The latter form the evoked (or consideration) set referred to in Figure 6.1. The subsequent choice between alternatives is further reduced to a choice set through exclusion or rejection. The final group of consumer decisions involves choosing, experiencing and appraising one item from those in the choice set. The model allows the reconsideration set to be updated at various decision stages, so that future selection takes past experience into account. This corresponds to the 'update evoked set' step in Figure 6.1.

Similar to the integrated model of consumer decision-making process (Figure 6.1), evoked sets and sequential choice theory do not explain why consumers choose the way they do. They focus on the process and make no distinction between highly tangible and highly intangible products, brands, the outlet or the supplier (Spiggle and Sewall, 1987; Brand and Cronin, 1997), although the theory can be applied to selecting one supplier from a set.

Bringing together models of consumer decision-making and sequential choice theory of evoked sets provides a better understanding of the process of supplier selection. However, this understanding is incomplete because highly intangible products necessitate different consumer evaluation processes from those used when assessing highly tangible products (Zeithaml, 1981). There are at least seven areas where this difference may lead to dissimilar evaluation processes.

1. *Information search* – regulation of professional advertising, difficulty in communicating experiences and eventual limitations in communication skills and funding available to suppliers may restrict consumers' access to external information sources about their offer.

2. *Perceived risk* – intangibility and limited information, coupled with heterogeneity of the product, fewer warranties or guarantees and a lack of personal technical knowledge limit consumers' ability to assess satisfaction even after consumption and increase consumers' perceived risk in selecting an alternative.

3. *Size and composition of the evoked set of alternatives* – together with home production, self-service and the offer of fewer brands by individual providers, fewer information sources may generate fewer alternatives for consumers to consider; the evoked set may be smaller for highly intangible than for highly tangible products (Davis, Guiltinan and Jones, 1979; Brand and Cronin, 1997).

4. *Adoption of innovation* – consumers may resist innovation because new products may be incompatible with existing values and behaviours.

5. *Brand loyalty* – consumers may have greater loyalty to providers because switching re-establishes perceived risk and may be costly (in terms of search, transaction and learning costs, savings related to repeated use, habit, emotional and time costs associated with cognition).

6. *Attribution of dissatisfaction* – inseparability relates to consumer involvement in the production process, such that some of the blame for an unsatisfactory outcome may be naturally appropriated by the consumer, whether the consumer is to blame or not (Bendapudi and Berry, 1997).

7. *Evaluative criteria* – the presence of all the above characteristics can lead to greater difficulty in assessing quality, satisfaction and, ultimately, establishing reliable evaluative criteria. Cues such as price and the physical context may be some of the necessary means available to judge quality and inform perceived value.

Linked to consumers' exchange decisions, perceived value is affected by the experiential nature of highly intangible products (e.g. services difficult to evaluate prior to purchase and delivery – a haircut); by co-production (influencing the evaluation of technical quality); and, by direct encounters with the supplier influencing evaluations of quality. Ultimately, these factors influence how consumers acquire information and consider alternatives, the criteria they use to choose between suppliers and how benefits are evaluated (McGuire, 1999).

In summary, the decision process model described by Figure 6.1 offers a general description without a particular focus. Different steps may be more or less important to individual consumers depending on that focus. For example, differences between highly tangible and highly intangible products explain the greater importance devoted by consumers of the latter to evaluation in the post-consumption stage, while consumers of the former concentrate on pre-consumption evaluation. Excluding situational circumstances, the decision to seek more or less new information can be argued to depend on consumer knowledge and experience, as well as on the type, complexity and importance of the buying task. This also applies to which sources are selected. Consumers' motivation and evaluation criteria can be expected to vary with the stage in the overall decision-making process and decision task. All decisions involving information search internalize other auxiliary decisions regarding what and how much information is necessary and sufficient, and from where it will be sourced.

6.4 How 'average' consumers select suppliers

Suppliers may operate with a single brand so that the selection of brand and supplier may involve one and the same decision. These associations may apply, for example, in deciding between generalist or specialist medical service activities (the product), followed by a decision about the specific supplier (both brand and supplier). These decisions may be separate, although not the procedure involved in these decisions.

What do these decisions entail? Drawing from perceived value theory, the average 'rational' consumer decides between alternative offerings by comparing respective net perceived values. These correspond to the difference between all the perceived benefits and all the perceived costs associated with each of the offerings. How many offerings are considered depends on how many different suppliers consumers are aware of (McGuire, 1999). Awareness is influenced by prior experience, marketing communications, providers' reputation and word-of-mouth recommendations, particularly in the case of products with high credence attributes. Consumers may research the market to identify evaluation criteria for particular products and to compare competitors.

Consumers' evaluation of the product during the consumption and post-consumption stages is likely to be guided by five particularly conspicuous elements of the experience, originally identified by Zeithaml, Parasuraman and Berry (1990) as follows.

1. *Tangibles* or *physical evidence* refer to the frontstage – whether physical facilities, equipment and appearance of the interacting personnel correspond to expectations.

2. *Reliability* (also *technical* or *functional quality*, or *expressed performance*) refers to the basic expectation that a supplier does what it promises in a dependable and accurate manner (Swan and Comb, 1976; Gronroos, 1991).

3. *Empathy* refers to the perception that the supplier actually cares about consumers' needs, beliefs and reservations.

4. *Assurance* refers to the perception that the supplier is knowledgeable and courteous.

5. *Responsiveness* refers to the perception that the supplier is consistently willing to help.

While these are criteria that suppliers need to address in developing marketing strategies, experience by consumers in respect to these criteria can be expected to

- help determine whether to switch suppliers;
- help form expectations about the product; and,
- provide indicators of performance to take into account during supplier selection.

This broad application of evaluation criteria is useful because consumers are deemed to evaluate products and suppliers by comparing expected performance with perceptions of actual performance. It is reasonable to assume that a criterion that has been used by suppliers to create expectations is used by consumers for subsequent evaluation (Keaveney, 1995). Ultimately, if perceptions match or exceed expectations the average consumer is likely to be satisfied and there may be no motivation for switching supplier.

Overall, the average 'rational' consumer can be expected to follow the various steps in the decision-making process more or less closely, depending on the decision unit, importance and complexity of the task and related consumer experience and knowledge. These require decisions that may challenge all consumers; however, how and why particular consumers or consumer groups actually do what they do is still a 'black box' that remains largely closed to our understanding (Lovelock, Patterson and Walker, 1998). The next section examines whether the basic process of supplier selection requires adaptation when applied to the case of ethnic minority consumers.

6.5   How ethnic minority consumers select suppliers

Market segmentation usually involves some level of critical mass that, in consumer markets, is unlikely to be met by any individual ethnic minority consumer, but may be at the reach of a minority ethnic group. An individual ethnic minority consumer becomes important, if at all, only when associated with other similar individuals, creating an identifiable, measurable and actionable group that is internally homogeneous in consumption and heterogeneous in relation to other groups. To be marketing relevant, individual ethnic minority consumers may need to rely upon, and behave similarly to other members of their minority ethnic group. The marketing relevance of the minority ethnic group depends on its membership mass and homogeneity, although its survival is separate from any one consumer. The minority ethnic group is a reference for ethnic minority consumers. Their importance as targets depends on their association with the group. In turn, the group's importance depends on the individual's identification with the group.

Some ethnic minority consumers change their status and behaviour over time. Return migration, relocation to areas outside the reach of practical group influence, acculturation to the host or other cultures and the consequent behavioural change, are examples that come to mind. Some ethnic minority consumers will leave a particular minority ethnic group and some new members will join. The consequence is that, in any given market and for any minority ethnic group, there are likely to be consumers with variable degrees of market knowledge. The more recent the arrival in the host country, the less the knowledge about the local market and the greater the difficulties faced, even for the satisfaction of common consumer needs.

Decision-making difficulties for ethnic minority consumers

Reaching ethnic minority consumers may not be easy given the existence of ethnic communications networks (Laroche, Kim and Clarke, 1997), marketers' difficulty in understanding different cultures (Hotchkiss, 1996), language barriers and consumers' preference for ethnic brands, limited exposure to printed media and difficulty reading English (Kaufman, 1991). The consequences of these difficulties are addressed with reference to Figure 6.3. The figure consists of an adaptation of the integrated model earlier depicted in Figure 6.1. It represents the process of selection of preferred suppliers

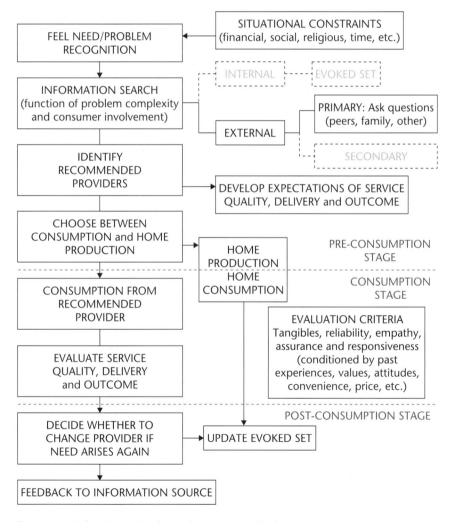

Figure 6.3 Preferred provider selection by inexperienced ethnic minority consumers

by inexperienced ethnic minority consumers and depicts steps likely to be emphasized. Again, the process invo'ves three stages (pre-consumption, consumption and post-consumption) separated in the figure by two broken lines.

Pre-consumption stage

All first-time potential purchasers of a product may face difficulties in learning about and appraising that product. Time and budgetary scarcities may limit available sources, and communication difficulties and limited knowledge of the marketplace may limit the ability to search for, and evaluate, product information. Inexperienced, communication-challenged ethnic minority consumers may experience greater difficulty in perusing product literature and evaluating 'new' physical products and brand names, as well as discomfort in consulting with service staff. Inability or increased difficulty in acquiring risk-reducing information increases the perceived risk from making the wrong decision, a consequence that may be compounded when products are highly intangible.

How might inexperienced ethnic minority consumers reduce perceived risk? Trial and error consumption is a solution for some products that are highly tangible. Home production is an option for some that are highly intangible (e.g. haircutting) as well as highly tangible (fruit and vegetables). Ethnic minority consumers may also look for providers with a presence in their home country (e.g. international brands such as McDonald's or the Body Shop) or seek to reduce risk by searching for familiar ethnic brands. The more general answer is that, for products difficult to appraise prior to consumption, perceived risk can be reduced by selecting providers based on information from sources that can be trusted.

Because similar others (in values, attitudes, etc.) trust and are more trusted compared to dissimilar others (Dwyer, Schurr and Oh, 1987), inexperienced ethnic minority consumers source consumption information from experienced similar others who can understand their needs and predicaments. Their recommendation may be adopted because it reduces perceived risk and because of the desire to conform to group behaviour.

For newly arrived ethnic minority consumers, information search is conditioned by a lack of personal knowledge and poor access and exposure to secondary external sources. Primary external sources (family, similar others) are the main, perhaps lone, source of information. Information gathered from family and similar others may be taken at face value, as if a consumer were to borrow their source's reconsideration set. Positive and negative past experiences are received as guidelines for consumption behaviour, together with a set of expectations that impacts on the inexperienced ethnic minority consumers' evaluation criteria. Indeed, it is unclear why consumers would choose not to follow the guidelines almost literally if the source is credible. Even if conflicting information is received from alternative sources about a particular provider, although this may affect the expectation set and evaluation criteria, to go outside the guidelines may increase perceived risk.

In using the reconsideration set of a trusted source, inexperienced ethnic minority consumers may become aware of providers other than the recommended one. Negative feelings about providers are also received and adopted by inexperienced ethnic minority consumers. Hence, the evoked set for inexperienced ethnic minority consumers may be the single recommended (and preferred) supplier.

Consumption stage

The consumption stage may be pivotal for understanding long-term or continued use of suppliers by ethnic minority consumers, particularly for products high in credence qualities and involving personal processing. Where production and consumption are inseparable, such as a diagnosis by a doctor, a haircut, or effective stain removal by a dry cleaner, satisfactory provision may depend on the consumer's specification, communication, and participation in its production. Inexperienced ethnic minority consumers may be challenged when their needs and wants have to be unambiguously communicated to suppliers, often in the presence of others. Perceived or real difficulties in communicating may be encountered, both in explaining their needs and responding to what may be required of them during their participation in the production process.

Communication difficulties involve more than language problems. Meaning and context are important in defining a 'normal' way of doing things, how staff and customers address each other, whether physical touch is allowed or how people with different ethnic backgrounds behave towards different others. By selecting the supplier recommended by experienced similar others, inexperienced ethnic minority consumers reduce the perceived risk of making a bad selection. In addition they are seen to conform to group behaviour. An additional and valued outcome for ethnic minority consumers may be the opportunity for social interaction with similar others.

From a different perspective, personal interaction with the supplier provides ethnic minority consumers with the opportunity to make their needs and preferences known, together with additional personal information. Suppliers may use such information for supplementing their core product. To the extent that the cultural awareness and sensitivity of the recommended supplier leads to responsiveness, customization and personalization may ensue. This involves adjusting the product so that it provides a better match for the particular needs of each customer at the time of delivery (Hartman and Lindgren Jr., 1993) as well as converting the commercial interaction into a de facto social interaction (Mittal and Lassar, 1996). Both create customer dependence on the preferred supplier (Bowen and Jones, 1986).

In terms of evaluation, intangibility, inseparability and heterogeneity create difficulties for all consumers. These may be greater for ethnic minority consumers due to home country-acquired expectations and evaluation criteria for similar products. Distinct expectations may emerge in the new market with new information sources. As a result, evaluation criteria may be less well articulated and appraisal of the value received in the service encounter much more subjective. In addition, ethnic minority consumers aware of their own communication difficulties may apportion at least part of the blame for unsatisfactory performance to themselves, contributing to performance ambiguity.

In summary, in addition to the search costs incurred in the pre-consumption stage, inexperienced ethnic minority consumers may invest considerable effort in the interaction process. Providers may be considered credible due to recommendation by similar others. Combined with buyer–seller interaction, communication difficulties:

- provide opportunities for customers' needs to be met more closely;
- convert commercial interactions into social interactions;
- possibly increase the risk of product delivery failure.

These possible outcomes also reinforce existing supplier credibility and promote customer dependence on that supplier, resulting in lower perceived risk, social involvement and consequent continued patronage, all combining to reduce any incentive to switch suppliers. Arguably, inexperienced ethnic minority consumers may be loath to change partners because to do so is to re-establish risk.

Post-consumption stage

Post-consumption evaluation takes all preceding evaluations into account and plays a major role in determining whether the supplier will have the consumers' continued patronage (Fisk, 1981). For inexperienced ethnic minority consumers the likelihood of switching suppliers may be very low. The consumption stage involves creation of perceived value through closer focus on customer needs via customization and personalization, culminating in increased customer dependence on a supplier with reinforced credibility. This outcome implies an alignment of perceptions with expectations and that the consumer is happy with the supplier. This leaves little incentive to switch. Continued customer satisfaction with supplier performance promotes that supplier to a preferred status. Preferred suppliers benefit from sustained ethnic minority consumer loyalty and a willingness by the ethnic minority consumer to recommend them to others, namely their minority ethnic group.

The preceding claims assume that consumers are rational in valuing risk and that the supplier is culturally aware, sensitive and, most importantly, responsive to customer needs. These assumptions can be defended because

- supplier recommendation is sourced from an experienced similar ethnic minority consumer; and

- to the extent that they are perceived as a preferred supplier to the minority ethnic group, suppliers may perceive that the long-term patronage of ethnic minority consumers is particularly worth investing in.

There will be suppliers that meet the above criteria and others that do not, just as there will be satisfied and dissatisfied consumers. Whatever the case may be, the consumption experience can be visualized to result in the updating of the consumer's various sets (e.g. rejection set, reconsideration set). In extreme negative or positive cases, there may be voluntary feedback to the original source.

Finally, inexperienced ethnic minority consumers do not remain inexperienced forever. Becoming experienced, they may pass their experiences, positive and negative, on to other ethnic group members, themselves potentially preferred sources of information for more inexperienced ethnic minority consumers.

Summary

This chapter has brought together into one framework relevant models of the consumer decision-making process and used it to help explain the decision-making processes of ethnic minority consumers. Ethnic minority consumers are likely to place greater reliance on some steps of the process, while other steps are addressed cursorily or simply skipped. The process of supplier selection relies heavily on pre-consumption evaluation, even in the context of products high in credence qualities. Therefore, the focus for marketers is to understand more clearly the information search phase of the decision-making process.

From the practitioners' point of view, ethnic minority consumers' reliance on references from similar others points to the minority ethnic group as the target for the marketing effort. Awareness and sensitivity of ethnic minority consumers' cultural characteristics arises as key factors to which marketers may need to respond. Responsiveness may be embedded in customized and personalized strategies designed to appeal to ethnic minority consumers.

Because of the interlinking of the individual within the group, the process of supplier selection can lead to ethnic minority consumers depending on a few suppliers bearing the group's imprimatur of enhanced perceived credibility. Customer satisfaction and low incentive to switch promote these suppliers to a preferred supplier status for both individual consumers and their group of affiliation. This process is potentially conducive to consumer loyalty and long-term relationships.

References

Ajzen, I. and Fishbein, M. (1973) 'Attitudinal and normative variables as predictors of specific behaviours', *Journal of Personality and Social Psychology*, 27(1): 41–57.

Bendapudi, N. and Berry, L. (1997) 'Customers' motivations for maintaining relationships with service providers', *Journal of Retailing*, 73(1): 15–37.

Bettman, J. (1979) *An Information Processing Theory of Consumer Choice*, Sydney: Addison-Wesley.

Bowen, D. and Jones, G. (1986) 'Transaction cost analysis of service organization–customer exchange', *Academy of Management Review*, 11(2): 428–41.

Brand, R. and Cronin, J. (1997) 'Consumer-specific determinants of the size of retail choice sets: an empirical comparison of physical good and service providers', *Journal of Services Marketing*, 11(1): 19–38.

Chan, R. and Lau, L. (1998) 'A Test of the Fishbein–Ajzen behavioural intentions model under Chinese cultural settings: are there any differences between PRC and Hong Kong consumers?', *Journal of Marketing Practice: Applied Marketing Science*, 4(1): 85–101.

Darby, M. and Karni, E. (1973) 'Free competition and the optimal amount of fraud', *Journal of Law and Economics*, 16 (April): 67–86.

Davis, D., Guiltinan, J. and Jones, W. (1979) 'Service characteristics, consumer search and the classification of retail services', *Journal of Retailing*, 55(3): 3–23.

Dwyer, F., Schurr, P. and Oh, S. (1987) 'Developing buyer–seller relationships', *Journal of Marketing*, 51(2): 11–27.

Engel, J., Kollat, D. and Blackwell, R. (1968) *Consumer Behavior*, New York: Holt, Rinehart and Winston.

Engel, J., Kollat, D. and Miniard, P. (1986) *Consumer Behavior*, Hinsdale, IL: Dryden Press.

Fishbein, M. (1963) 'An investigation of the relationship between beliefs about an object and attitude toward that object', *Human Relations*, 16: 233–40.

Fisk, R. (1981) 'Toward a consumption/evaluation process model for services', in J. Donnelly and W. George (eds) *Marketing of Services*, Chicago, IL: AMA, pp. 191–5.

Gronroos, C. (1991) 'Strategic management and marketing in the services sector', *Studentlitteratur*, Lund, Sweden.

Hartman, D. and Lindgren Jr., J. (1993) 'Consumer evaluations of goods and services: implications for services marketing', *Journal of Services Marketing*, 7(2): 4–15.

Hawkins, D., Neal, C., Quester, P. and Best, R. (1994) *Consumer Behaviour: Implications for Marketing Strategy*, Sydney: Irwin.

Hotchkiss, D. (1996) 'Weaving cultural sensitivity into marketing', *Journal of Bank Marketing*, June: 26–33.

Howard, J. and Sheth, J. (1969) *The Theory of Buyer Behavior*, New York, NY: Wiley.

Kaufman, C. (1991) 'Coupon use in ethnic markets: implications from a retail perspective', *Journal of Consumer Marketing*, 8(1) (Winter): 41–51.

Keaveney, S. (1995) 'Customer switching behaviour in service industries: an exploratory study', *Journal of Marketing*, 59 (April): 71–82.

Laroche, M., Kim, C. and Clarke, M. (1997) 'The effects of ethnicity factors on consumer deal interests: an empirical study of French–English–Canadians', *Journal of Marketing Theory and Practice*, Winter, 5(1): 100–11.

Lovelock, C., Patterson, P. and Walker, R. (1998) *Services Marketing – Australia and New Zealand*, Sydney: Prentice-Hall.

McGuire, L. (1999) *Australian Services: Marketing and Management*, Sydney: Macmillan.

Mittal, B. and Lassar, W. (1996) 'The role of personalization in service encounters', *Journal of Retailing*, 72(1): 95–109.

Narayana, C. and Markin, R. (1975) 'Consumer behaviour and product performance: an alternative conceptualization', *Journal of Marketing*, 39 (October): 1–6.

Nelson, P. (1970) 'Advertising as information', *Journal of Political Economy*, 81 (July–August): 729–54.

Nicosia, F. (1966) *Consumer Decision Processes*, Englewood Cliffs, NJ: Prentice-Hall.

Shaw, E. and Pirog III, S. (1997) 'A systems model of household behavior', *Journal of Marketing Theory and Practice*, Summer: 17–29.

Sheth, J. (1974) *Family Decision-Making Model, in Models of Buyer Behavior: Conceptual, Quantitative and Empirical*, New York: Harper & Row, pp. 17–33.

Sheth, J., Newman, B. and Gross, B. (1991) *Consumption Values and Market Choices: Theory and Applications*, Cincinnati, OH: South-Western Publishing Co.

Shocker, A., Ben-Akiva, M., Boccara, B. and Nedungadi, P. (1991) 'Consideration set influences on consumer decision-making and choice: issues, models, and suggestions', *Marketing Letters*, 2(3), Kluwer Academic Publishers, 181–97.

Spiggle, S. and Sewall, M. (1987) 'A choice sets model of retail selection', *Journal of Marketing*, 51 (April): 97–111.

Swan, J. and Comb, L. (1976) 'Product performance and consumer satisfaction: a new concept', *Journal of Marketing*, 40 (April): 25–33.

Zeithaml, V. (1981) 'How consumer evaluation processes differ between goods and services', in J. Donnelly and R. George (eds) *Marketing of Services*, Chicago, IL: American Marketing Association, pp. 39–47.

Zeithaml, V., Parasuraman, A. and Berry, L. (1990) *Delivering Quality Service*, New York: Collier Macmillan.

Gambling and time in multicultural South Africa

Gabriel Rousseau*

RN 6.1 Introduction

South Africa is a multicultural society. The divergent composition of the South African population – in terms of income, education, needs, values, expenditure and communication – provides ample opportunity for market and media segmentation based on research. Two areas that recently became a focus of researchers in South Africa are gambling and time perception. Both these areas have serious marketing implications for businesses in the gaming industry and service organizations.

RN 6.2 Gambling research

Political changes in South Africa over the last decade have increased gambling opportunities dramatically. Research suggests that a third of South Africans gamble, with the state lottery being the most popular, followed by slot machines and casinos. It is further estimated that more than 40 per cent of Lotto ticket purchasers earn an average family income of between $133 and $667 per month while 11 per cent earn less than $133 per month, supporting anti-Lotto lobbyists assertion that lotteries are a poor man's tax.

Another survey focused on consumer attitudes towards gambling amongst various socio-demographic groups in Port Elizabeth. This study was instigated by the opening of a casino in the centre of an up-market residential suburb in the city which caused divergent views amongst the general public on the

---

* Professor of Industrial and Organizational Psychology, University of Port Elizabeth, Republic of South Africa.

appropriateness of such a development. A sample of more than 600 respondents were drawn in two separate surveys, comprising of English-, Afrikaans- and Xhosa-speaking residents in the city.

Results confirmed significant differences between socio-demographic groups observed in a pilot study regarding attitudes towards gambling. Cultural influences deduced from home language and religion influenced gambling attitudes; in particular older English-speaking females in the upper income groups with a tertiary education were most in agreement about the economic reason for gambling whilst Xhosa-speaking respondents were more sceptical about the economic, hedonic and symbolic motives for gambling. They perceived gambling as a potential danger, possibly due to their lack of experience with gambling as a form of entertainment.

These findings suggest that casinos should focus on gambling motives in their efforts to create awareness of the potential of problem gambling amongst all cultural groups. Casinos need to also abstain from targeting 'high risk' problem gamblers such as elderly women or pensioners as these customers may damage the gaming industry's image of providing healthy recreational entertainment, should they become compulsive gamblers. The findings of this study further provided guidelines for implementing socially responsible marketing strategies for the gaming industry in South Africa.

RN 6.3 Time perception research

Setting service standards for local government has come under pressure in recent years, not only in South Africa but also abroad. Public services such as those provided by municipalities display the same characteristics of intangibility, heterogeneity and inseparability as most other services. Thus their performance cannot be tested in advance; it may be influenced by the service recipient and is open to the influence of several factors outside the control of the service provider such as waiting, queuing and attendance duration. In South Africa customers often experience long queues at traffic departments and Home Affairs, waiting for vehicle licensing, issuing of drivers' licences, identification documents or passports.

A study was conducted in Port Elizabeth to investigate perceived cultural differences in the perception of time and reactions to waiting amongst a sample of 336 respondents, representative of various socio-demographic groups. The study was motivated by negative press reports about service delays at municipal departments in the city. English-, Afrikaans- and Xhosa-speaking respondents participated in the survey. The results showed significant differences between language, age and education groups on various factors of time perception and reactions to waiting.

Of particular importance was the finding that language groups differed in their assessment of service quality at municipality departments, as well as on emotional experiences while waiting in queues for service at these departments. The fact that English- and Afrikaans-speaking respondents were less positive about service quality at these departments may be due to their being representative of Eurocentric cultures which are more task-oriented. Xhosa-speaking respondents on the other hand were less concerned about waiting for service delivery. This may be due to their being representative of Afrocentric cultures which are more collective and relationship-orientated. They experience the passage of time as less urgent in terms of punctuality.

The study demonstrated that time perception does have an impact on service evaluation, especially when the cost of waiting in queues for service come into play. Results further suggest that emotions affect service evaluation amongst different cultural groups. Serious consideration should therefore be given to time perception of customers, representative of various cultural groups if service organizations strive to enhance their service quality and corporate image. One way of neutralizing potential negative emotions is by providing explanations for delays.

RN 6.4 Conclusion

Multiculturalism within the context of globalization is a new paradigm which no company can afford to take for granted, whether its focus is domestic or foreign markets. Multiculturalism means cultural diversity. Even in traditional, homogeneous domestic markets, subcultures are formed due to the influx of foreigners which bring with them new values, needs and customs. Marketers must sensitize themselves to ethnic diversity if they want to survive in the new world order of globalization.

Further reading

Du Plessis, P. J. and Rousseau, G. G. (2003) Buyer Behaviour: *A Multicultural Approach*, 3rd edn., Cape Town: Oxford University Press.

Rousseau, G. G. and Venter, D. J. L. (2002) 'Measuring consumer attitudes towards gambling: a follow-up study', *Management Dynamics*, 11(3): 24–32.

Rousseau, G. G. and Venter, D. J. L. (2003) 'A multicultural investigation into consumer time perception', *Management Dynamics*, 12(2): 24–32.

CHAPTER 7

Competitive advantage and consumer loyalty in ethnic markets

7.1 Chapter objectives

The preceding chapter brought out the close interrelationship between ethnic minority consumers and their identification with the minority ethnic group. The group has its preferred suppliers and group members, whether new arrivals or long-established residents, benefit from using these preferred suppliers. Search processes are truncated while the endorsement and use by many group members also has the potential to strengthen social bonds between members.

Becoming a preferred supplier may be a source of competitive advantage for businesses over other competing suppliers. Moreover, this competitive advantage is likely to be sustainable and tied to consumer loyalty. Provided the preferred business continues to meet its target group's needs and preferences, consumer loyalty may make it difficult for other business to gain even a testing of their product. Even in situations involving relatively small minority ethnic groups (that is, with relatively few members), creating a strong loyalty involving a willingness to repeat purchase can increase market attractiveness far greater than is suggested by the numerical strength of the group.

This chapter addresses how, having identified an ethnic segment, a business can proceed to develop a competitive advantage that ensues from the achievement of a preferred supplier status, with strong long-term loyalty by the group and its membership. Achieving sustainable competitive advantage is a desirable objective for most businesses, including those active in marketing to ethnic groups. The process requires the use of effective segmentation, targeting and positioning analysis, combined with specific supplier skills including cultural awareness, sensitivity and responsiveness. Concepts of loyalty are explained and related to the possible sources of sustainable competitive advantage that can be used to build ethnic minority consumer loyalty. Possible reasons for switching are also discussed.

7.2 Sources for a sustainable competitive advantage

Sustainable competitive advantage requires a business taking a position in the market different from its main competitors, that will be considered, first, more attractive to the target market than competitors' offers and second, difficult for competitors to emulate (Porter, 1996). Minority ethnic groups constitute groups of consumers with different needs and preferences from other groups. To win and hold members of a minority ethnic group requires that a business find the differences that matter to members of that group, positioning itself to offer those differences in the value proposition – the promise to the target group that encapsulates the differences sought.

A sustainable competitive advantage can be claimed when the target customers perceive the value proposition is superior relative to competitors'. That perception of superiority may arise from many possible bases for distinctiveness that a business may seek to develop, including:

- product quality;
- special product features;
- reputable brands;
- product innovation;
- strong relationships with suppliers and customers;
- special capabilities.

Price or lowest cost is missing in this list because, in general, it means offering the same as your competitors, only cheaper, and is rarely sustainable for a long period.

Distinctiveness may combine several of these bases. For businesses successful in ethnic markets competitive advantage will often be found in their strong relationship with the minority ethnic group and, through the group, with the individual consumer, as well as in the special capabilities required of a relationship-based approach. In turn, if developed and nurtured, these bases for competitive advantage create a loyal customer base that increases the difficulty of entry for potential competitors.

Relationship marketing

In targeting consumers, relationship marketing is concerned with identifying, maintaining and growing a network of individual consumers over time. The network should be interactive and of mutual benefit to the business and the network (Shrivastava and Kale, 2003). While business may gain from a loyal network of repeat customers, the issue a business must address in targeting ethnic minority consumers is: what is the benefit to the consumer?

A useful starting premise for relationship marketing is a presumption by a business that most consumers are in, or would like to be in, a relationship. This applies with stronger force to ethnic minority consumers. Referring to the problems of ethnic minority consumers, especially those newly arrived, discussed in the preceding chapter, the minority ethnic group is central to the creation of a relationship with many types of businesses that ethnic minority consumers deal with. Ethnic minority consumers create a relationship with their minority ethnic group. Through the group they create a relationship with preferred businesses. It is this relationship that justifies the 'preferred' qualifier.

Why does this relationship arise? Because customers make relationship-specific investments of time and effort to identify suppliers and develop relationships with them. These investments range 'from informing a hairdresser about one's personal style and preferences . . . to gathering financial records and participating in a series of in-depth discussions to educate a personal financial planner' (Bendapudi and Berry, 1997: 24).

These relationship-specific investments involve not only information, but also time, effort and money, all of which, from an economic perspective, are taken into account by consumers when considering switching providers (Shaw and Pirog III, 1997).

In addition, ethnic minority consumers' communication difficulties might reduce their ability to pass and retrieve information. Particularly where products are high in interpersonal contact and credence, customization, responsiveness and personalization have the potential to differentiate the exchange further. This is likely to result in the dual effect of increasing switching costs and reinforcing customer dependence upon the supplier. Greater dependency fosters relationship maintenance (Ganesan, 1994).

The link between ethnic minority consumers and their minority ethnic group is likely to support a long-term relationship with businesses, provided experiences are not negative; that is, that suppliers remain credible. Inexperienced ethnic minority consumers benefit from the support of their group through lower perceived risk. Through their identification with that group, they become important to suppliers.

The implication from the dependence on the group is that continued group membership requires consumers' behaviour to conform to the group's values and attitudes. Self-ascription to a minority ethnic group may not be sufficient; it may be necessary to be seen to belong to that group. This supports Johnson's (1982) argument that, in addition to economic costs, switching costs also need to account for social or psychological costs, leading to a relationship that is constrained by a member's conformance to the group.

Customers may stay in a relationship because of the constraints just noted or as a result of customer satisfaction, which may be attributed to the adoption by business of customer-oriented strategies (Bendapudi and Berry, 1997). Customer satisfaction by itself is rarely sufficient to maintain a long-term relationship. Continued support for and referral to a specific business by a minority ethnic group implies consistently positive experiences, together with switching constraints. Hence, the combination of the uniqueness of ethnic groups and difficulties in evaluation may result in ethnic minority consumers' loyalty. The discussion of loyalty in the next section shows that loyalty will not be strong and enduring unless further actions by the business are undertaken.

7.3 Concepts of loyalty

The viability of ethnic market targeting can be increased through suppliers taking active steps to ensure a high retention of their target customers. If a business has a high customer retention rate it may sometimes mistakenly believe that this comes from a strong relationship and customer loyalty. Sure enough, the underlying reasons for high retention may be related to loyalty emerging from a nurtured relationship between ethnic minority consumers and their preferred suppliers. However, high retention may also emerge through the creation of switching cost, where the satisfaction of customers with the business is far less, but the relatively high costs of switching hold the customer. There is a need to understand the drivers that cause ethnic minority consumers to switch because both elements need to be considered in the retention strategies available to businesses targeting ethnic consumers.

Customer loyalty is often cited as an important determinant of long-term growth and profit margins (Doyle, 2000). Unfortunately, there are some differences in the marketing literature regarding its definition, forms, and determinants (Dick and Basu, 1994; Dekimpe *et al.*, 1997; Ewing, 2000; Curasi and Kennedy, 2002). In this book we follow Oliver (1999), possibly the leading authority on the concept's use in marketing. Loyalty is 'a deeply held commitment to rebuy or repatronize a preferred product/service consistently in the future, thereby causing repetitive same brand or same brand-set purchasing, despite situational influences and marketing efforts having the potential to cause switching behavior'. In this definition loyalty is both a socio-emotional attitude and a behavioural outcome – the act of consuming. This concept of loyalty does not presume customer satisfaction, an outcome of consumption that results in pleasurable fulfilment. Loyalty, the psychological meaning of what drives the customer to return to the same supplier, extends beyond attaining a satisfying experience, although satisfaction is an obvious building block of loyalty.

Consumer behaviour may be moderated by social norms such as role requirements, and situational factors such as perceived opportunities (Dick and Basu, 1994). A consumer's consumption history and the physical and social setting in which consumer behaviour takes place may also moderate the link between attitude and behaviour (Foxall, 2002). Consequently, a lot more needs to be known about the influences on the continuing use by ethnic minority consumers of a particular brand or a particular supplier. Continuing use of the same supplier and reluctance to switching does not provide much insight into an ethnic minority consumer's strength of attitude versus social position and situation as an influence on choice.

In this context, the linking of attitude and behaviour together in a model of loyalty by Oliver (1999) also provides insight into how, to hold the loyalty of ethnic minority consumers, the business must satisfy their group's needs and preferences. Loyalty may range from the relatively superficial to a very strong positive affect accompanied by action, as indicated in Table 7.1. In this model loyalty is not static but dynamic and changing, in a positive way if nurtured by the business.

The first stage of loyalty development is *cognitive loyalty*. Here, loyalty is based primarily on belief rather than personal experience. Cognition may be based on information about the brand or supplier and credence is given to that information. For a recently arrived ethnic minority consumer, this information may well come from the minority ethnic group and its information network. If the transaction does not require any significant involvement, then loyalty developed by the consumer may remain shallow and undeveloped. Counterargument and competitive blandishments may cause switching because little affect or emotional ties are developed.

For loyalty to develop to the next stage of *affective loyalty* requires that satisfaction with the experience be processed. Liking for the provider grows based on cumulative satisfying usage occasions. There is both cognition and affect, but not necessarily strong commitment, hence switching is a strong possibility as the consumer remains open to offers from competitors.

Table 7.1 Stages in loyalty development

Step	Type of loyalty	Based on	Requires	Switching due to	Potential switching
1	Cognitive	Belief	Cumulative satisfaction	Counterargument and competitive blandishments	Strong
2	Affective	Satisfaction	Liking the supplier	No commitment	Strong
3	Conative	Increasing commitment; cumulative satisfaction	Intention to future repurchase	Intentions can be diverted	Weaker but still likely
4	Action or ultimate	Build-up of resistance to switching motivations	Immunity to competitors' claims; group preference	Lack of social relationship	Unlikely

Conative loyalty reflects a deepening commitment to a brand or supplier, with the reinforcement of previous satisfying experiences motivating an intention to repurchase in future. Again, switching is still likely because conative loyalty is essentially an intention that can be diverted.

The highest level of loyalty is *action loyalty*, where motivated intention is carried through into a preparedness to act. It encompasses both readiness to act and the desire or preparedness to overcome obstacles that could prevent the intention becoming an action. This means the consumer is willing to overcome situational influences and marketing efforts that have previously caused him or her to switch. It leads to inertial rebuying because situational influences do not dissuade the action.

Nevertheless, loyalty can be undermined in all four stages, including action loyalty. For action loyalty to be maintained consumers must be immune to claims from competitors and induced dissatisfaction creation that might entice them to try another brand or supplier. To achieve this state of immunity, or *ultimate loyalty*, as Oliver (1999) calls it, requires the building of a social relationship between consumers and the provider. Businesses that become preferred suppliers of minority ethnic groups are in a strong position to win ultimate loyalty, providing a strong sustainable competitive advantage based on incumbency.

Table 7.2 brings out the social role of consumption and loyalty that is missing from individually focused concepts of loyalty, using a simple matrix based on the individual consumer's determination to stay with a brand or supplier, and the degree of social support that may assist in that endeavour.

Individual fortitude refers to the strength of will of a consumer in resisting attempts by competing businesses to switch. That fortitude is high when the

Table 7.2 Dimensions of loyalty

	Community/Social support	
Individual fortitude	Low	High
Low	Product superiority	Village envelopment
High	Determined self-isolation	Immersed self-identity

Source: Oliver (1999)

consumer is, for example, exhibiting action loyalty because there is inertia to competitors' offers. Community or social support recognizes the social role of consumption and the importance of social approval. The community with which a consumer identifies can provide varying impetus for consumer loyalty, passively or proactively. Both dimensions are examined, for simplicity, in terms of being either high or low.

Low individual fortitude and low community or social support is likely to correspond to a situation where only cognitive loyalty is generated. An individual may have a high fortitude towards a particular brand, although community social support is relatively low. While this cell (determined self-isolation) reflects individual resistance to overtures from competing brands, this is likely to be difficult without the support of the individual's community.

The two cells on the right of Table 7.2, corresponding to situations of high community or social support, suggest that strong community support is a key element in building ultimate loyalty. Consider a newly arrived ethnic minority consumer in a strange land needing to find a wide range of suitable providers. Internal fortitude will necessarily be low. Social support and guidance in selection of suppliers will largely come from the ethnic group with which the new arrival identifies. The preferences of new arrivals for particular providers will be shaped by those of their community, as suggested in Chapter 6. This is a situation of 'village envelopment', in which 'the primary motivation to become loyal on the part of each consumer is to be one with the group and the primary motivation of the group overseers is to please their constituency' (Oliver, 1999). The group includes the consumer in its social and economic network and protects this consumer from outside influences when individual fortitude is relatively low. The extreme case of this social environment, with its recommendation of preferred providers and what to consume, is that the consumable sought by the group members is not the purchased product but the social relationships or camaraderie of the minority ethnic group.

Immersed self-identity, involving high individual fortitude for a brand or supplier combined with community/social support provides a case where there is both individual and social integration with the brand or provider. 'The consumable is a part and parcel of the consumer's self-identity and his or her social identity.' Belonging to a religious sect or cult is used by Oliver (1999) to illustrate this outcome.

While action loyalty is a strong form of loyalty that businesses can develop through their relationships, businesses that target ethnic minority groups are able to tap into the social side of consumption, building a stronger loyalty based on group recommendation and the importance of the group to the individual.

7.4 Building loyalty

Can ultimate loyalty be created through ethnic marketing regardless of the type of business? How can businesses create this ultimate loyalty? Ultimate loyalty requires product superiority, customers who have a strong desire to consume and defend the brand or provider, reinforced by a strong community support of this provider. This is unlikely to be available to all suppliers for all types of goods and services.

Type of product

The types of business activities that are most able to apply an ethnic marketing strategy are discussed in Chapter 9 (Marketing Services). From the perspective of the potential for loyalty creation, businesses need to be aware of the implications arising from the varying tangibility of products. All products can be classified relative to the degree of dominance of their tangibility element (Rathmell, 1966; Shostack, 1977; Lovelock, 1996), and distributed into search, experience and credence groups, following Zeithaml and Bitner (2000: 31). Tangible dominant products are likely to be high in search qualities that can be predetermined before purchasing takes place. Products that involve characteristics that can only be discerned after purchase or during consumption are likely to be high in experience qualities (Nelson, 1970). At the highly intangible end of the continuum, products difficult to evaluate even after consumption are said to be high in credence qualities (Darby and Karni, 1973). In general, products high in experience and credence qualities are likely to prove the most amenable to the stronger forms of loyalty creation although even search products can engender cognitive loyalty.

Loyalty and switching costs

Many retention reasons are not loyalty-based. These can be discussed using a switching costs typology identified by Burnham, Frels and Mahajan (2003). Switching costs are the one-time costs that customers using a particular supplier perceive as likely to be incurred in switching to another supplier, and that would not be incurred if they stayed with the current supplier (Porter, 1980), a definition widely used in the marketing literature that embraces all costs, monetary or otherwise (Jones and Sasser, 1995; Jones et al., 2000; Sharma and Patterson, 2000; Kiser, 2002).

Eight types of switching costs are identified by Burnham, Frels and Mahajan (2003). *Economic risk* costs include the perceived risk of poor performance, often an accompanying financial risk and the inconvenience of changing. *Evaluation costs* are the costs (often in time and effort) incurred in information collection and evaluation of alternative suppliers. *Learning costs* are the costs of acquiring new skills and knowledge required to use the new supplier. Adaptation to a new system or rules is often a part of the change to a new supplier. *Set-up costs* are different, addressing the *establishment costs* of moving to a new supplier, such as installation and configuration of a software program. *Benefit loss costs* arise from the loss of economic benefits in switching to a new supplier, for example the loss of loyalty points or discounts for cumulative purchases. *Monetary loss costs* are exemplified by one-time financial outlays, such as a deposit, that may be required to initiate service provision. *Personal relationship losses* are created, from the breaking of bonds or ties with people with whom the customer has interacted. These may be employees but, drawing on Oliver's (1999) village envelopment concept, will also include other patrons who may provide a social attraction to use that provider. *Brand relationship losses* are affective, arising from the breaking of a bond with the brand or business itself.

These costs can be grouped into three higher order types: procedural (economic risk, evaluation, learning and set-up costs); financial (benefit–loss and financial costs); and relational (personal relationship loss and brand relationship loss costs). Having chosen their first supplier on arrival, ethnic minority consumers are likely to be particularly susceptible to many types of procedural switching costs, hence the importance of the ethnic group in the choice of providers. However, creating procedural and financial cost is not the way for a supplier to win the loyalty of ethnic minority consumers. The creation of *perceived relational costs* is the thrust of loyalty building. These costs are likely to have particular relevance for ethnic minority consumers with supplier loyalty built on the village envelopment or immersed self-identity (Oliver, 1999). Stronger forms of loyalty (and higher relational switching costs) may be obtainable for businesses providing services that are high in experience and credence properties (Colgate and Hedge, 2001).

Attraction to particular brands or suppliers in these categories may well be based on elements of cultural affinity that ease the acculturation process. Staying with a supplier because of both communication ease and pleasure arising from the provision of ethnic language services, familiarity and perhaps identification with employees, the socialization provided by widespread use by others of the same group (similar others), as well as good service, all suggest that ethnic minority consumers may incur a loss of identity and a breaking of bonds causing psychological and/or emotional discomfort in switching providers (Burnham, Frels and Mahajan, 2003). Conversely, developing these bonds with an ethnic group provide the basis for Oliver's (1999) loyalty dimensions.

Building cultural affinity

Building a strong loyalty requires addressing a minority ethnic group's needs and preferences, as well as evaluative criteria before, during and after consumption. The range of cultural variables that are likely to distinguish minority ethnic groups from the mainstream can be expanded beyond those previously outlined. Many are communication-based and require business targeting ethnic groups to tailor a communication strategy recognizing these differences, a matter developed further in Chapter 11. By seeking to address these often valued cultural differences, a village envelopment that bonds the group and the individual to a business can be constructed.

A multicultural or multiethnic society is based on a collection of different ethnic groups alongside a majority 'national' group (Yinger, 1976). This gives rise to many forms of cross-cultural interaction difficulties because the influence of a culture creates a product made out of a residue of behaviours, ideas and beliefs with which people are comfortable and which they consider 'proper' or the right way (Brislin, 1981), although this product may appear overly personal or time inefficient to others. The resulting cross-cultural interaction difficulties ensue from communication complexity. Particularly important is the degree of reliance on non-verbal cues (Weiss and Stripp, 1998) that will influence the capacity of a person from a different cultural background to appraise information provided by alternative service providers framed in a different cultural context. Further, within a relationship with a supplier, barriers to switching are created by communication complexity. More search and other procedural costs, as well as relational costs, may need to be incurred compared with a mainstream consumer of the same service.

The importance of context

Hall and Hall (1990) elaborate on the dimensions (of context, space and time) that can create favourable or unfavourable interactions between persons from different cultures. Context is the information that surrounds an event and is bound up with the meaning of an event. Events and contexts are in different proportions depending on the culture. As a generalization, persons immersed in a low-context national culture generally need more information when making a business decision than persons from a high-context culture. Low-context people may be at a loss when high-context people do not provide enough information, while high-context people may react to excessive, unsought information. An appropriate level of context is needed for each situation because too much information may lead people to feel they are being talked down to, while too little may alienate them. However, faced with a 'new enterprise' to which they have not been contexted, high-context persons may require more information than low-context persons in order to reach their own synthesis of meaning rather than accepting this synthesis from another foreign party. Hence, within a low-context national culture, persons from a high-context culture may be attracted to and retained by a supplier with the most suitable contextual communication strategy.

The importance of space and time

Space and time can also create dissonance between cultures. Space is perceived by all the senses. Spatial changes give tone to communication, accent it and may override the spoken word. Time is also structured differently between cultures and can influence the customer–supplier relationship (Hall and Hall, 1990). In addition to communication complexity from these elements other differences also operate, including risk-taking propensity; the bases of trust; concern with protocol; the nature of persuasion (reason or emotion); and whether the form of agreement is implicit or explicit (Weiss and Stripp, 1998).

The minority ethnic group and its relationship with a preferred provider also reduces the perceived risk of purchase for the individual consumer. Building loyalty involves the business in assessing the sources of perceived risk. Perceived risk is a situational and personal construct (Dowling and Staelin, 1994) that has been defined in several ways. Mitchell (1999) suggests the weight of empirical research has favoured a definition that has two components: the probability of a loss and the subjective feeling of the unfavourable consequences (Cunningham, 1967).

Perceived risk pertains primarily to pre-decision consumer choice and information search (Dowling, 1986). The greater or more likely the actual purchase experience differs from the purchase goals, the higher the perceived risk. By Cox and Rich's (1964) description, risk is a function of the amount at stake and the subjective certainty of the outcomes. For each purchase decision, the consumer will have a set of buying goals, or expected outcomes of the purchase. Therefore, perceived risk is a reflection of the possible or expected dissatisfaction with a purchase, based on the consumer's buying goals.

As previously mentioned, the perceived risk of incurring procedural costs may be high for ethnic minority consumers, leading to newly arrived consumers taking risk-reducing actions through the ethnic group. The quality of the long-term relationship that the consumer's ethnic group, drawing from its collective experience, maintains with suppliers is the important interaction for the supplier to focus on. The current exchange is not viewed necessarily as the last. It is part of a process of exchange that is likely to continue. This will influence the expectations and relationship between the two parties. Ethnic consumers can draw on the exchange experiences of similar others as a preferred source of market information. This dependence will influence the maintenance of customer relationships with the group (Sheth and Parvatiyar, 1995) and strengthen the propensity to maintain a long-term relationship with a particular provider (Brand and Cronin, 1997). This means that in seeking to build loyalty with a particular minority ethnic group or groups, a business will need to monitor each target group relationship rather than the customer base as a whole, to ensure that the group does not perceive increased risk in the preferred relationship.

7.5 Why ethnic consumers may switch

Although ethnic consumers may form close relationships with preferred businesses and this can be developed into strong forms of loyalty, competition for ethnic consumers, even if not targeted as a group, requires close attention to their switching behaviour. Service quality failure and dissatisfaction are reasons contributing to switching suppliers (Grace and O'Cass, 2001; Mihelis *et al.*, 2001), but consumers who switch may not be dissatisfied with their provider, while those that do not may not be wholly satisfied. Other factors, such as better deals from competitors or a desire for a change (Fournier and Yao, 1997) can also play a role. A study by Keaveney (1995), developed from critical incidents, addresses why retention may fail. Pricing, inconvenience, core service failure, service encounter failure, employee response to service failure, attraction by competitors and ethical problems are reasons why customers switched providers in this study.

Switching motivations are likely to vary depending on the type of product, with higher switching rates in search products than the other classes of credence and experience. In Keaveney (1995) 'inconvenience' was found to be important (20 per cent of respondents) but not the major switching motivation. For ethnic minority consumers, inconvenience is also likely to be important but mainly in search-type products. It is likely to be far less important as a switching motivation for products high in credence qualities.

For newly arrived ethnic consumers, improved market knowledge is likely to be an important switching reason for products in the experience and credence classes. Improved market knowledge encompasses a growing awareness of other suppliers and is indicative that the preferred supplier recommended by the group has failed to develop a strong loyalty strategy. It may also reflect that individual ethnic consumers have acculturated away from their ethnic group over time.

'Pricing' is also an important switching motivation in Keaveney's study. Price-driven switching is likely to be more important for products in the search class, compared with the experience and credence classes. 'Core service failure' and 'service encounter failure' were respectively the largest and second largest switching motivations in the Keaveney study. These are clearly at the core of relationship and loyalty development with an ethnic group, while dissatisfaction with the provider's service is likely to be a major reason for the minority ethnic group seeking alternative providers. Because of group dynamics, rather than the business facing a slow attrition from customers' switching, the ethnic group link to individual consumers may cause a large and rapid loss of the target group. Having targeted and attracted the patronage of an ethnic group, there is also an economic imperative for the business continually to address and monitor the relationship.

7.6 Summary

An ethnic marketing strategy needs to address provider retention by what may be, numerically, a small target group. In targeting a minority ethnic group the aim is to develop a strategy that will give the targeting business a sustainable competitive advantage over its close competitors, thus retaining hard-won customers. This chapter has addressed how this can be done.

Competitive advantage has been linked to the building of a strong relationship, but this in turn requires special capabilities, especially implementing cross-cultural awareness and practices. Relationships are at the core of successful ethnic marketing. These involve both the relationship between the ethnic group and the individual ethnic consumer, and the relationship between the group and the preferred provider recommended to group members. The close interlinking of the three parties has mutual benefit for each.

It is this mutual benefit that helps to develop consumer loyalty to the business over time. Satisfaction, by itself, is not sufficient to engender loyalty. Loyalty is best considered to be dynamic and varying in its possible strength. The model proposed by Oliver (1999) classifies four stages or phases of loyalty development. Beyond action loyalty, ultimate loyalty requires a socio-emotional involvement to which the ethnic group contributes as a social network. Successful relationship marketing requires the consumer to derive benefit from the relationship. In the case of ethnic consumers the growth of what Oliver calls village envelopment generates this benefit in many ways ranging from the reduction of perceived risk for individual members to the social ties formed.

The elements of constructing a strategy that will lead to a high retention of ethnic consumers attracted by targeting strategy may also include the creation of perceived procedural and financial switching costs. These are not, however, elements of a loyalty strategy and may well engender group dissatisfaction that undermines a loyalty strategy.

References

Bendapudi, N. and Berry, L. (1997) 'Customers' motivations for maintaining relationships with service providers', *Journal of Retailing*, 73(1): 15–37.

Brand, R. and Cronin, J. (1997) 'Consumer-specific determinants of the size of retail choice sets: an empirical comparison of physical good and service providers', *Journal of Services Marketing*, 11(1): 19–38.

Brislin, R. (1981) *Cross-cultural Encounters*, New York: Pergamon Press.

Burnham, T., Frels, J. and Mahajan, V. (2003) 'Consumer switching costs: a typology, antecedents and consequences', *Journal of the Academy of Marketing Science*, 31 (Spring): 109–26.

Colgate, M. and Hedge, R. (2001) 'An investigation into the switching process in retail banking services', *International Journal of Bank Marketing*, 19: 201–12.

Cox, D. F. and Rich, S. U. (1964) 'Perceived risk and consumer decision-making: the case of telephone shopping', *Journal of Marketing Research*, 1 (November): 32–9.

Cunningham, S. (1967) 'The major dimensions of perceived risk', in D. F. Cox (ed.) *Risk Taking and Information Handling in Consumer Behavior*, Boston, MA: Harvard University Press, pp. 82–108.

Curasi, C. and Kennedy, K. (2002) 'From prisoners to apostles: a typology of repeat buyers and loyal customers in service businesses', *Journal of Services Marketing*, 16: 322–41.

Darby, M. and Karni, E. (1973) 'Free competition and the optimal amount of fraud', *Journal of Law and Economics*, 16 (April): 67–86.

Dekimpe, M., Steenkamp, J., Mellens, M. and Abeele, P. (1997) 'Decline and variability in brand loyalty', *International Journal of Research in Marketing*, 14: 405–20.

Dick, A. and Basu, K. (1994) 'Customer loyalty: towards an integrated conceptual framework', *Journal of the Academy of Marketing Science*, 22: 99–113.

Dowling, G. R. (1986) 'Perceived risk: the concept and its measurement', *Psychology and Marketing*, 3: 193–210.

Dowling, G. R. and Staelin, R. (1994) 'A model of perceived risk and intended risk handling activity', *Journal of Consumer Research*, 21 (June): 119–34.

Doyle, P. (2000) *Value-based Marketing*, Brisbane: John Wiley.

Ewing, M. (2000) 'Brand and retailer loyalty: past behavior and future intentions', *Journal of Product and Brand Management*, 9: 120–7.

Fournier, S. and Yao, L. (1997) 'Reviving brand loyalty: a reconceptualization within the framework of consumer–brand relationships', *International Journal of Research in Marketing*, 14: 451–72.

Foxall, G. (2002) 'Marketing's attitude problem – and how to solve it', *Journal of Customer Behaviour*, 1: 19–48.

Ganesan, S. (1994) 'Determinants of long-term orientation in buyer–seller relationships', *Journal of Marketing*, 58 (April): 1–19.

Grace, D. and O'Cass, A. (2001) 'Attributions of service switching: a study of consumers' and providers' perceptions of child-care service delivery', *Journal of Services Marketing*, 15: 300–21.

Hall, E. T. and Hall, M. (1990) *Understanding Cultural Differences*, Yarmouth, ME: Intercultural Press.

Johnson, M. (1982) 'The social and cognitive features of the dissolution of commitment relationships', in S. Duck (ed.) *Personal Relationships: Dissolving Personal Relationships*, New York: Academic Press, pp. 51–73.

Jones, M., Mothersbaugh, D. and Beatty, S. (2000) 'Switching barriers and repurchase intentions in services', *Journal of Retailing*, 76: 259–69.

Jones, T. and Sasser, E. (1995) 'Why satisfied customers defect', *Harvard Business Review*, 73 (Nov.–Dec.): 88–99.

Keaveney, S. (1995) 'Customer switching behavior in service industries: an exploratory study', *Journal of Marketing*, 59 (April): 71–92.

Kiser, E. (2002) 'Predicting household switching behavior and switching costs at depository institutions', *Review of Industrial Organization*, 20: 349–65.

Lovelock, C. (1996) *Services Marketing*, 3rd edn., New Jersey, NJ: Prentice-Hall International.

Mihelis, G., Grigoroudis, E., Siskos, Y., Politis, Y. and Malandrakis, Y. (2001) 'Customer satisfaction measurement in the private bank sector', *European Journal of Operational Research*, 130: 347–60.

Mitchell, V. (1999) 'Consumer perceived risk: conceptualization and models', *European Journal of Marketing*, 33(1/2): 163–95.

Nelson, P. (1970) 'Advertising as information', *Journal of Political Economy*, 81 (Jul.–Aug.): 729–54.

Oliver, R. (1999) 'Whence consumer loyalty?', *Journal of Marketing*, 63: 33–44.

Porter, M. (1980) *Competitive Strategy*, New York: Free Press.

Porter, M. (1996) 'What is strategy?', *Harvard Business Review*, November–December.

Rathmell, J. (1966) 'What is meant by services?', *Journal of Marketing*, 30: 32–6.

Sharma, N. and Patterson, P. (2000) 'Switching costs, alternative attractiveness and experience as moderators of relationship commitment in professional, consumer services', *International Journal of Service Industry Management*, 11(5): 470–83.

Shaw, E. and Pirog III, S. (1997) 'A systems model of household behavior', *Journal of Marketing Theory and Practice*, Summer: 17–29.

Sheth, J. and Parvatiyar, A. (1995) 'Relationship marketing in consumer markets: antecedents and consequents', *Journal of the Academy of Marketing Science*, 23: 255–71.

Shostack, L. (1977) 'Breaking free from product marketing', *Journal of Marketing*, 41 (April): 73–80.

Shrivastava, S. and Kale, S. (2003) 'Philosophizing on the elusiveness of relationship marketing theory in consumer markets: a case for reassessing ontological and epistemological assumptions', *Australasian Marketing Journal*, 11(3): 61–71.

Weiss, S. and Stripp, W. (1998) 'Negotiating with foreign business persons', in S. Niemeier, C. Campbell and R. Driven (eds) *The Cultural Context in Business Communication*, Amsterdam: John Benjamin's Publishing Company.

Yinger, J. M. (1976) 'Ethnicity in complex societies', in A. Lewis *et al.* (eds) *The Uses of Controversy in Sociology*, New York: Free Press.

Zeithaml, V. and Bitner, M. (2000) *Services Marketing: Integrating Customer Focus Across the Firm*, Sydney: McGraw Hill.

You need more than a road map

Karen Benezra*

Reaching out to the multicultural marketplace, whether in the USA or abroad, requires more than a phrase book and a road map. More often, it means relying on culturally attuned experts who can guide marketers through language gaps and other hurdles. 'There are bonds within ethnic groups that connect all the members into a cohesive marketplace that go beyond having a common language', said Yuri Radzievsky [a New York Agency that specializes in multi-cultural accounts].

With nationalism and cultural pride on the upswing, immigrant communities that one time tried to shed their native languages or style of dress and blend in with the American scene are now proud to identify themselves as Russian–American or Chinese–American. Despite the growing diversity, community opinion holds great sway over individuals on issues like brand preference. 'Newcomers ask friends and neighbours which refrigerator to buy, or how to call abroad', Radzievsky said. Thus, winning over one consumer means winning over all of them.

When looking for other common threads in the ethnic marketplace, media is an important link. Telemundo and Univision are key conduits to Hispanic audiences here, but Asian–Americans cling to newspapers as their primary medium.

QUESTIONS

1. How can marketers create bonds that tie them to such ethnic communities?
2. What are the other types of hurdles?

---

* *Brandweek*, 17 July 1995.

CHAPTER 8

Identifying and reaching an ethnic market: methodological issues

8.1 Chapter objectives

Information about ethnic groups doesn't come cheaply. Even using basic indicators such as country of birth or nationality, establishing relatively straightforward dimensions about ethnic groups, such as group size, is often a very difficult task to accomplish. Difficulties compound when behavioural perspectives of ethnicity are preferred.

Defining ethnic group dimensions is, nevertheless, a task that needs to be done. This chapter presents a methodology for businesses and researchers to acquire information necessary for, first, profiling a minority ethnic group, and second, establishing a workable and reliable interface with the group. Both are fundamental for sound decision-making in ethnic marketing.

8.2 Why it is difficult to profile minority ethnic groups

Consideration of the difficulties inherent to the process of ethnicity-based segmentation within culturally diverse markets, in Chapter 5, pointed to the use of ethnic group resources (or more precisely their existence, variety and number) as proxies for a minority ethnic group's potential substantiality. Positive expectations of substantiality justify businesses' investment in the process of profiling the specific minority group, as a prerequisite for deciding about its targeting and in what way.

Assessing the importance of an ethnic group for marketing purposes requires the development of a clear profile of the group, including information about networks of communication, location, concentration, demographic make-up, substance, consumption pattern, as well as unsatisfied needs, preferences and evaluative criteria before and after consumption. The gathering of this information may not be an easy task to accomplish in a culturally diverse society.

Developing a profile for a minority ethnic group may be difficult due to informational, attitudinal and methodological limitations, listed in Table 8.1.

Table 8.1 Limitations on the development of minority ethnic group profiles

Informational limitations	■ Group boundaries are difficult to establish due to lack of information
	■ Published statistics about the group may not be readily available
	■ Past studies about the specific group, or other ethnic groups that could be used as a reference, are lacking
	■ Inability to assess substantiality acts as a moderator on the research effort
Attitudinal limitations	■ Cultural ethnocentricity, past and present, does not encourage ethnic group research
	■ Affiliates of minority ethnic groups may have limited acculturation to social enquiry
Methodological limitations	■ Market cultural diversity, and the need to research many ethnic minority groups, may be too demanding on available resources
	■ The cultural and linguistic skills required to communicate effectively with the group may not be readily available
	■ A framework for ethnic marketing research is currently lacking

A lack of information about group boundaries, of readily available group statistics and of past studies about the group, or other groups that may be used as a reference, may curtail the profiling effort, particularly when the potential payoff is not known. From an attitudinal perspective, an apparent disregard traditionally afforded to minority ethnic groups by business and by researchers justifies a corresponding lack of social inquiry into these groups, including ethnic group profiles. In turn, the lack of social inquiry limits ethnic group members' exposure and acculturation to the social inquiry process. As a process, acculturation to social enquiry depends on exposure to data gathering exercises and on researchers' experience in dealing with possibly reluctant participants. This contributes a dynamic element that justifies that information gathering may be both cumulative and easier at later stages of the process. Affiliates of invisible minority ethnic groups are likely to be less acculturated to social enquiry.

Relative to methodological limitations, researchers need to develop appropriate protocols and to communicate effectively with ethnic minorities in a culturally diverse and cosmopolitan environment. Skill and resource limitations may combine with uncertainty about the best methods to reach and research specific groups, themselves probably uncomfortable and reluctant subjects. This may divert attention to aggregates of groups, in any case limiting the availability of specific ethnic group profiles. The case of Newham Council (England), Case 6 (page 161), is a good illustration for these limitations. As expressed by Sills and Desai (1996): '[T]he size and diversity of Newham's ethnic population, together with the range of languages they speak, presents enormous problems for a council committed to listening to its public.' The same difficulties applied to the researchers outsourced by the council, 'whose task [was] to facilitate the listening process'. Such difficulties included information inadequacies and lack of a methodological precedent, to guide how to proceed.

Last but not least, a lack of ethnic group research means that there is no knowledge of what works and what does not, no examples to follow and no known pitfalls to avoid. But the lack of a framework for ethnic marketing research clearly constrains more than the development of minority ethnic group profiles. The constraint extends, first, to comparative evaluations among minority ethnic groups, as part of the target selection process, and second, to the design of effective strategies for the selected markets, due to the lack of knowledge of the needs, preferences and evaluative criteria valued by the minority ethnic consumers being targeted.

8.3 Using conventional research methods to identify ethnic groups

To be effective, market segmentation must focus on achieving homogeneous and unique reactive consumption behaviour to marketing stimulus, over a period of time long enough for the marketing action to reach and generate a response in the targeted population. That is, the population needs to be identifiable, measurable, actionable, unique, stable and homogeneous in the relevant characteristics. This prescription is even more inflexible in the realm of ethnic marketing, since there is no ethnicity-based rationale for the aggregations of resident ethnic communities (the emic-etic distinction), often based on language similarity, so typical in the marketing literature.

As explained in Chapter 4, to aggregate some highly homogeneous minority ethnic groups may prove advantageous for discrete marketing purposes (like achieving critical mass and economies of scale). But the abuse of group aggregations may be an unwarranted pragmatic reaction to perceived difficulties in identifying and dimensioning individual minority ethnic groups (the population), and in sampling that population in a reliable and convenient way. This has potential implications for the use of conventional research methodology, because the methodological precedent that was lacking in the case of Newham Council is still missing.

Other possible explanations for the lack of studies dealing with single, narrowly defined, minority ethnic groups include:

- perceived irrelevance of these groups for marketing research purposes, as claimed by subscribers to the linear assimilation model, discussed in Chapter 3. This clearly ignores the potential marketing opportunities afforded by the continuing existence of ethnic groups within advanced economies;

- cultural ethnocentricity, past and present, which did not and does not encourage research of narrowly defined minority ethnic groups;

- lightly elaborated calls for aggregation of sub-cultures;

- insufficient evidence of the importance of these groups for marketing, as an incentive for the marketing research effort;

- the fact that individual minority ethnic groups with relatively few members may remain invisible within common information sources. This may link to a lack of public exposure and consistent reporting on the realities, problems, activities and celebrations of these groups, as compared with others, perhaps with larger numbers of affiliates. For market researchers and practitioners alike, inclusion of a minority ethnic group in this category may be indicative of lack of critical mass or substance;

- processes of continuous acculturation influence behaviour by ethnic minority consumers and their group of affiliation. Simple explanations of acculturation are challenging because the acculturation process is potentially more dynamic for individuals than for groups. By the same rationale, acculturation effects are likely to be stronger for individual minority ethnic groups than for aggregates of groups; hence the preference for studies with a focus on the latter.

Ultimately, the focus on aggregates of ethnic groups combines with the noted lack of a methodological precedent and of a framework for ethnic marketing research, to justify a need for qualitative exploratory research methods when studying individual minority ethnic groups.

A method for conducting exploratory qualitative research of an ethnic group, for which little published information is available, is subsequently discussed. For objectivity, the discussion draws on a research project conducted in February 2000 with a focus on the Portuguese community in Sydney, Australia (basic information about the community is provided as Case 5 in this chapter). This project provides extensive coverage of the issues that researchers can expect to face in identifying and reaching an 'invisible' minority ethnic group and how these were resolved.[1] The proposed methodology involves a symbiosis of *symbolic interaction* (the understanding of group lived experience and the meanings that are imminent in the interactions that occur within this group) with *phenomenological description* (understanding the individual through understanding of the group that provides the individual's context) that yields rich information about the group. Both of these are at the basis of grounded theory (Horn, 1998; Byrne, 2001).

8.4   Project research design[2]

The research design was qualitative, aimed at exploring meanings of social phenomena as experienced by individuals themselves in their natural context (Miles and Huberman, 1994). The project was deliberately limited to only one minority ethnic group in order to avoid disparate qualitative information, possibly in different languages, as well as to reduce problems such as sample design, recruitment and moderation problems resulting from the problematic aggregation of ethnic groups using qualitative research (Sills and Desai, 1996).

Data collection relied on a written survey to be distributed to individuals self-ascribed to the community as of February 2000.[3] Limited availability of secondary sources of information introduced an element of uncertainty that exposed the need for *exploratory* research. How would the target individuals react to the request for information about their behaviour as consumers? How should the participation request be addressed and structured to induce a response? How to overcome the complexities inherent to research involving persons inexperienced in participating in research projects and unsure about any implications from their participation? Were there any actions, words or images to be avoided to reduce the risk of alienating the respondents? No clear responses to these and other similar questions were found in the literature.

Table 8.2 Process used for initial selection and probing of experts

- Identify gatekeepers to the community being studied, gathering sufficient information to personalize the contact
- Telephone each gatekeeper informally
- Offer to converse in the gatekeeper's preferred language
- Explain the broad aims of the research project, emphasizing potential benefits for the community
- Explain how the gatekeeper was chosen, how she/he can contribute and the importance of that contribution for the project and, ultimately, for the community
- Probe the gatekeeper about her/his willingness to participate in a depth interview
- Probe the gatekeeper about her/his willingness to participate in a focus group
- Ask the gatekeeper to name other experts on the community who should be contacted, or to ask them to contact the researcher

Experience surveys and selection of experts

The project used experience surveys, also called expert opinion surveys, to gain background information and guidance from individuals thought to be knowledgeable on the issues relevant to the research problem, namely those relating to accessibility to the community for the purposes of gathering the desired information (Bradburn, 1983; Burgess, 1986; Streiner and Norman, 1995; Burns and Bush, 2000). The selection and probing of experts can facilitate the gathering of useful information, although it does not allow for any considerations of representativeness in relation to the population being studied. The process used for selecting and probing experts is summarized in Table 8.2.

Similar to the research projects carried out by Anzul *et al.* (2001) involving Portuguese-speaking parents of special needs students with severe disabilities, and Sills and Desai (1996) for Newham Council (England), the process of selection of experts was an iterative one, mostly governed by the identification of gatekeepers to the community, a role made important for its referential qualities.[4] Gatekeepers invariably have a better knowledge of their local community and, if consulted at an early stage of the research design, can help to define the population, feasibility of the proposed sample, administration method and so on. In the case of a minority ethnic group the gatekeepers may be individuals (including employers, teachers, providers of religious services and other professional services providers, community officials and dignitaries) as well as institutions and their representatives (consulate personnel, community support, welfare and recreational organizations, and so on). As noted in Chapter 5, the depth of this extant network is a potential indicator of group strength.

Experts were informally contacted by telephone and, having been given the choice, opted for interaction in the Portuguese language. A brief explanation of the broad aims of the study, of why they were selected and of how they could contribute was given at the outset. Experts were then probed about their availability for an interview and for partaking in a focus group discussion. Finally they were asked either to name other experts on the community who should be contacted, or to pass the researchers' contact to the potential gatekeepers, for contact at their leisure.

In-depth interviews and contextual embedding

Face-to-face interviews were informal, unstructured and taped. The tapes were then analysed for content to identify recurring themes, useful for preparing the agenda for the ensuing focus group session. This strategy allowed the gathering of information about the interviewees' opinions on the research problem, as well as the perspective of the community on a range of issues, ranging from literacy to attitudes to participation in social inquiry. The information gathered was instrumental in both the design of a draft questionnaire and in deciding about the method for questionnaire administration.

The interviews revealed the crucial importance of an adequate appreciation of the contextual embedding of the Portuguese community for the success of the project. Group affiliates were described as

- largely inexperienced as participants in research studies;
- reluctant participants due to a possible element of suspicion about undisclosed motivations for the questioning;
- reluctant participants due to a fear of not being able to give the 'right answers';
- possibly limited in their ability to participate due to an alleged relatively low level of schooling.

It was apparent that this information had to be taken into account in designing the questionnaire and in deciding on its promotion, distribution and other action conducive to elicit participation, cognizant of the need to avoid any discomfort to the potential participants.[5]

A draft questionnaire was prepared based on the propositions derived from conceptual analysis and the insights from the interviews (Singh *et al.*, 1990). The aim was to develop questions that respondents could and would answer whilst yielding the desired information, to minimize incompleteness and non-response due to respondent boredom, fatigue and effort, and to minimize response error arising from inaccurate answers by respondents or misanalysis of the answers by the researcher (Malhotra *et al.*, 1996). A tabulation format for collecting this information was initially used because it allowed the questionnaire to be limited to just six pages, but this had to be modified following the first pre-test that took place during the focus group session.

Because participants had been interviewed and were, therefore, aware of the issues to be explored, the focus session proved useful in confirming the issues noted during the interviews, rather than as a source of new issues. Participants reiterated their belief that the survey would obtain very few responses regardless of the survey instrument or method of administration, due to the contextual embedding of the community discussed above. This strengthened the decision to use a qualitative and exploratory research design. It was apparent that the use of conventional quantitative research methods needed to be carefully evaluated before application to a narrowly defined and research inexperienced group. Use of a multi-item scale often used in quantitative research would be necessarily limited by the respondents' ability to use it effectively.

The focus session indicated the need to modify the format (including several open-ended questions and revising the options provided in limited choice questions) and wording of the questionnaire, and to produce it in Portuguese and English versions. This was an important event to note because it suggests that questions of meaning and interpretation are not limited to cross-cultural research involving different languages.

8.5 Reducing respondents' reluctance

Endorsed surveys

Participants in the focus group were asked, and agreed, to complete and comment on the reformulated questionnaire. In addition, as a means of reducing the reluctance of the members of the community in completing the survey, participants were asked to endorse and promote the project, to distribute the questionnaire to individuals they identified as members of the Portuguese community, and to identify other community members that could distribute the questionnaire. Such endorsement by the experts, gatekeepers to the community, was an important asset for the research, given evidence in the literature of a positive impact on response rates (Rochford and Venable, 1995).

Changes to the questionnaire

Pre-testing of the questionnaire indicated that the tabulation format was inadequate for the population to be examined. Fewer pages resulted in crowding and increased complexity, working as a deterrent for respondents. The tables were interpreted as involving the simultaneous consideration of 16 different services and the determination of the appropriate cell to fill was an extra difficulty.

Revising the questionnaire in line with the comments required major changes to its length and structure, simplicity, error avoidance mechanisms and respondent orientation, as explained below.

■ *Length and structure* – The revised questionnaire was much larger than the original and clearly repetitive in its structure. It was divided into sections. Following a page of general instructions, the first section repeated a set of questions for each of the 16 types of services, one page per service. Each page was divided into two parts. The questions in the first part referred respondents to their first preferred provider of the service in Australia. The questions in the second part referred respondents to their current preferred provider of the same service. It was apparent that asking the same questions, in the same order, over 16 consecutive pages, could result in order or position bias.[6] However, randomization of the questions would introduce difficulties in terms of maintaining a context that flows from question to question and, importantly, would increase the degree of complexity perceived by respondents. This could conceivably result in a lower participation rate, particularly given the length of the survey instrument.

■ *Simplicity* – Since the questionnaire confined all the questions for each service to a page, respondents were given the option to tick a single box in the top line of each page to indicate they had never used the particular service. In addition, by simply ticking one box separating Part 1 (first provider) and Part 2 (current provider), respondents could indicate that the providers were one and the same, avoiding the need to complete the questions in Part 2.

■ *Error avoidance* – The questionnaire asked respondents to remember moments in their past, related to their selection of the first provider for the different service activities. In order to avoid errors of omission, telescoping and creation, instructions asked respondents to proceed to a designated question number, if they could not remember.[7]

■ *Respondent orientation* – Versions of the revised questionnaire were developed in English and in Portuguese. The objective was to increase the number of responses by providing potential respondents with a questionnaire in their preferred language. The two versions mirrored each other in organization and contents, although some adaptation was required in the Portuguese version to account for context.

The two versions of the revised questionnaire were posted to the experts who had participated in the focus group discussion. Phone contact was made 48 hours later to make sure that the questionnaires had been received and to agree on a date for their feedback. This feedback resulted in simpler and more comprehensive instructions to assist in the completion of the questionnaire, as well as in the enlargement of the font.

Once the questionnaires had been fully revised and tested, the two versions were printed in a booklet with 22 pages, in itself a possible deterrent for some potential respondents.[8] But it was hoped that creating a questionnaire visually appealing and easy to complete, in the preferred language, would lessen this effect.

The final questionnaire was constructed with simple, short, structured questions that respondents could answer in most cases by simply choosing a selection or selections and ticking the corresponding boxes. Little writing was required. This was particularly important because the questionnaire was to be self-administered. Options of the type 'Other (please justify)' were included in the structured questions to provide respondents with the chance to answer when other options seemed inadequate. Although this may not always produce the desired results because it is easier for respondents to tick one of the available boxes than to write their own answer, sole use of a list of possible answers for respondents can produce biased responses (Bishop, 1987). Trials indicated that it would take respondents between 20 and 45 minutes to complete the questionnaire, but distribution of the questionnaire as a mail survey gave respondents time to answer the questionnaire at their own pace (Ferber and Kraus, 1984).

8.6 Population definition

In seeking to identify and target a particular minority ethnic group, definition of the population by parameters such as language or birthplace can only provide an approximate starting point because membership is often self-ascribed (Barth, 1969). Using the parameters of language and/or birthplace, the Portuguese community in Sydney was defined as including all persons who either spoke Portuguese at home, or did not speak Portuguese at home but whose parents (mother or father or both) were born in Portugal (or any of the Portuguese ex-colonies, including Brazil). Defined in this way the population may exclude those who self-ascribe to this particular community and include those who do not ascribe. Sampling from this population may encounter respondent unwillingness and sampling frame errors that need to be controlled (Malhotra *et al.*, 1996). In the case of this study, the respondents were subject to self-screening, to screening by questionnaire distributors, and, finally, to screening in the data entry phase.

It is apparent that the difficulty in defining population boundaries when studying minority ethnic groups for marketing purposes is a primary and major problem in attempting to profile these groups, and to assess their marketing relevance. This is particularly important because the canonical procedure for generalization in statistically driven studies requires the random selection of a sample from a population, as a condition for determining levels of probability regarding the relationship between findings on the sample and the population from which it is randomly selected (Eisner, 1997). This applies to any population and there is no apparent justification for exception in the case of minority ethnic groups. The process of defining population boundaries, as well as the gathering of other information needed for effective profiling, requires applied research at the group level, as illustrated in the method used in 2000 to study the Portuguese community in Sydney.

8.7 Sampling process

The lack of a precedent for a sampling process effectively applied to a minority ethnic group justifies the use of an exploratory research design. In the case of the Portuguese community in Sydney, identifying a sample representative of the population was complicated by the lack of reliable lists documenting group affiliation, although several databases were located, including client databases at official and community welfare agencies, and memberships of two major recreational community clubs. Some of these databases were either outdated and unreliable, or operationally inaccessible because of confidentiality laws. Ethical concerns also applied to the use of lists of club members. The possibility of using the White Pages directory (electronic version) for creating a database of the community was explored and abandoned after a phone trial showed the sample to be highly unreliable and uncontrollable.[9] After an assessment of available resources a strategy with nine steps was devised for sampling the population. Table 8.3 details the nine steps making up this strategy.

Step 1 consisted of the creation of a working database of individuals and institutions linked to the Portuguese community in Sydney. This list was compiled from publicly available community newspapers and internet listings prepared by the Consulate of Portugal in Sydney. The major institutions in the database, notably the two major recreational community clubs, were visited as part of **Step 2**, to obtain institutional endorsement and support, as

Table 8.3 Strategy used for sampling the population

Step 1	Create a working database of individuals and institutions linked to the population to be examined
Step 2	Visit major institutions in the database to obtain their endorsement and support in the distribution of the survey
Step 3	Use community information channels to create awareness and interest in the study and encourage participation
Step 4	Make contact with individuals in the working database to request their own participation and support as distributors
Step 5	Promptly mail out data collection packages to all distributors
Step 6	After seven days, renew contact with distributors for feedback and reappraisal of needs
Step 7	Promptly mail out additional data collection packages required
Step 8	Make phone contact for debriefing with distributors on completion of the distribution effort
Step 9	On completion of the study, mail out to all distributors a 'thank you' letter together with a synopsis of results

well as assistance in the proposed community enquiry. This involved endorsement and distribution to members of the survey instrument that would be used to collect information.

Step 3 involves the use of community information channels to create awareness and interest in the information-gathering exercise. The use of credible communication channels is important in reducing possible lack of acculturation to social enquiry, hence encouraging participation. In this particular instance, a press release about the study was distributed to community newspapers and radio, aimed at creating awareness and interest within the community. As a result, the press releases were publicized in the newspapers and the Portuguese radio stations dedicated time to the study.

In **Step 4**, selected individuals in the working database were contacted by telephone. Contact involved a brief overview of the study and an inquiry about their availability for completing the survey themselves and for distributing the survey to other individuals affiliated with the Portuguese community. Those that agreed to distribute the survey (23 in total) were asked how many questionnaires they would be able to distribute. In **Step 5**, data collection packages were provided to the recruited distributors. Each data collection package included the questionnaire, an addressed reply-paid envelope, and a 'thank you in advance' letter, each copy signed by the researcher and emphasizing the guarantee of respondents' anonymity.

After seven days, phone contact was again made with distributors, thanking them for their effort, obtaining feedback and inquiring about any further support that they might need for distributing the questionnaires. This action, **Step 6** in the table, was important because:

- it demonstrated the researcher's interest and appreciation for the distributor's efforts;
- it allowed the supply of questionnaires to be adjusted to the distributing capacities of the distributor;
- it encouraged a proactive attitude by the distributor within the set time frame; and,
- it revealed elements of the distribution process that had not been taken into account.

In **Step 7**, additional data collection packages were immediately posted to the distributors, as requested. A final phone contact with distributors was made once the distribution period had elapsed (**Step 8**). All distributors were contacted and thanked for their contribution. Finally, **Step 9** in the strategy involved a final mailing to all distributors of a formal 'thank you' letter together with a synopsis of results.

A word of caution is in order at this point. The tabulation of the stepped strategy used for sampling the population needs to be kept in perspective. Each minority ethnic group, given its different characteristics, is likely to require some adaptation and 'recipes do not necessarily guarantee excellent outcomes' (Morse, 2001, p. 147).

The role of the distributors

Direct identification and distribution to other respondents by selected distributors may result in demographic and psychographic characteristics that are more similar to the distributors than would occur by chance. Some members of the Portuguese community not connected to the distribution system may not be sampled, and distributors' opinions may bias the respondents' answers. For example, some distributors possibly overcame respondents' reluctance and/or literacy limitations by reassuring them and assisting them in completing the questionnaires. To the extent that these de-facto 'untrained field workers' contributed some of their opinions to the respondents' answers, there was a potential *distributor bias* involved. Although clearly undesirable, this potential bias was perceived as a minor cost to pay for responses that otherwise could not have been obtained. No corrective action was taken, other than tactfully asking distributors to separate themselves from the actual answers of the respondents they assisted.

Choice of individuals and organizations for the working database took this situation into account. Using the two major community clubs for distributing the questionnaires complemented the use of Portuguese mass media so as to reach a large number of members of the Portuguese community.

Snowball sampling

It is apparent that the described nine-step sampling strategy is inconsistent with probability sampling (Burdess, 1994) and it does not precisely fit techniques commonly described in the literature. Non-probability sampling is described as involving selection of sampling units by judgement, convenience or quota, rather than using a strictly random process (Sudman and Blair, 1998). Judgement sampling requires the use of judgement in assessing the representativeness of each respondent. In the study used for illustration of the sampling process, judgement was necessary in Step 1, when the original working database was created.[10] However, the actual selection of respondents involved no judgement by the researcher. Because the number of observations to be gathered was not predetermined, the quota technique also does not apply. The sample technique used is more closely identified with snowball sampling, which involves the random selection of an initial group of respondents, asking them to identify others who belong to the population of interest (Malhotra *et al.*, 1996).

Comparison of the resulting self-ascribed sample and the community profile based on specific parameters, using Table 8.4, illustrates the need to identify such groups, for marketing purposes, by means other than 'objective' measures. The distributions are similar in terms of gender and age, marital

Table 8.4 Characteristics of the sample and of the Portuguese community profile, Sydney, selected indicators

		Sample (2000) %	Community profile (1996) %
Gender	Male	50.2	50.8
	Female	49.8	49.2
Age	18–25	11.3	20.0
	26–45	56.2	47.6
	> 46	32.5	32.4
Marital status	Single	10.3	31.8
	Married/De Facto	79.3	58.2
	Separated/Widow	10.4	9.8
Income	< $25,000	30.6	66.9
	$26,000–$40,000	52.2	19.9
	> $41,000	17.2	13.2
Australian citizenship	Yes	60.6	75.1
	No	35.0	22.9
	Unsure	4.4	2.0
*English proficiency**	Not good	45.4	76.5
	Good or very good	50.7	21.5

Note: Community Profile statistics (1996) were compiled from Ethnicity Thematic Profiles specially prepared by the ABS (Australian Bureau of Statistics) using the 1996 Census of Population and Housing. * 8 respondents (3.9 per cent) who declared to be unsure are not included.

status and citizenship. However, income and English proficiency were areas of notable difference. Incomes less than $25,000 were indicated by 30.6 per cent of the sample, contrasting with 67 per cent reported for the community. In terms of self-perceived English proficiency, over 50 per cent of the sample rated it as good or very good, compared with only 21.5 per cent reported in the community profile.

Finally, the sample method used yielded valid responses from 203 respondents. All completed questionnaires used the Portuguese version. A thousand questionnaires were printed (700 in Portuguese and 300 in the English version) and sent out for distribution. Approximately 70 questionnaires in Portuguese were returned unused.[11] On the available numbers the research process produced an indicative-only response rate of 32 per cent (203/630).

8.8 Limitations

The methodology discussed in this chapter was developed based on preliminary conceptual elaboration. The adoption of an exploratory and qualitative research design, as well as the use of snowball sampling, was justified by limitations regarding the choice of a strategy for effectively gathering data from a small, difficult to identify minority ethnic group, for which little information is readily available.

The invoked strategy has limitations for sample size (linked to sampling error) and, more importantly, representativeness (linked to sample bias).[12] While the population to be studied was defined, there were limitations in obtaining a sampling frame for that population because the population boundaries were ambiguous in their definition of valid individuals. Additionally, valid individuals could not be easily identified in a cost-effective manner. It was not possible to identify every population unit. The solution resides in the development of quality control mechanisms, in the analysis of current practices and in a continued effort to assess the extent of the problem and to think about the best ways to rectify it. It appears unlikely that some recipe can be concocted to apply to ethnic group research in general. Each group will have its circumstances that need to be taken into account.

Notes

1. The Portuguese community in Sydney was a convenient choice for the project, given its geographical proximity and, foremost, the ethnic background of the researcher, Portuguese by birth. This allowed the contribution of some degree of inside perspective into the project (Mayall, 1991), whilst avoiding the complications associated with the use of interpreters and translators (Edwards, 1998; Esposito, 2001). The researcher's background and proximity to the group required the effect of the researcher to be taken into account to avoid subjectivity (Malterud, 2001), but reflexivity bias was reduced due to a reliance on propositions derived from conceptual analysis and the use of a narrative approach in reporting.

2. The research problem was to understand the process used by ethnic minority consumers to select their providers of services in a culturally diverse society (Pires, 2001). Preliminary conceptual elaboration included the development of a model, derived from an integration of general models of the consumer decision-making process (Pires and Stanton, 2000), subsequently elaborated upon for its particular applicability to ethnic minority consumers. Additional to greater reliance on some steps of that process, analysis of the model suggested that the key issue was an apparent interdependence of the individuals with their group of affiliation, indicating the need for researchers to use ethnic group resources for reaching group members. Hence the project sought to establish the impact of the minority ethnic group and its resources (particularly their sources of information), on the criteria used by affiliates to select providers of specific types of service activities.

3. There is, therefore, an element of self-identification in operation, raising operational concerns regarding the status of the targeted subjects as consumers affiliated to the Portuguese community in Sydney. These concerns were minimized by clearly divulging the requirement to potential participants. As no reward, pecuniary or otherwise, was offered for participation, there is no reason to presume participation by persons not affiliated with that community.

4. There was a deliberate attempt to gather information about each gatekeeper in order to enable some degree of personalization during interactions.

5. Two of the participants had previously conducted community consultations in the context of their professional activities in welfare organizations and were, therefore, relatively experienced.

6. Order or position bias occurs when a respondent tends to check an alternative merely because it occupies a certain position or is listed in a certain order (Payne, 1951; Krosnick and Alwin, 1987).

7. Errors of omission, telescoping, and creation may result from attempts by respondents to overcome possible inability to answer any of the questions that refer to events that occurred some time ago (Cook, 1987).

8. Respondents' willingness to answer a large questionnaire may be reduced if the effort to answer is seen as excessive, hence limiting the efficiency of the questionnaire (Malhotra *et al.*, 1996).

9. The process involved the identification of listings using potential Portuguese surnames. Over 5000 listings were identified. Many listings were outdated, addresses were either wrong or incomplete, and many surnames belonged to non-Portuguese people.

10. It also applied at the time of data entry, when respondents were screened for validity.

11. Distributors indicated that all questionnaires had been distributed, but this could not be verified. Similarly it was not possible to ascertain whether several questionnaires were distributed to the same individual.

12. Sample bias is controlled by defining the population of interest before drawing the sample, selecting a sample that represents the entire population in a fair manner, and obtaining a high response rate from that sample (Sudman and Blair, 1998).

References

Australian Bureau of Statistics (ABS) (1998) *1996 Census of Population and Housing, Ethnicity Thematic Profile Service*, http//www.abs.gov.au/Websitedbs/D3310108.NSF? OpenDatabase (accessed 15 October 2003), Canberra: ABS.

Anzul, M., Evans, J., King, R. and Tellier-Robinson, D. (2001) 'Moving beyond a deficit perspective with qualitative research methods', *Exceptional Children*, 67(2) (Winter): 235–48.

Barth, F. (1969) 'Ethnic groups and boundaries' (extract from *The Social Organization of Ethnic Groups and Boundaries*, Boston: Little, Brown) reprinted in J. Hutchinson and A. Smith (eds) *Ethnicity* (1996), Oxford: Oxford University Press.

Bishop, G. (1987) 'Experiments with the middle response alternative in survey questions', *Public Opinion Quarterly*, Summer: 220–32.

Bradburn, N. (1983) 'Response effects', in P. Rossi, S. Wright and A. Anderson (eds) *Handbook of Survey Research*, New York: Academic Press.

Burdess, N. (1994) *The Really Understandable Stats Book*, Sydney: Prentice-Hall Australia.

Burgess, R. (ed.) (1986) *Key Variables in Social Investigation*, London: Routledge.

Burns, A. and Bush, R. (2000) *Marketing Research*, New Jersey, NJ: Prentice-Hall International.

Byrne, M. (2001) 'Grounded theory as a qualitative research methodology', *Association of Operating Room Nurses (AORN) Journal*, 73(6) (June): 155–6.

Cook, W. (1987) 'Telescoping and memory's other tricks', *Journal of Advertising Research*, Feb.–Mar.: 5–8.

Edwards, R. (1998) 'A critical examination of the use of interpreters in the qualitative research process', *Journal of Ethnic and Migration Studies*, 24(1): 197–209.

Eisner, E. (1997) 'The new frontier in qualitative research methodology', *Qualitative Inquiry*, 3(3) (September): 259–74.

Esposito, N. (2001) 'From meaning to meaning: the influence of translation techniques on non-English focus group research', *Qualitative Health Research*, 11(4): 568–79.

Ferber, R. and Kraus, R. (1984) 'Upgrading benchmark studies: how multivariate analysis can enrich survey findings', *Journal of Business Marketing*, 69(4): 96–103.

Horn, J. (1998) 'Qualitative research literature: a bibliographic essay', *Library Trends*, 46(4) (Spring): 602–11.

Krosnick, J. and Alwin, D. (1987) 'An evaluation of a cognitive theory of response–order effects in survey measurement', *Public Opinion Quarterly*, Summer: 201–19.

Malhotra, N., Hall, J., Shaw, M. and Crisp, M. (1996) *Marketing Research: An Applied Orientation*, Sydney: Prentice-Hall Australia.

Malterud, K. (2001) 'Qualitative research: standards, challenges, and guidelines', *The Lancet*, 358(9280), 11 Aug.: 483–92.

Mayall, B. (1991) 'Researching childcare in a multi-ethnic society', *New Community*, 17(4): 553–68.

Miles, M. and Huberman, A. (1994) *Qualitative Data Analysis: An Expanded Sourcebook*, 2nd edn., Thousand Oaks, CA: Sage Publications.

Morse, J. (2001) 'Steps and strategies', *Qualitative Health Research*, 11(2): 147–8.

Payne, S. (1951) *The Art of Asking Questions*, Princeton, NJ: Princeton University Press, p. 141.

Pires, G. D. (2001) 'The selection of service providers by ethnic minority consumers in a culturally diverse society', unpublished doctoral thesis, University of Newcastle.

Pires, G. D. and Stanton, J. P. (2000) 'Service provider selection by ethnic minority consumers (EMCs)', in *Proceedings*, Multicultural Marketing Conference, Hong Kong, China, September.

Rochford, L. and Venable, C. (1995) 'Surveying a targeted population segment: the effects on mail questionnaire response rate', *Journal of Marketing Theory and Practice*, Spring: 87–96.

Sills, A. and Desai, P. (1996) 'Qualitative research amongst ethnic minority communities in Britain', *Journal of the Market Research Society*, 38(3) (July): 247–66.

Singh, J., Howell, R. and Rhoads, G. (1990) 'Adaptive designs for Likert-type data: an approach for implementing marketing surveys', *Journal of Marketing Research*, 27: 304–21.

Streiner, D. and Norman, G. (1995) *Health Measurement Scales: A Practical Guide to Their Development and Use*, 2nd edn., Oxford Medical Publications, Oxford: Oxford University Press.

Sudman, S. and Blair, E. (1998) *Marketing Research: A Problem-Solving Approach*, Sydney: McGraw-Hill.

The Portuguese community in Sydney, Australia

The Portuguese community in Sydney has been studied as a part of a wider study of the ability to target a small ethnic group (Pires, 2001). Portuguese migration to Australia, either direct or from third countries, has been so small as not to be recorded separately in published Australian statistics. A search based on the Australian 1996 Census (ABS 1996) to establish the potential size of the community based on links with either the Portuguese language, Portugal or former Portuguese colonies (including Brazil) drew less than 41,000 persons (Table 8.5). Of these less than 17,950 resided in the Sydney metropolitan area, predominantly in inner western suburbs.

The diverse nationalities that may identify with this community are apparent in the place of birth of the Sydney residents. Only 44 per cent were born in Portugal, 30 per cent in Australia, and the rest elsewhere. Neither nationality nor race or birthplace defines the community. The attractions to settle within the Portuguese community in Sydney are many. The community assists new arrivals'

Table C5.1   Profile of the Portuguese community in Australia, 1996

	Persons	%
Spoke Portuguese at home	24,594	60.3
Did not speak Portuguese at home but whose parents (both) were born in Portugal or ex-colonies	6,053	14.8
Did not speak Portuguese at home but whose mother was born in Portugal or ex-colonies and father born elsewhere	4,607	11.3
Did not speak Portuguese at home but whose father was born in Portugal or ex-colonies and mother born elsewhere	5,507	13.6
TOTAL	**40,761**	**100.0**

Source: Compiled from ABS (1996) Census of Population and Housing, Ethnicity Thematic Profile Service.

habituation to their new environment and in establishing and maintaining socioeconomic ties within the close-knit community, assistance that is particularly important when poor English proficiency and low skills reduce employment opportunities on arrival (Gonçalves, da Silva and Seniuk, 1986: 1). While the existence of the community cannot be questioned, its sustenance from immigration from Portugal is decreasing over time. The rate of inflow, as a percentage of the Sydney community, was 6.7 per cent between 1986 and 1990, dropping to only 1.5 per cent in 1996.

Identification of the Portuguese community in Sydney for marketing purposes needs to consider the role of ascription and self-ascription in the formation of the group. The group needs to be researched (profiled) and the links that maintain it as a community well understood in order to achieve actionability, once appropriate strategies are designed. The framework that has developed to help maintain this community is reflected in a dense social network. The community is served by two newspapers, round-the-clock Portuguese language radio programmes, a television channel received directly from Portugal, two major recreation and sporting clubs and many commercial enterprises within the community, in a wide range of activities. The community is also serviced by a number of schools and churches of four denominations each with a Portuguese priest or pastor. Casual observation suggests that the Portuguese community in Sydney is well adjusted, rather than acculturated, to the Australian way of life. It uses major shopping centres, as does the mainstream population, but still retains its various specialty stores and, particularly important in the marketing context, it retains recommendation from like others in the selection of many service providers (Pires, 2001).

Given adequate preparatory research, this relatively small community in Sydney meets four requirements for effective market segmentation (identifiability, measurability, actionability and stability). As for substantiality, its assessment needs to be considered at product level taking the relevant business objectives into account. The test of substance is essentially an exhortation to evaluate the value of the segmentation opportunity and needs to be consistent with achieving these objectives (Stanton and Pires, 1999). *Ex ante*, even small ethnic groups may be substantial for particular businesses.

Common features of an ethnic group include a common proper name, fictive kinship or ancestry, perceived shared memories of a common past, one or more elements of a common culture, an often symbolic link with a homeland, and a sense of solidarity by at least some sections of the population. These are usually subscribed to with varying intensity (Hutchinson and Smith, 1996). While ethnicity-based segmentation should produce segments that are unique, the boundaries, community links with other groups, internal interdependence and the degree and form of social control of members can vary significantly between communities and over time (Bentley, 1981). For example, self-ascription by Brazilian-born individuals to the Portuguese community in Sydney may be caused by perceived cultural proximity to this community, given that a Brazilian community lacks critical mass. Focusing on the Brazilian group alone would be inadequate, a conclusion that supports the view that, at least for discrete marketing purposes (like achieving critical mass and economies of scale), it may prove advantageous for marketers to aggregate some highly homogeneous ethnic groups (Pires and Stanton, 2000). This variability, together with potential methodological inadequacies associated with group aggregations, recommends that behavioural differences across ethnic groups be tested to ensure effective market segmentation and an efficient allocation of resources, given business objectives. A similar response to a tailored marketing stimulus is required from ethnic group members.

It is important to emphasize the role of business objectives in ethnic market segmentation, but it is not the only role. The Portuguese community in Sydney illustrates the propriety of using market segmentation, even in the case of a small ethnic group, itself including smaller groups arguably lacking critical mass. Yet there are instances where even smaller ethnic minority populations (possibly dismissed by marketers for their presumed lack of substance) are identified for segmentation purposes, as illustrated in the context of the Newham Council, England (Case 6).

References

Australian Bureau of Statistics (ABS) (1996) *Census of Population and Housing, Ethnicity Thematic Profile Service*, Canberra: ABS.

Bentley, G. (1981) *Ethnicity and Nationality, A Bibliographic Guide*, Seattle: University of Washington Press.

Hutchinson, J. and Smith, A. (eds) (1996) *Ethnicity*, Oxford: Oxford University Press.

Gonçalves, A., da Silva, E. and Seniuk, S. (1986) *The Portuguese Community in the Illawarra*, Regional Migrant Health Centre, State Health Publication No. (ILR) 86-071, Sydney.

Pires, G. (2001) 'The selection of service providers by ethnic minority consumers in a culturally diverse society', unpublished doctorial thesis, University of Newcastle.

Pires, G. and Stanton, J. (2000) 'Ethnicity and acculturation in a culturally diverse country: identifying ethnic market segments', *Journal of Multilingual and Multicultural Development*, 21(1): 42–57.

Stanton, J. and Pires, G. (1999) 'The substantiality test: meaning and application in market segmentation', *Journal of Segmentation in Marketing*, 3(2): 105–15.

Non-profit objectives: Newham Council, England

Sills and Desai (1996) report on the endeavours of a London borough council, Newham, to listen to the views of their customers in order to ensure that local government services were delivered to residents in accessible and acceptable ways. This was a complex task, given problems with qualitative research amongst ethnic groups, the size and diversity of the ethnic population, and the range of spoken languages. These problems challenged service delivery in terms of cultural acceptability and sensitivity. While an essential part of the research programme was to include a variety of communities so that the council could assess the similarities and differences between its ethnic minority groups, the more communities included, the more costly the research and the less the depth of understanding gained about each community.

The problem was which communities to include. While each community was internally diverse (reminiscent of the earlier discussion about group heterogeneity), the material and cultural resources it could mobilize as a community needed to be taken into account. For example, the Chinese community, with a membership below 2000, was a small, but significant group given the council's objectives, so it was included in the research. Other ethnic minority communities included in the research programme were Indians (27,656 individuals), Pakistanis (12,504), Bangladeshis (8152) and Somalis (very small size, not reported). The Pakistanis were perceived as a well-established community group that benefited from some statutory provision of services, while the Bangladeshis relied more on voluntary groups. The Somalis had very little statutory provision of services and a limited community network. Clearly, ethnic group size alone was not an adequate guide for segmentation, given the Council's objectives.

The cases of the Portuguese community in Sydney, Australia and the Newham Council in the UK, contradict the view that decreasing migration and small group size renders moot the case for ethnic market segmentation.

Reference

Sills, A. and Desai, P. (1996) 'Qualitative research amongst ethnic minority communities in Britain', *Journal of Market Research Society*, 38(3) (July): 247–66.

Korean rotating credit associations in Los Angeles

Ivan Light, Im Jung Kwuon and Deng Zhong*

Rotating credit associations (RCAs) are informal social groups whose participants agree to make periodic financial contributions to a fund which is 'given in whole or in part to each contributor in rotation'. RCAs represent cultural resources that support the consumption, home purchase, and commercial enterprise of groups endowed with the tradition.

The rotating credit association has a centuries-long history in Korea. Koreans call their RCA *kye* (pronounce keh). The word means 'contract' or 'bond', but is often translated as voluntary associations. Nearly all Korean kye participants were and are women. Although Korea is a patriarchal society, women customarily manage family finances in Korea. Korean women use RCAs to save and invest.

Reviewing research on Korean RCAs in Los Angeles and elsewhere in the United States, Light and Bonacich reported that kye was a frequent practice among Korean–Americans. Kyes were so widespread in Los Angeles' Korean–American community that Korean banks developed kye-like savings plans in order to compete with them.

Researching kye participation in the USA has proved difficult. Finding respondent suspicion and hostility unbearable, one Korean–American ethnographer prematurely terminated his research assignment. Another researcher concluded that survey research could not elicit intimate and honest response regarding the kye from respondents.

Reluctance has been attributed to the following:

---

* *Amerasia*, 1990, 16(1).

- Many Koreans regard kyes as archaic.
- Many believe that kyes are illegal in the USA.
- Few kye participants reported their interest income and thus avoided tax.
- Interest rates prevailing typically exceed statutory maxima.
- Question wording in surveys posed another methodological problem.

Learning from these problems, the authors undertook their own survey. This was a self-administered questionnaire of ten items, with an explanatory letter of introduction, explaining the research importance and that the activity was not illegal. The questionnaire was translated into Korean, pre-tested, revised and mailed to an entire Korean–American industry association. It accompanied the association newsletter and also had a letter of endorsement from the Association's director. The end result was a relatively poor response rate of 29.9 per cent.

The authors explain the strength and persistence of kyes in the USA in terms of embeddedness theory. Embeddedness theory claims that 'structures of social relations' always influence economic behaviour to the extent that overlooking their influence is a grave error. Its stress is upon the continuing influence of social relationships upon economic action even in fully modern societies.

The authors found that Korean entrepreneurs drawn from the industry association targeted used kyes more in the USA than in Korea. Ignorance of financial alternatives was ruled out as a cause of their enhanced utilization.

The Korean immigrant community institutionalized social trust to an extent that kyes continued to offer some Korean entrepreneurs a useful tool for saving and borrowing. Conceivably, acculturation of Korean immigrants will erode their community solidarity. If so, kye's obsolescence would occur. So long as social trust exists, kye enjoys a permanent transaction cost advantage relative to bureaucratic institutions. In turn, this transaction cost advantage supports the premodern social trust that makes kyes possible. Like ethnic business generally, kyes encourage the ethnic solidarity they require.

QUESTIONS

1. Think of ways you could have used to identify a target group and also increased the response rate.
2. Can you give other reasons why response rates tend to be poor when seeking to reach an ethnic group?
3. Given the discussion in the text about acculturation paths, do you agree with the authors that such institutions will necessarily wither? Why may they be sustained?

CHAPTER 9

Ethnic marketing in practice – marketing services

9.1 Chapter objectives

Because of the characteristics of services, there is considerable scope to use ethnic marketing. Although all consumers confront difficulties in evaluating services, not all services offer the same opportunities and ethnic marketing strategies need to vary between different types of services. This chapter examines specific characteristics of services, how they foster evaluation problems for ethnic minority consumers, and how this influences the process of selecting and purchasing services. Particular attention is given to explaining how differences in service–product tangibility influence that process. Ethnic minority consumers, in addressing their evaluation problems, are likely to develop relationships with, and dependence upon, service suppliers preferred and recommended by their reference minority ethnic group. This strengthens the loyalty generation process discussed in Chapter 7. Discussion of marketing implications focuses on the benefits that may ensue from developing strategies for marketing services to minority ethnic groups.

9.2 Dimensions of services

Newly arrived ethnic minority consumers face a foreign environment that may condition their market exchanges. At least in the short to medium term, time and budgetary scarcities combine with communication difficulties and limited knowledge of the marketplace to condition their ability to search for information about products and suppliers, and their consequent evaluation. Over time, this conditioned behaviour may be gradually contained by consumer acculturation, improved communication skills and some degree of acculturation to the host society in general, if not necessarily to the host dominant group.

Perceived risk

Limited ability to search for information about products and suppliers, and their consequent evaluation, increases the risk perceived by ethnic minority consumers in making consumer decisions. As discussed in Chapter 3, this provides an incentive for these consumers to draw on the experience of, and recommendation from similar others, in particular members of the minority ethnic group to which they affiliate. This is an important factor because marketers targeting ethnic minority consumers may abstract from the volatility inherent to the individual, to focus their attention on the minority ethnic group. Provided the conditions for effective segmentation are met, marketers targeting ethnic minority consumers will be well advised to adapt their programmes to the special needs, preferences and evaluation criteria of these consumers' minority ethnic groups. Consideration may need to be given to the financial, functional, social, psychological, physical or safety and time components of consumer perceived risk (Bednall and Kanuk, 1997).

Targeting ethnic minority consumers and their groups is not without difficulty. First, marketers' knowledge of the referred special needs, preferences and evaluative criteria requires the development of community profiles (an involved process discussed in Chapter 8), as these usually are not readily available. Second, the difficulty of ethnic minority consumers learning about and appraising market offerings illustrates the challenge faced by marketers in communicating their offerings to this group.

Service-products

'Market offerings' may refer to physical goods or intangible services performances. In the discussion that follows all products (hereafter service-products) can be visualized as a continuum from pure goods (without intangible elements), to pure services (without a tangible element) (Rothmell, 1966; Shostack, 1977). This is depicted in Figure 9.1.

The figure illustrates a distribution of 16 service-products consistent with distributions suggested by Zeithaml (1981) and endorsed by Zeithaml and Bitner (2000: 31) and Lovelock (1996: 18). Because the position of any one service-product on the continuum is a function of the dominance of the tangible element over the intangible element, exchange difficulties may be presumed to increase with intangibility.

Independent of the service-products being offered, marketers' ability to reach ethnic minority consumers is often constrained by:

- language barriers between marketers and consumers;
- marketers' difficulty in understanding different cultures (Hotchkiss, 1996);

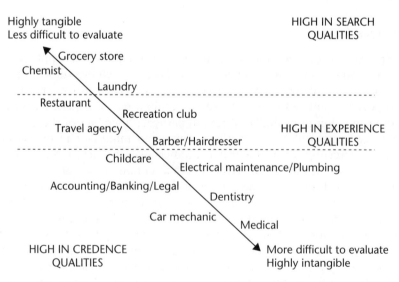

Figure 9.1 Distribution of service-products in a continuum with reference to tangibility and ease of evaluation

- marketers' lack of familiarity with ethnic communications networks (Laroche *et al.*, 1997);

- consumers' limited exposure to mainstream printed media (Kaufman, 1987);

- language difficulties limiting consumers' exposure to mainstream mass media;

- consumers' preference for ethnic communications networks;

- consumers' preference for ethnic brands (Kaufman, 1987).

Since perceived risk is higher for services (Murray, 1991) and is determined by the consumer's willingness and ability to acquire risk-reducing information, the impact of these constraints on ethnic minority consumers and marketers can be inferred to be highest for intangible dominant service-products. This is because intangibility makes it difficult to understand what is being offered, to identify potential suppliers, and to evaluate alternatives (Legg and Baker, 1987). Arguably, the unique characteristics of service-products necessitate distinct consumer evaluation processes and require distinct marketing techniques (Zeithaml, 1981; Zeithaml *et al.*, 1985).[1]

Logical thinking would suggest that, the higher the hurdles faced by consumers, the better the opportunities at the reach of alert marketers for winning these consumers over through perceived value creation. However, the analysis of minority ethnic groups in a services framework is a clear gap in the marketing literature, in some way reflecting the limited attention given to such opportunities.[2] One of the few exceptions, borrowed from sociology, is the case of a study of Korean Rotating Credit Associations in Los Angeles (Light *et al.*, 1990), included in this book as Case 7. The case discusses how 'ethnic minority entrepreneurs, who lack credit ratings, collateral, or are the victims of ethno-racial discrimination' obtain loan capital from their ethnic group of affiliation, circumventing 'the slow, unfriendly, and bureaucratic channels of banks and insurance companies, the mainstream financial institutions of market societies' (p. 35). Another exception, marketing-oriented, is the work developed by Pires and Stanton, extensively discussed in this book.

9.3 Service characteristics and consumer inexperience

The uniqueness of intangible dominant service-products is commonly grounded on four main characteristics: intangibility, simultaneity, heterogeneity and perishability (Lovelock, 1983). These characteristics are examined below, in order to explore how they increase evaluation problems for newly arrived, market-inexperienced ethnic minority consumers. In addressing these problems it is argued that word-of-mouth communications may play a significant role, crucial for the development of necessary relationships by ethnic minority consumers with their group of affiliation and the group's preferred suppliers.

Tangibility: harder to get risk-reducing information

Intangibility emphasizes service-products as performances resulting in experiences. In contrast, tangibility refers to the physical nature of the core product, the basic, generic central thing that is exchanged (Levitt, 1973). Physical goods may be displayed and examined by prospective purchasers, often without interaction with the supplier being necessary. Indeed,

> retail stores generally display a number of company brands and a variety of models for each brand name. This arrangement provides the consumer with the opportunity to make physical comparisons and to set standards on which to make purchase decisions.
>
> (Hartman and Lindgren Jr., 1993: 12)

Even when the service-product is tangible dominant, physical comparison may not always be sufficient for conclusive evaluation by inexperienced mainstream consumers, or for supporting their choice between brands. Reassurance may be sought from service personnel in these cases, and free trials, or the promise of a 'satisfaction or money back guarantee' may reduce perceived risk and help resolve evaluation and purchase difficulties. When considering inexperienced ethnic minority consumers with communication limitations, tangibility facilitates physical comparisons across off-the-shelf service-products. However, if these consumers need to interact with suppliers, as when learning how to use or consume a particular service-product, they may experience difficulties. Inability to peruse appropriate literature and/or problems in consulting with service staff may result in discomfort and higher levels of perceived risk among ethnic minority consumers than among mainstream consumers (Murray, 1991).

Service-products also can be distinguished by three evaluative qualities, search, experience and credence, which are perceived to vary with the tangibility of the service product (Figure 9.1). Highly tangible service-products high in search qualities associated with some characteristic (such as appearance, colour or smell) that can be predetermined before purchasing takes place, hence involve less risk. These service-products are relatively easy to evaluate. Service-products that involve characteristics that can only be discerned after purchase or during consumption (such as taste or ease of handling) are said to be high in experience qualities (Nelson, 1970), involve more perceived risk and are relatively more difficult to evaluate. At the highly intangible end of the continuum, service-products may be impossible to evaluate even after consumption. These service-products involve the highest levels of perceived risk and are said to be high in credence qualities (Darby and Karni, 1973). Hence, it may be more difficult for inexperienced ethnic consumers to acquire risk-reducing information for all service-products, but especially for the more intangible ones. This information is likely to be highly valued once a reliable source is found. That value is likely to be attributed by the consumer to the source. It could be a service supplier that, cognizant of the consumer's liabilities and requirements, recommends culturally sensitive suppliers for other needed service-products. The most likely sources of information are, however, family and friends, and the consumer's minority ethnic group with its communications channels, including the ethnic press.

As long as the consumer feels they can rely on the information, there is no incentive to search for new information sources. Service suppliers may achieve high consumer retention and develop a source of competitive advantage by supplementing their core product with this information. Indeed, consumers with less market expertise, as would be the case with inexperienced ethnic minority consumers, 'may be loath to change partners because to do so is to reestablish risk' (Bendapudi and Berry, 1997: 25). The implication is that service supplier credibility may be of crucial importance, particularly in the case of service-products high in credence qualities. Inexperienced consumers, by definition, have no apparent grounds to assess service supplier credibility.

Simultaneity and inseparability: chance for responsiveness and personalization

Simultaneity (and inseparability) implies that service production generally occurs at the same time as service consumption and the consumer is often an active participant in the production process. As a performance that results in a service experience, intangible dominant service-products may be argued 'to have no existence apart from the interaction between the people, both provider and consumer, who experience the service together' (Friedman and Smith, 1993). This consumer–supplier interaction provides the opportunity for consumers to make their individual needs and preferences known to suppliers. Hence, depending on supplier responsiveness, inseparability provides the opportunity to match each consumer's particular needs more closely, by adjusting the service-product (Hartman and Lindgren Jr., 1993). This opportunity may not apply equally to all consumer groups.

Inexperienced ethnic minority consumers may be challenged in situations where their needs and preferences have to be unambiguously transmitted to suppliers, often in the presence of others. The consumption of intangible dominant service-products may be particularly challenging because of consumers' perceived or real difficulties both in explaining their needs and in responding to what may be required of them during their participation in the production process. These difficulties have two important outcomes. One is that consumers may apportion part of the blame for service failure resulting from incorrectly provided instructions or faulty participation. The other refers to the opportunity that is created for the supplier to create value for consumers through personalization – the social content between consumer and supplier (Mittal and Lassar, 1996) – encouraging ethnic minority consumers' loyalty. This is because of an increased opportunity cost of switching suppliers and because the social interaction is, in itself, a possible shopping motive (Hawkins *et al.*, 1994).

Heterogeneity: meaning and context

Heterogeneity or variability ensues from active human involvement in the production/consumption of service-products. This involvement limits the perfect reproduction/re-experience of the service-product in subsequent service encounters, and suppliers' ability to meet consumers' expectations. Personalization and the difficulty of replicating service performance can be expected to make service quality evaluation more difficult (Mittal and Lassar, 1996).

Since consumer satisfaction and retention may be determined solely by the quality of the personal encounter (Solomon *et al.*, 1985), the greater the evaluation difficulty the greater the importance of perceived supplier credibility. For example, measuring quality for medical service-products (Figure 9.1) is likely to be more difficult than for childcare service-products, thus implying the need for greater supplier credibility in the first case. Intangible service-products, therefore, create evaluation difficulties for all consumers, even those with substantial market knowledge. At least on two grounds, these difficulties may be greater for inexperienced ethnic minority consumers:

1. While mainstream consumers may rely on what they have learned from past service encounters, probably with similar-others, inexperienced ethnic minority consumers have no significant past in the new market and may need to interact with different-others.

2. 'Consumer evaluative criteria are less well articulated and the appraisal of the value received (in the service encounter) is much more subjective' (Mittal and Lassar, 1998: 178). Hence, consciousness about communication difficulties reinforces the effect of simultaneity, pushing inexperienced ethnic minority consumers into accepting part of the blame for service failure and contributing to performance ambiguity (Bendapudi and Berry, 1997).

As discussed in Chapter 11, communication difficulties may involve more than language problems. Meaning and context are important in defining a 'normal' way of doing things, as are the way consumer service personnel and consumers address each other, whether physical touch is allowed, how people with different racial backgrounds behave towards different others (e.g.

discrimination, paternalism, stereotyping) or, in a nutshell, how culturally aware and sensitive are the parties to the service delivery.

Similarity is the extent to which members of a dyad share personal attributes and characteristics. These may include one or all of life stage, gender, culture, ethnic background, work attitudes and personality. Interaction with others who have similar attitudes, values, activities and experiences is easier and less cognitively challenging (Smith, 1998).

Individual exchanges of service-products are not assessed in isolation, but within a continuation of past exchanges likely to continue in the future (Bendapudi and Berry, 1997). As ethnic minority consumers with communication difficulties have a reduced ability to receive and convey risk-reducing information that might compensate for intangibility, they are likely to experience greater difficulties than mainstream consumers when choosing suppliers, in consuming service-products and in evaluating their quality. Hence, risk-reducing information is likely to be highly valued once a reliable source (such as the minority ethnic group) is found, particularly for intangible service-products.

Perishability: limits experience and awareness

The challenges associated with intangibility are also relevant in the context of perishability. Intangible dominant service-products cannot be produced today for tomorrow's consumption. This is a reinforcing characteristic of services because consumers associate intangibility with availability, reducing their awareness about services (Hartman and Lindgren Jr., 1993). Perishability supports the proposition that consumers engage in more post-purchase than pre-purchase evaluation when selecting and consuming services (Friedman and Smith, 1993). As post-purchase evaluation involves a consumer's recollection of his or her experience throughout the service encounter, the consequences for inexperienced ethnic consumers may be linked back, for example, to service quality issues identified in discussing heterogeneity.

Distribution channel

The four main characteristics discussed are not universally applicable to all service-products. For example, intensive consumer–supplier interaction is not always required. The result of this lack of universality has been a fragmentation into other generalizations, themselves limited in their scope.

One such generalization, potentially relevant in the present context, refers to the structure and nature of distribution channels. Service activities requiring consumers to visit (or to be visited by) a service point for the delivery process to take place may use tangible elements and create scenarios (such as physically appealing front-stages) in order to impress and inform consumers. However, poorly targeted tangibilizing elements can be expected to have a negative impact on consumers' evaluation of what is supplied and of the supplier. For example, using national flag colours (red, white and blue) to appeal to Australian consumers may be elusive to ethnic consumers from other countries, such as Italy (red, white and green) or Greece (white and blue). What appeals to one group may fail to cause an impression on another.

The conclusion from this discussion is that inexperienced ethnic minority consumers, particularly those with communication difficulties, are likely to experience significantly greater difficulties than mainstream inexperienced consumers in the selection of service suppliers and in consuming service-products. This is the result of a reduced ability to receive and convey risk-reducing information. Understanding of these greater difficulties and their implications requires recognition of the role that minority ethnic groups may play as a reference for inexperienced ethnic consumers and, by implication, the appraisal of word-of-mouth communications, 'the primary means by which consumers gather information about services' (Clow *et al.*, 1997: 232).

9.4   Reliance on word-of-mouth from similar others

Consumers obtain their information from internal and external sources. Internal sources rely on scanning their past experiences and are less important in the present context because consumers are assumed to be inexperienced. External sources range from marketer-dominated to personal and impersonal. Studies of usage of service-products in a pre-purchase context, hence by inexperienced consumers, reveal that the consumption of intangible dominant service-products relies on personal sources (Murray, 1991; Friedman and Smith, 1993). Ultimately, word-of-mouth emerges as the most important source of risk-reducing information, with an emphasis on opportunities for clarification and feedback. Word-of-mouth is particularly valued when conveyed by family and friends, as well as opinion leaders and reference group members credible for their previous use of the service-product. In the case of inexperienced ethnic minority consumers, reliance may be on word-of-mouth conveyed by their minority ethnic group of affiliation.

Earlier, in Chapter 4, we showed that, for marketers entertaining ethnic marketing objectives, individual ethnic consumers are important as members of the ethnic group with which they identify. However, belonging to an ethnic group is not enough; it is necessary to be seen to belong. Individual ethnic group members must exhibit needs and preferences *mostly* coincidental with those of the group, as well as similar evaluative criteria before and after consumption. It is this requirement that ensures that the ethnic group is internally homogeneous and its consumption behaviour predictable. The implication is that inexperienced ethnic minority consumers are likely to obtain consumption information from similar others more knowledgeable about the marketplace, particularly in relation to intangible service-products and their suppliers. Ultimately, a recommendation from similar others is likely to be adopted because it reduces perceived risk. The positive or negative experiences feed back to the group, reinforcing or weakening group preference.

It is apparent that the interaction between ethnic minority consumers and suppliers of intangible service-products is influenced by

- the consumers' relative inexperience within the marketplace;
- the quality of the long-term relationship that the consumers' ethnic group, drawing from their collective experience, maintains with those suppliers.

Individual exchanges of service-products are not assessed in isolation but as a continuation of past exchanges likely to continue in the future. Ethnic minority consumers draw on the experiences of similar-others as a preferred source of market information and this dependence influences the maintenance of consumer relationships for the long term (Sheth and Parvatiyar, 1995; Brand and Cronin, 1997).

9.5 The impact of experience (market knowledge)

Service-product type and information sources

What links ethnic minority consumers to their group is not a case of 'blind dependence'; rather it is a behavioural response constructed on the value perceived by consumers from their proximity to the group.

In general terms, a desire to conform to the behaviour of their ethnic group of affiliation, together with perceived liabilities ensuing from intangibility and supplier credibility, justifies that inexperienced ethnic minority consumers might rely on information from similar others. This reliance may depend on whether the service-product is characterized by search, experience or credence qualities, as indicated in Table 9.1.

Table 9.1 Information sources used by inexperienced ethnic minority consumers by type of service-product

	Search	*Experience*	*Credence*
Valuation of risk-reducing information	Low	High	Highest
Reliance on information from similar others	Low	High	Highest
Reliance on information from ethnic non-personal sources (radio, TV and press)	Low	High	Highest
Attention to price and convenience	Highest	High	Low
Attention to language, observed similar others' behaviour	Low	High	Highest

Evaluation of highly tangible service-products (high in search qualities) may depend less on supplier credibility and reputation than evaluations of highly intangible service-products (high in credence qualities). Perceived risk is lower for these service-products and the need to seek and rely on information from similar others may also be lower. Hence, other selection criteria may be relatively more important for ethnic minority consumers where tangibility is dominant. Criteria such as price or convenience may substitute for referral by similar others when service-products are high in search qualities. In contrast, when service-products are high in either experience qualities or credence qualities, the greater need for ethnic minority consumers to communicate and interact with suppliers may justify their use of evaluation criteria such as language, observed similar others' behaviour, information from ethnic sources (press, radio, television) and recommendation by similar others.

Over time, ethnic minority consumers lose their 'inexperience'. If they are satisfied with their suppliers there is a lack of incentive to search for new information sources or new suppliers, because to change partners is to re-establish risk. But there will be cases where they may consider switching suppliers:

1. Consumers may need to switch from the supplier originally selected. Business closure or relocation, change in ownership, reduced perceived quality and satisfaction are examples of reasons requiring reconsideration. Dependence on information from similar others may be less important in these situations (even for service-products high in credence qualities) due to greater knowledge of the market.

2. Consumers may become disappointed with a supplier performing below expectations. In this case the perceived net value of retaining the supplier will be reduced. Whether the consumer will switch is a matter of comparing the new perceived value relative to the net values of available alternatives. Endorsement by the minority ethnic group, for example, may suffice to deter switching. But the decision to switch may also inform the group perception about the particular supplier. While one consumer's switching may not be enough to check the group's preference for a supplier, similar feedback by other members may result in the supplier losing its status.

3. Consumers may have limited use of ethnic resources for daily living necessities. Some will acculturate, or even assimilate to the mainstream ethnic group, although there is some suggestion that the ethnicity bond may not be easily lost. Desire to comply with the group may deepen the meaning of dependence in the group. An article in *National Geographic* discussing New York's Chinatown described Chinese settlers, including accountants and beauty technicians, as coming 'to

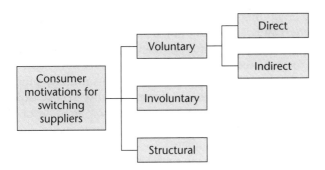

Figure 9.2 Types of switching motives

> Chinatown to escape loneliness, to meet other Chinese people, to eat the best Chinese food, to remind themselves of where they came from . . . Cultural pride is evident in Chinese Americans who live among non-Chinese neighbours . . . but come to Chinatown on weekends to give their children what they call "a Chinese experience . . . It's nostalgic. You go even if you don't need anything, and you always pick up something that reminds you of home" . . . To keep their sense of the mother culture strong . . . , parents send their children to Chinese-language, or "Saturday", schools in Chinatown' (Swerdlow, 1998: 64–71).

Switching motives

The relationship between loyalty creation and switching motives was discussed in Chapter 7 in a general fashion; here we discuss the motives that encourage consumers to switch service providers as represented in Figure 9.2.

Switching motives may be voluntary (a decision by the consumer), involuntary (the supplier ceases activity) and structural (the consumer no longer needs the service activity, as in the case of childcare). Voluntary motives may be direct, if they are triggered by perceived supplier misbehaviour (such as poor service, or failure to remain competitive on price), or indirect, if they are not related to the quality of the immediate interactions that the consumer maintains with the supplier. Indirect motives may ensue from switching preferences by the ethnic group (resulting, for example, from negative feedback by other consumers affiliated to the same group), or as a result of the market acculturation process, with consumers possibly becoming aware of additional suppliers, some of whom may be more conveniently located (closeness to the locality of residence or workplace) or be more accessible (after hours, weekends, online).

Suppliers that gain the preference of the minority ethnic group may compromise this status if they become condescending about their performance and cease to meet group expectations. Preferred supplier status is aligned to the perception by the group that those distinguished are the best suppliers of net value. Responsiveness and personalization, for example, may be attributes that clinch the 'preferred supplier' status through customer-oriented strategies. But, as in most market situations, the good performance of the core service in a competitive fashion cannot be compromised. Continued support and referral by the ethnic group implies consistently positive service experiences, together with switching constraints. Hence, the combination of the uniqueness of minority ethnic groups and services marketing may result in greater loyalty by ethnic minority consumers.

The relative importance of the various motives may vary with service-product class, although the combination of market acculturation and convenience is endogenous to the supplier selection process. Inexperienced consumers rely on word-of-mouth by similar others or on ethnic resources to reduce the perceived risk inherent in making decisions with limited information. These consumers are then subject to market acculturation and, importantly, to possible logistic incentives related to their residence and workplace. They may relocate their homes or change jobs and may need to adjust consumption patterns to the new day-to-day reality. Since convenience, with its many facets, is an element inextricably intertwined with assessments of perceived value, switching decisions may follow.

In addition to adequately accounting for minority ethnic group needs, preferences and evaluative criteria when developing their value propositions, suppliers may develop service delivery systems designed to overcome eventual logistic liabilities, such as home delivery and pick-up (for possession processing service activities, such as car repair and car detail, dry cleaning, video hire) or home delivery (for personal processing service activities, such as health care, hair care, financial planning, banking).

There is some similarity in the experience and credence classes regarding the use of information sources and primary criteria used in selecting current suppliers. However, switching motives and valuation of supplier attributes suggest there are differences that require each class to be treated separately for strategy purposes. For example, it may be worthwhile for credence-based service suppliers to target consumer perceptions regarding service quality and perceived value. While ethnic minority consumers may rely on supplier credibility as a major selection criterion, they are not passive when faced with poor service, inconvenience and/or over-pricing.

In the search class, price needs to remain competitive, since consumers can easily shop around and compare essentially tangible service-products, even before they make a purchase. In contrast, service-activities in the credence class are complex and difficult to evaluate even after consumption, suggesting that price is much less important. This is not necessarily so, since minority ethnic consumers condition their price evaluations in this class on their assessment of service quality. If the performance is perceived positively, there may not be consideration of price. If the performance is perceived negatively, then price provides an excuse for switching suppliers, even when the consumer lacks the technical expertise to assess performance quality (Pires, 2000).

The selection of new suppliers is the culmination of the switching process, unless the particular service activities are no longer required. Three points to bear in mind are:

1. There is no reason to expect that motivations for switching be in the selection criteria for new suppliers. Since ethnic minority consumers are now acculturated, there may be differences in the criteria used for selecting new suppliers.

2. Switching does not question the continued importance of the minority ethnic group.

3. In addition to economic costs, switching costs also need to account for social or psychological costs, leading to a relationship that is constrained by a member's conformance to the group (Johnson, 1982).

Valued supplier attributes

To some extent, motivations for switching may indicate which attributes are most valued by ethnic minority consumers in their preferred suppliers. That is, inconvenience as a switching motivation might indicate that convenience is a valued attribute of current preferred suppliers. But this is not always the case. For example, language difficulties are not a common motivation for switching suppliers because this is one of the requirements taken into account in selecting the current supplier. However, it is likely to remain an important attribute in the profile of currently preferred suppliers, particularly in the experience and credence classes. In contrast, repeat contacts with a particular supplier become a relationship, characterized by a common history and shared knowledge of the parties to the relationship.

Relationships

Relationships are the result of a process, not a deliberate ex-ante outcome. The existence of a relationship may constitute a most important attribute in the preferred service supplier. The time and effort to identify service providers and develop a relationship with them, as discussed in Chapter 7, may involve considerable costs that are taken into account by consumers when considering switching.

The concept of the 'family doctor' is a good illustration. If a doctor is friendly, he or she may be viewed also as being skilled. In addition to not querying the quality of this provider of a credence-based professional service activity, there are perceived switching costs associated with the doctor's knowledge of the person's past medical history. Using the same doctor makes it easy to participate in service encounters and reduces the time required to receive the service performance. Switching doctors could conceivably result in a time-intensive and painful process, while the relationship benefits would be lost, if not the past medical history. Similar consideration would apply to lawyers, solicitors and accountants, bank managers and tax consultants, and many other professional or technical service activities.

To know and to be known by a supplier are, therefore, valued supplier attributes in the credence and experience classes. Use by similar others will still be valued by experienced consumers, both as a facilitator for socialization and a confirmation of the preference by the group. As for convenience, it is a lower ranked criterion, although there is no lack of evidence demonstrating that ethnic minority consumers are often willing to be inconvenienced to access their preferred supplier. '"Only a Chinese person can cut my hair", says a young Chinese American who lives in Connecticut but whose barber works in Chinatown [New York]' (Swerdlow, 1998: 62).

Finally, the attributes valued by ethnic minority consumers in suppliers of service-products high in search qualities cannot be expected to differ strongly from those of mainstream consumers. Convenience, competitive price and good quality service are the top attributes, although usage by similar others and language may still be valued, as demonstrated by the proliferation of Hong Kong-style shopping malls in Vancouver, small stores catering for Mexican–Americans in the United States, the French quarters in Montreal and Chinatowns in most major cities of the world.

9.6 Implications

Examining the characteristics of services consumption and how these may impact on supplier selection by ethnic minority consumers clearly supports the need for ethnic marketing. Ethnic minority consumers confront a range of specific difficulties that, evaluated strategically, offer excellent opportunities for business.

The major issues uncovered in the discussion of services consumption by ethnic minority consumers are summarized in Table 9.2.

The various issues ensue from ethnic minority consumers' inability to draw on past experience as well as differences in meanings and contexts. It may be difficult to read product literature and discomfort may arise in consulting with service staff and different others. In addition, perishability results in reduced awareness and ability to assess provider credibility, while greater difficulty in obtaining information from available sources and limited sources of information may increase perceived risk. The assessment of value and quality is also subjective and it is often difficult for ethnic minority consumers to participate in service encounters. As a result of such difficulties, potential implications include increased post-purchase evaluation; less information

Table 9.2 Ethnic minority consumers and services consumption

Typical problems	Immediate implications	Second-tier implications	Outcome
Limited exposure to a different cultural context	▪ Discomfort in participating in service encounters ▪ Differences in meanings and contexts	▪ Acculturation to minority ethnic group ▪ Use ethnic resources	▪ Selects preferred suppliers to the group of affiliation
Communication limitations	▪ Difficult to obtain information from available sources ▪ Difficult to read product literature ▪ Discomfort in consulting with service staff and different others ▪ Difficulty in participating in service encounters	▪ Fewer information sources ▪ Use ethnic resources	▪ Increase perceived risk ▪ Less incentive to search for information ▪ Greater dependence on preferred suppliers ▪ Less incentive to switch suppliers ▪ Greater loyalty
Market inexperience	▪ Inability to draw on past experience ▪ Less awareness about alternatives due to perishability	▪ Fewer information sources ▪ Subjective assessment of value and quality ▪ Difficult to assess supplier credibility	▪ Less information gathering from the front-stage ▪ Increase post-purchase evaluation ▪ Increase dependence on service providers

gathering from the front-stage; an increased dependence on service providers; a decreased incentive to search for information and to switch service providers; and possible greater loyalty (Pires and Stanton, 2000).

Ethnic minority consumers and minority ethnic groups face consumption problems that may generate marketing opportunities for all businesses, particularly those offering intangible dominant propositions. Because these consumers are dependent on service suppliers and likely to invest in long-term relationships, perhaps the most attractive opportunity is to invest in the establishment of rewarding long-term relationships that will maximize customer lifetime value (Bolton, 1998).

Customer loyalty is not easy to achieve, particularly where the subjectivity of intangible experiences is compounded by customer–provider interactions for which consumers may not be prepared. The business problem then must be to determine how to provide ethnic minority consumers with memorable service experiences and positive value perceptions that they will evoke every time the need for the service arises.

Customization, responsiveness and personalization are marketing tools that may be particularly effective in reaching ethnic minority consumers of services. Effective use of these tools, however, depends on the skill of service personnel to interact with consumers. Business must encourage internal cultural sensitivity and awareness to bridge the understanding gap between culturally different actors. Possible avenues include training and, in some cases, reducing dissimilarity through the employment of ethnically identified service personnel (Danowski, 1993).

Progress towards a relationship depends on the participants' characteristics, on the quality of the service encounters and on the adoption of a customer orientation (supplier responsiveness). The service encounter may determine overall satisfaction with the service. For ethnic consumers, satisfaction may also be influenced by the setting of standards (expectations regarding performance) and ethnic group recommendation.

Service encounters often occur in a front-stage that may be strategically designed to appeal to customers. In addition, culturally sensitive and responsive service personnel may reduce consumers' perceived risk by developing user-friendly service delivery systems. Service supplier-initiated activities that succeed in reducing perceived risk may promote goodwill towards the supplier. Arguably, it is the service experience that distinguishes one service organization from another (Booms and Nyquist, 1981). Combined with lower perceived risk, higher switching costs stimulate customer dependence on the supplier that may convert into competitive advantage.

Information can also be a strategic tool. Ethnic minority consumers rely mostly on ethnic information sources (similar others and ethnic communication channels) for selecting their suppliers. These channels have been identified as a barrier, however there is no apparent reason why they should not be used to communicate business offerings.

Finally, the crucial issue in marketing services to ethnic minority consumers is that businesses seek to deal with the minority ethnic group. Marketing strategies such as sponsorship of, and conspicuous participation in, important community events, together with social bonding and endorsement of ethnic group societal attitudes and concerns may help shape a business profile to a status of credible perceived similar other (Bendapudi and Berry, 1997), fostering close long-term relationships and competitive advantage. However, the targeting will ultimately be ineffective if service encounters with individual ethnic consumers are allowed to deteriorate. Business must match and preferably exceed consumer expectations, ensuring that the feedback to the group is positive. Positive customer experiences trigger positive feedback that strengthens perceived supplier reliability, 'the most influential determinant of overall service quality or of customer satisfaction with the service' (Mittal and Lassar, 1998: 180).

Notes

1. Enis and Roering (1981) emphasize the benefits provided by services, rather than service classifications based upon hypothetically unique characteristics. Hartman and Lindgren Jr. (1993) use three 'simplifying evaluative dimensions' of goods and services (customization, evaluation and delay). Nevertheless, the proposition that services are different from goods remains largely undisputed.
2. A search of the wider literature dealing with ethnic marketing revealed a variety of anecdotal references about the target marketing of specific ethnic groups by particular service firms, mostly in the Canadian and the United States financial industries. These references generally originate in commercial multicultural marketing (read advertising) agencies. They tend to be prescriptive in nature, proposing some set of generalizations about some minority ethnic groups or their aggregate and offering recommendations about 'how to' be successful in targeting ethnic communities (Holliday, 1993; McCullough, 1995; Svendsen, 1997).

References

Bednall, S. and Kanuk, W. (1997) *Consumer Behaviour*, Sydney: Prentice-Hall.

Bendapudi, N. and Berry, L. (1997) 'Customers' motivations for maintaining relationships with service providers', *Journal of Retailing*, 73(1): 15–37.

Bolton, R. (1998) 'A dynamic model of the duration of the customer's relationship with a continuous service provider: the role of satisfaction', *Marketing Science*, 17(1): 45–65.

Booms, B. and Nyquist, J. (1981) 'Analyzing the customer/firm communication component of the services marketing mix', in J. Donnelly and W. George (eds) *Marketing of Services*, Chicago, IL: AMA.

Brand, R. and Cronin, J. (1997) 'Consumer-specific determinants of the size of retail choice sets: an empirical comparison of physical good and service providers', *Journal of Services Marketing*, 11(1): 19–38.

Clow, K., Kurtz, D., Ozment, J. and Ong, B. (1997) 'The antecedents of consumer expectations of services: an empirical study across four industries', *Journal of Services Marketing*, 11(4): 230–48.

Danowski, A. (1993) 'Ethnic markets', *Journal of Bank Marketing*, Nov.: 65–6.

Darby, M. and Karni, E. (1973) 'Free competition and the optimal amount of fraud', *Journal of Law and Economics*, 16: 67–86.

Enis, B. and Roering, K. (1981) 'Services marketing: different products, similar strategy', in J. Donnelly and W. George (eds) *Marketing of Services*, Chicago, IL: AMA, pp. 1–4.

Friedman, M. and Smith, L. (1993) 'Consumer evaluation processes in a service setting', *Journal of Services Marketing*, 7(2): 47–61.

Hartman, D. and Lindgren Jr., J. (1993) 'Consumer evaluations of goods and services: implications for services marketing', *Journal of Services Marketing*, 7(2): 4–15.

Hawkins, D., Best, R. and Coney, K. (1994) *Consumer Behavior: Implications for Marketing Strategy*, 5th edn., Boston, MA: Irwin.

Holliday, K. (1993) 'Reaching ethnic markets', *Journal of Bank Marketing*, Feb.: 35–7.

Hotchkiss, D. (1996) 'Weaving cultural sensitivity into marketing', *Journal of Bank Marketing*, 28 (June): 26–33.

Johnson, M. (1982) 'The social and cognitive features of the dissolution of commitment relationships', in S. Duck (ed.) *Personal Relationships: Dissolving Personal Relationships*, New York: Academic Press, pp. 51–73.

Kara, A. (1996) 'Ethnicity and consumer choice: a study of Hispanic decision processes across different acculturation levels', *Journal of Applied Business Research*, 12(2): 22–34.

Kaufman, C. (1987) 'Coupon use in ethnic markets: retailers' perceptions within the marketing channel', in *Proceedings*, AMA Workshop on Cultural and Subcultural Influences in Consumer Behavior and Marketing, Chicago, IL: AMA.

Laroche, M., Kim, C. and Clarke, M. (1997) 'The effects of ethnicity factors on consumer deal interests: an empirical study of French–English–Canadians, *Journal of Marketing Theory and Practice*, 5(1): 100–11.

Legg, D. and Baker, J. (1987) 'Advertising strategies for service firms', in C. Surprenant (ed.) *Add Value to Your Service*, Chicago, IL: AMA, pp. 163–8.

Levitt, T. (1973) 'What's your product and what's your business?', in *Marketing for Business Growth*, New York: McGraw-Hill, p. 7.

Light, I., Kwuon, I. and Zhong, D. (1990) 'Korean rotating credit associations in Los Angeles', *Amerasia*, 16(1): 35–54.

Lovelock, C. (1983) 'Classifying services to gain strategic marketing insights', *Journal of Marketing*, 47: 9–20.

Lovelock, C. (1996) *Services Marketing*, 3rd edn., Englewood Cliffs, NJ: Prentice-Hall.

McCullough, M. (1995) 'Nailing the niche: four marketers tap into the power of the Chinese market', *Marketing Magazine*, September 19: 17.

Mittal, B. and Lassar, W. (1996) 'The role of personalization in service encounters', *Journal of Retailing*, 72(1): 95–109.

Mittal, B. and Lassar, W. (1998) 'Why do customers switch? The dynamics of satisfaction versus loyalty', *Journal of Services Marketing*, 12(3): 177–94.

Murray, K. (1991) 'A test of services marketing theory: consumer information acquisition activities', *Journal of Marketing*, 55: 10–25.

Nelson, P. (1970) 'Advertising as information', *Journal of Political Economy*, 81: 729–54.

Pires, G. D. (2000) 'The selection of service providers by ethnic minority consumers in a culturally diverse society', unpublished doctoral thesis, University of Newcastle.

Pires, G. D. and Stanton, J. P. (2000) 'Marketing services to ethnic consumers in culturally diverse markets: issues and implications', *Journal of Services Marketing*, 14(7): 607–18.

Rothmell, J. (1996) 'What is meant by services?', *Journal of Marketing*, 30(4): 32–6.

Shaw, E. and Pirog III, S. (1997) 'A systems model of household behavior', *Journal of Marketing Theory and Practice*, Summer: 17–29.

Sheth, J. and Parvatiyar, A. (1995) 'Relationship marketing in consumer markets: antecedents and consequents', *Journal of the Academy of Marketing Science*, 23: 255–71.

Shostack, L. (1977) 'Breaking free from product marketing', *Journal of Marketing*, 41: 73–80.

Smith, J. (1998) 'Buyer–seller relationships: similarity, relationship management, and quality', *Psychology & Marketing*, 15(1): 3–21.

Solomon, M., Surprenant, C., Czepiel, J. and Gutman, E. (1985) 'A role theory perspective on dyadic interactions: the service encounter', *Journal of Marketing*, 49: 99–111.

Svendsen, A. (1997) 'Building relationships with microcommunities', *Marketing News*, 9 June 13.

Swerdlow, J. (1998) 'Chinatown', *National Geographic*, August: 60–77.

Zeithaml, V. (1981) 'How consumer evaluation processes differ between goods and services', in J. Donnelly and R. George (eds) *Marketing of Services*, Chicago, IL: American Marketing Association, pp. 39–47.

Zeithaml, V., Parasuraman, A. and Berry, L. (1985) 'Problems and strategies in services marketing', *Journal of Marketing*, 49(2): 33–46.

Zeithaml, V. and Bitner, M. (2000) *Services Marketing: Integrating Customer Focus Across the Firm*, Sydney: McGraw-Hill.

Verizon targets minority customer base

Kevin Fitchard*

In a speech at the National Hispanic Publishers' Conference last month, Eduardo Menasce, president of Verizon Communications' Enterprise Solutions Unit, declared that the RBOC's future is tied directly to Hispanic communities throughout the USA. He showed that Hispanics spend more than $20 billion annually and are one of the fastest growing segments of internet users.

'These numbers are getting bigger as Hispanic buying power and population size continue to grow faster than the national average', Menasce told the assembled publishers. 'So when we say your future is our future, it's not an exaggeration, it's a fact.'

With the demographic makeup in the USA quickly changing, carriers are starting to wise up about who their customers are. Minorities represent not only massive voting blocs in states such as New York, California, Florida, Illinois and Texas, they're becoming significant consumer blocs that often spend more on telecom services than the mass market.

And it's not just the Hispanic community that Verizon is courting. Verizon and its fellow carriers are seeing the same growth in spending and population size in the African–American and Asian communities as well as the smaller minority groups comprising the cultural polyglot of metropolitan areas. 'I want a customer to see Verizon and say we understand all of the cultural nuances and geographical differences in our customer base', said Ed Miller, Verizon's executive director of multicultural marketing. 'We understand that different minority groups want to communicate differently and have different needs than the mass market.'

While Verizon's territory contains some of the most ethnically diverse cities in the USA – including New York, Boston and Washington, DC – the carrier's minority makeup is consistent with the national average: 14 per cent Hispanic,

* *Telephony*, 7 April 2003, 243(7):

12 per cent African–American and 4 per cent Asian. 'But those combined communities spend, on average, 23 per cent more on telecom services than mass-market consumers', Miller said. 'Hispanic and Asian consumers generally spend much more on international long-distance, Asian customers are much earlier adopters of Internet and DSL services, and African–American customers are among the most avid consumers of enhanced voice features such as caller ID and three-way calling', Miller said.

Not only do they spend more, their ranks are rapidly expanding. In some states, Hispanics have surpassed Caucasians as the single largest ethnic group. For instance, in California minority groups account for 55 per cent of the state's total population.

Verizon has consequently launched aggressive minority and multilingual marketing campaigns in many of its more diverse markets. In New York alone, Verizon markets in eight languages. In addition, it targets marketing campaigns to English-speaking sub-groups, using different 'cultural cues' to address African–American, gay and lesbian, and disabled consumers. Miller, however, pointed out that Verizon's marketing efforts go far beyond advertising in different languages; its sales and support forces are multilingual as well. A Russian living in New York can call a Verizon customer service rep and expect to hear a Russian voice.

Not only does Verizon market services differently to different groups, it makes specific cultural accommodations for specific minorities. For example, among Chinese, the number four is very unlucky and its pronunciation in Chinese is almost identical to the word 'death'. Miller said Verizon's Chinese marketing team tries to expunge the number from all its marketing materials to the point that every call-in customer service and support line doesn't require Chinese customers to dial the number four.

Verizon is definitely on the right track, but there is only so far a major market carrier can go with segmented marketing, said Derek Gietzen, CEO of Vycera, a long-distance provider and CLEC that sells solely to Spanish-speaking consumers in major US markets.

'All the big telecom companies have ethnic marketing departments, but they're always boutique departments', Gietzen said. 'While Verizon has the right idea marketing toward minorities directly, it's still offering the same basic services it's offering the mass market. Different ethnic communities have different telecom needs.'

QUESTIONS

1. What are the communication differences between cultures that need to be addressed by a telephony company?
2. Do you agree or disagree with Gietzen's opinion, expressed in the last paragraph?

Ethnic marketing in practice – HRM issues

10.1 Chapter objectives

This chapter examines human resource management (HRM) problems that may hinder adoption of ethnic marketing strategies, namely limited skills tied to deficient understanding of ethnic markets. It explains that businesses tend to deal with these limitations by undertaking cultural awareness training as a means of managing cultural differences. Alternatively, or in addition to this training, there are instances where firms elect to employ ethnic staff as a means of overcoming skills shortages. However, these hiring tactics may be counterproductive.

10.2 The cultural challenge

Awareness of 'ethnocentrism', the tendency to consider one's own culture superior to others (Czinkota *et al.*, 1994), is a recurring theme in international business, arising in the discussion of strategy formulation (the strategy works successfully in my home market, it should work in foreign markets); marketing (if the marketing mix worked at home, it should work abroad); and human resource management (why should the workforce practices and training be any different to those at home?). Given the tardiness of businesses to recognize and act on cultural diversity within national boundaries, very little attention has been given to the practice and consequences of ethnocentrism within national boundaries, although similar consequences from its practice may well arise.

While an ethnocentric approach may be successful, a prior requirement for this choice is that the professional who aspires to do business abroad is internationally adept and culturally aware (Bonvillian and Nowlin, 1994). Cultural awareness in this context has two sides: awareness of how another person's culture affects their behaviour; and self awareness of the decision-maker of how their own culture affects their behaviour (Beamish *et al.*, 1997). In seeking to win and hold an ethnic minority market within a national boundary, similar awareness must be developed as the basis for creating the most favourable environment for dealing with customers.

An increasing visibility of minority ethnic groups has heightened business awareness of the opportunities offered by 'new' markets based on ethnicity within national borders (Exhibit 10.1). Targeting of these markets is challenging for business, not the least because of the cultural differences that may need to be understood and bridged if the encounter is to result in a loyal customer. If a business can pinpoint an ethnic audience and talk to it in its own language, it can create a special bond and perhaps get a jump on the competition (Schumackler, 1995).

The cultural challenge is also a challenge for human resource management because business demand for the skills that facilitate effective communication and interaction with ethnic communities may influence the criteria that are used in employee selection, as well as the need for, extent and nature of, staff training. One possible way to shed some light on the important issues is to draw from the international cross-cultural environment.

10.3 Managing differences abroad

A study of language use and practice in the context of the internationalization process to be followed by European business indicated the need to deal with linguistic and cultural obstacles in foreign markets. Most important in the present context, the process integrates product-based decisions with

... sensitivity to Canada's cultural diversity is on the rise. As more immigrants arrive and our major cities' multicultural communities mature, so too does the marketing industry. Marketers and agencies are hiring more people of various ethnic backgrounds, especially Chinese and East Indian, and advertising reflects the country's diversity more than ever ... Manyee Juli Lui, president of Manyee Research Associates Inc. of Toronto, says ... an increasing number of marketers are hiring people of specific cultural backgrounds who can advise them on marketing ... *'There's absolutely less reservation to hire (minorities),'* she says. *'As a matter of fact, it's going in the opposite direction.'* Airlines, financial institutions, telecommunications companies and retailers are looking at their customer databases, realizing the weight and buying power of these cultural groups, and are compelled to learn more about them.

Martin Glynn, CEO of the Vancouver-based Hong Kong Bank of Canada, says 25% of the company's 115 Canadian branches are Chinese branches, and the company is now developing Mandarin Centres, staffed by people ready to give assistance to people from Taiwan, China and Singapore. *'The traditional two solitudes of Canada are breaking up,'* he says. *'There are whole subsets opening up. Marketing along ethnic lines is a growth market.'*

Peggy Sum, vice-president Asian markets at Bank of Montreal, says her bank *'is changing ...'.* The bank has hired three Chinese executive VPs for the Chinese market, a senior-staff person for the Korean market, and a senior manager for the Indo-Canadian market; overall, more than 25 people from visible minorities have been hired to middle- and senior-management positions in the last couple of years.

Source: Excerpt from Pollock (1997).

decisions about hiring local staff, handling foreign enquiries and operating effectively in the local language and culture (Hagan, 2000).

Effective operation in the local language and culture arguably requires expatriate managers to have a number of skills. These skills (identified and explained in Table 10.1) consist of interpersonal skills, linguistic ability, cultural curiosity, tolerance for uncertainty and ambiguity, flexibility, patience and respect, cultural empathy, strong sense of self and sense of humour (Schneider and Barsoux, 2003, pp. 190–5).

Formal training programmes to foster cultural sensitivity and acceptance of new ways of doing things are widely practised by firms that use an expatriate workforce. Programmes can vary considerably in terms of rigour, involvement and cost. At one extreme are area briefings and lectures that largely provide factual information. Context, in which to use the facts, can be added using scenario analysis in which trainees must respond to specifically constructed

Table 10.1 Skills required by expatriates to function effectively internationally

Interpersonal skills	The ability to form relationships
Linguistic ability	Since having total command of the other language may not be feasible and may be less important than trying to develop a feel for what matters to others
Cultural curiosity	Genuine interest in other cultures
Tolerance for uncertainty and ambiguity	Information is often insufficient, unreliable and conflicting
Flexibility	In responding to customer needs and preferences
Patience	Learning new ways of doing things takes time; indeed, different cultures may hold distinct horizons
Respect	Non-ethnocentric approach
Cultural empathy	Focused learning and a non-judgmental approach
Strong sense of self	Allows for cross-cultural interaction without losing one's identity
Sense of humour	As a mechanism for coping with a sometimes hostile and always different environment, and for relationship building

situations in specific countries. At the other extreme of cost and involvement is actual field training under supervision (Czinkota *et al.*, 1994).

Businesses targeting minority ethnic groups within a country ultimately face the same sort of challenges in their preparedness to handle enquiries by, interact and arrive at an understanding with ethnic minority consumers. There is, therefore, no apparent reason why the skills in Table 10.1 would not apply here. In fact, those skills may need to be even more strongly required on two accounts:

1. There may be a perceived power shift from the customer to the supplier.
2. Customers from different minority ethnic groups may be in each other's presence when interacting with a business.

That is, business employees may need to deal with a variety of cultures simultaneously. The moderating factors may be the consumers' effort to fit with the mainstream way of doing things and, through simultaneity and inseparability in service encounters, the partial appropriation by customers of the responsibility for poor interactions.

One way to deal with these difficulties is to employ individuals that identify themselves with the target minority ethnic group. This is a common practice adopted by businesses targeting minority ethnic groups in many culturally diverse countries. Often these businesses advertise in the ethnic press, using the ethnic language and naming some employee that can be recognized by her/his 'ethnic' name, and exhibit prominent signs.

The lesson from cross-cultural marketing experience is that language and cultural differences among countries result in different vocabularies for the interpretation of things and different behaviours. Together with the skills required to manage differences abroad, language skills and intercultural understanding may facilitate interactions and agreement with ethnic minority consumers, reduce transaction costs (eventually making new business opportunities viable) and foster business relationships, leading to enhanced competitiveness.

10.4 Managing differences domestically

Language skills and cultural understanding are fundamental internal elements in the process of defining organizational capabilities necessary for ascertaining customer needs and preferences and, ultimately, for achieving competitive advantage (Cravens and Piercy, 2003). This is, slowly but surely, being understood and acted upon by business. In Canada and the United States, for example, there are many examples of businesses in the financial services sector attempting to deal with diversity, other than more universal attempts to reach ethnic communities with problematic translations of mainstream advertising. The anecdotes, more or less humorous, of cultural misunderstanding so created are abundant in the marketing literature. Notwithstanding, how to bridge the cultural gap separating businesses and ethnic consumers remains an area for research. The banking sector provides a lead.

In 1995, a study of the Chinese market in Canada noted that specific programmes for marketing to the Chinese community were rare or non-existent in many industries, in contrast with the banking industry where they were proliferating. As an example the study noted the launching by the TD Bank, in 1992, of the Chinese information phone line – a spin-off of the English/French Green Line it pioneered in 1984. In 1995 the line handled about 300 calls per month in Cantonese and Mandarin, justifying the introduction of more lines. The lines are used to provide information on TD products and to build relationships with callers, steering them to specific branches and specific sales personnel (Haman, 1995). Reliance on front-stage personnel with special skills is also reported in marketing agencies such as Ad Impact, of Toronto, which caters especially to Chinese, Italian, Portuguese, Spanish and Greek clients, with in-house experts from those communities (Pollock, 1992).

In the USA, and also in 1995, the Bank of America recognized the economic potential of the 'new' niche markets and was in the process of targeting several distinct ethnic populations (Nagy and Lepley, 1997). At the same time, 'savvy bankers' were 'refining financial marketing tactics to better bridge the language and lifestyle barriers that often impede relationships with minority communities.' Reportedly, banks serving Asian–Americans, such as the Atlanta-based Summit National Bank, were prospering with their growing populations. Over 50 per cent of employees were bilingual and the bank transacted business in 11 languages, including Chinese, Vietnamese, Japanese, Korean, French, German and Spanish.

In the broadly defined Hispanic market, the cardinal rule allegedly is to provide customer service in Spanish. Hence, in predominantly Hispanic areas, over 90 per cent of the customer service personnel of Coral Gables Federal, a financial institution serving central and southern Florida markets, are Spanish (Holliday, 1993). Given the language and cultural diversity of the Hispanic market, it is not surprising that cultural misunderstandings will continue to occur.

The attempt to deal with cultural diversity by banks and financial institutions in the USA is well illustrated in Exhibit 10.2, relating the case of the Hmong, a minority ethnic group residing cross-nationally in Indo-China, many of whom were displaced by the Vietnam conflict and ended up in the USA. Contrary to current common practices of segmenting the ethnic marketing based on similarities, the Hmong illustrate that the Asian–American market cannot be approached as a single segment.

The cultural gap and communications limitations between bank employees and Hmong customers, as well as customer tactics to assemble with friends and family to overcome their English limitations, caused bank employees to feel intimidated. Instead of hiding the challenges of segment uniqueness in the 'too hard basket' of the aggregation of Asian–Americans, the study concluded that the language barrier was a primary source of problems that might be reduced through involvement with the community, through training on communicating with those having limited English skills, and by employing bilingual personnel.

Language skills

The noted miscommunication problems between bank employees and Hmong customers emphasize the inability of those ethnic minority consumers to communicate effectively in the mainstream language. Providing employees with ethnic language training, or indeed the hiring of bilingual employees recruited from the minority ethnic group, are means to help manage the cultural gap. But the importance of language skills is not confined to consumers' limitations.

Even if consumers are bilingual and effective users of the mainstream language, there are reasons for business to use the ethnic language instead. While communicating in the mainstream would be adequate, businesses may need to go beyond 'adequate', in line with a simple message – 'Speak the

EXHIBIT 10.2: **Satisfying customers who are members of new ethnic groups**

Over the past two decades, northeastern Wisconsin has had a large inflow of Hmong immigrants who come from a tribal culture indigenous to areas of Laos and other Southeast Asia countries. Serving such a new market segment can be especially difficult, given the differences in cultural and linguistic norms between these people and the existing customer base and financial institution employees in the area . . . While there may be significant opportunities for bankers in ethnic markets, there are equally significant challenges in reaching these consumers . . . The Asian–American market cannot be approached as a single segment . . . Although some Americans might try to lump Asians together for marketing purposes, 29 major – and distinct – ethnic groups exist between the Indian subcontinent and the Pacific Ocean.

. . . Casual observation suggest(ed) that the Hmong customers were responding differently than their non-Hmong counterparts . . . In order to explore (this) further, we assembled a focus group of bank employees. These people represent the personnel on the front lines with whom the banks' customers have the most direct contact and who therefore produce important parts of the customer's impression of the bank . . . In the discussion, all of the employees recalled instances of miscommunication or cultural misunderstanding involving Hmong customers. Many noted that many Hmong names could be difficult to pronounce; also, husbands and wives often do not share the same last name . . . Most of the institutions represented in the focus group had few, if any, Hmong employees on hand to bridge language and cultural differences. As one participant noted, 'This is a tragic waste, since Hmongs represent 4 to 5 per cent of our customer base.'

Often, according to the participants, Hmong customers bring relatives or friends with them when applying for a loan or trying to resolve a problem. This no doubt provides an efficient way for recent immigrants to pool their relatively scarce English-speaking skills. But, the bank employees reported a feeling of intimidation when confronted with such large numbers of people together . . . The language barrier is most certainly a primary source of problems . . . (I)nstitutions can provide better training on communicating with those having limited English skills. . . .

Source: Excerpt from Nagy and Lepley (1997).

language, get the business' (Pollock, 1993: 13). Communicating in the ethnic language earns respect and attention. Following Hotchkiss (1996), there are many Hispanics who speak Spanish as well as English. If a business communicates with these consumers in Spanish, there is an emotional attachment as well as a moral obligation in operation – 'There is a company that is trying to reach me in a way I see as positive. Therefore, I want to do business with them' (p. 31). More generally, businesses may show their sensitivity towards ethnic minority consumers by communicating in their language, which is rewarded with their custom (Medcalf, 1993). This sensitivity may be heightened if the use of the ethnic language is complemented by ethnic employees who are aware of the customer's cultural make-up, and by their involvement with the minority group.

Involvement with, and hiring of ethnic minority consumers

Refocusing attention on the banking industry, many financial institutions hire members of minority ethnic groups. Because most people, if given their choice, will gravitate toward community groups with traits similar to their own, these employees are encouraged to be active in civic and business groups within the ethnic community. Hence the recommendation that financial institutions should demonstrate 'involvement with the Hmong community by actively recruiting qualified employees from that community and cultivating communication between the Hmong community and the population at large' (Nagy and Lepley, 1997: 40).

The proposition that most people will willingly gravitate toward community groups with traits similar to their own is supported by the combination of similarity-attraction theory, social identity theory and self-categorization theory. The argument is that individuals prefer and support relationships with similar others in order to reinforce their self-esteem and maintain balance or congruity in social-identity. A large body of literature in interpersonal relationships has established that similar others are more attractive, liked better, and more trusted compared to dissimilar others. Attitudinal and value similarity promote trust toward the other (Dwyer, Schurr and Oh, 1987). Accordingly, interaction is easier and less cognitively challenging with others who have similar experiences, attitudes, activities or values.

Similarity-attraction and self-identity

Value similarity can play a critical role in extending perceptions of similarity from an individual employee to the business, an idea that is aligned to the proposition sustained in this book that the importance of ethnic minority consumers is pegged to the cohesion, strength and ultimate marketing relevance of the minority ethnic group. Rather than individual focus, targeting should be largely through that group, including the process of perceived value creation and innovation. This focus on the group rather than the individual is illustrated, for example, in Coca-Cola sponsoring the planting of trees in Egypt as a means to sell cola to individuals (Fadiman, 1986), or its reported capturing of the American ethnic market by virtue of a social policy based on values such as diversity and non-discrimination, reflected in the company's support of the civil rights movement in the 1960s.

If involvement of a business or a brand with a minority ethnic group, for example through sponsorship of community events, may be warranted, misbehaviour to individuals, however, can also be penalized by the group. Coca-Cola became a victim of its lack of coherence when the value of non-discrimination was not apparent in its employment policies. Because African–American employees were perceived as underpaid and never promoted, Coca-Cola faced a boycott organized by some of its old allies such as the civil rights movement (Breton, 2000). Customers who patronize (or boycott) a business for supporting (or opposing) a favoured cause are responding to the perceived value similarity of the business. In a relationship, similar partners are proposed to signal their greater likelihood of facilitating the other party's goals.

Value similarity and similarity-attraction theory explain why ethnic minority consumers may be strongly predisposed to specialty shops and business establishments owned by members of their group of affiliation, and enter into personal relationships with shopkeepers (Parissis and Helfinger, 1993). The importance of the 'personal' factor justifies further elaboration in considering human resource skills.

'Personalization' – the social content of interaction between service employees and their customers – is distinct from customization and responsiveness, both of which can be offered with total lack of personalization. If there is a human encounter in a business transaction, the manner in which employees relate to their customers can be expected to play a significant role in business success. Personalization is the reason why customers seek familiar, likable, friendly service providers and retail clerks.

The customer's interaction with a supplier can be intra- or extra-role. Extra-role interactions involve social bonds that may develop outside the business relationship. For example, ethnic minority consumers interact with fellow group members in social or sporting activities organized by community social clubs. Some of these fellow members may be the bank clerk or the electrician preferred by the community. Indirect social interaction may also occur through business links to individuals (as in the case of a doctor that has treated a family over the years) or with institutions that the customer identifies with (such as the community church). The influence of family, friends and reference groups on purchase behaviour and relationship maintenance is well documented in the consumer behaviour literature (Childers and Rao, 1992; Sheth and Parvatiyar, 1995).

Ultimately, personalized interactions may provide customers with social support – consisting of social interactions which offer psychological comfort and elation to a person. Support outcomes can range from alleviation of mild boredom to ventilation of anxiety or personal thoughts, confirmation of personal opinions, receiving comfort in grief, or the satisfaction of being liked.

Self-categorization

The social aspect of self-identity is also developed through self-categorization along a variety of attributes, such as age, sex, race, or personality, and by making in-group and out-group contrasts to others. Social identity is promoted or enhanced by making favourable attributions to in-groups (those of personal interaction or psychological attachment) and unfavourable attributions to out-groups. This self-enhancement motive promotes in-group solidarity, cooperation and support, communications, trust and reciprocity, and greater satisfaction in, and perceived performance of, relationships.

10.5 The challenge of domestic diversity

The case of the targeting of Hmong consumers illustrates the need to overcome the language and cultural gap. This becomes a crucial human resource management issue because, in addition to special culture skills training in language and communication and training employees to deal with ethnic customers, similarity attraction recommends hiring ethnic employees who will be better equipped to identify and address subtle cultural nuances (Danowski, 1993). Avon, for example, openly aims its segmentation strategies to the alignment of organizational values with those of the customers, via ethnic identified personnel (see Exhibit 10.3).

Employing persons identifying with a particular ethnic group may be counterproductive if there is a lack of fit between the employee's culture and that of the employer. That is, if a business hires individuals from a particular minority ethnic group to be able to relate better to that group, there are questions that need to be asked:

- How well will the employee relate to the employer? With employees from distinct ethnic groups?
- Will the socialization of the employee be easy?
- How will performance be appraised and training given? (Schneider and Barsoux, 2003, 151, 157, 164).

For example, if a person is employed by a Japanese business for her/his language skills in dealing with the Portuguese community, will this person be seen the same as other employees? On the other hand, when high power-distance is involved, as in the case of the Portuguese, is there a risk that the employee becomes a gatekeeper to the organization, rather than a gateway to the community? Can this gatekeeper bully customers, as a means of getting perceived power within the community? If special control measures are implemented, these may be misunderstood for discrimination.

EXHIBIT 10.3: Avon – money left on the table

CEO James E. Preston credits diversity for helping Avon's financial perform-ance since 1990. The company's customer diversity management approach has been achieved through segmenting the market and developing strate-gies and tactics based on values, trends, and buying patterns of consumers in ethnic markets.

Avon conducted extensive market research to understand how ethnic consumers make their buying decisions. A major underlying tenet was the importance of values – specifically the alignment of organisational values with those of the customers. This premise is repeated by marketing man-agers and it ensures continuity of marketing strategy with corporate vision.

Avon also introduced 'Money Left on the Table', a training program to help sales managers understand the company's diversity strategy. The program is designed to change perceptions about consumers, by demonstrating who they are in terms of potential sales dollars and by providing information on how to address the ethnic markets. The training focuses on misconceptions about ethnic minority consumers' lack of money to buy products and on demonstrating that competition is intense, such that if Avon does not meet consumers' needs, someone else will.

The Avon sales representative is an independent contractor. Although the company does not know to whom the representative sells, it knows that the customers' cultural background mirrors that of the representatives.

Avon's CEO is committed to managing diversity and he is visible in the ethnic community. In culturally diverse markets, a business must create trust and be a good corporate citizen in the community. The key is to approach the ethnic minority customer with the same respect, in-depth analysis, support and quality that are brought to the mainstream market.

Source: Extract adaptation from Chapman and McFarland (1995).

Furthermore, in a culturally diverse market, businesses may deal with customers from many different minority ethnic groups, simultaneously and in a manner conspicuous to the different customers. Two consequences may arise from this circumstance. The first, quite extreme but nevertheless very common, compels businesses to overlook minority ethnic groups for market-ing purposes, for fear of backlash reprisal behaviour by mainstream consumers (Hemphill and Haines, 1998). The second refers to the fact that culture skills training in language and communication may need to account for all the different cultures embodied by their customers. This makes learn-ing all their diverse customs, attitudes, tastes and preferences a tremendously difficult task, if at all accomplishable.

If employees are hired based on ethnic similarity with the target groups, any problems from a lack of fit to the business culture (and the questions listed above) multiply. A solution could be only to hire employees from the most important ethnic customer groups. Importance, however, is a relative and dynamic concept and excluding a particular group may have unintended consequences. For example, the impact of employing a South African to reach that community may question not employing a Chinese to reach the Chinese; hence lack of respect and care for the Chinese community.

Whether ethnic group-affiliated employees are used or not, developing front-stages where members from a particular minority ethnic group feel welcome and comfortable doing business also requires, first, providing employees with extensive cultural training, in order to develop an understanding among employees of the different groups' unique needs and perspectives and, second, using physical evidence to match customers' attributes closely. This is a very complex task to accomplish because the diverse clientele will possibly be sharing the front-stage, requiring well-developed interaction skills by personnel.

Overall, the marketing opportunities offered by minority ethnic groups in culturally diverse markets are potentially challenging for businesses. Importantly, in the present context, the role played by people is crucial to the ability of the business to ensure positive and productive interactions with customers. Businesses need to develop cultural competencies and to manage cultural differences effectively.

10.6   Developing cultural competencies

Managing cultural differences may involve a number of alternatives, from the segregation of ethnic minority consumers, to the adoption of a standard or global approach to dealing with cultural differences or, indeed, to simply ignoring the differences. Businesses may also opt for developing cultural competencies, either by employing bilingual ethnic personnel or through appropriate skills training of existing staff.

The means for cultural competency may depend on a variety of factors and needs to take the context into consideration. Factors that need to be considered include the number of minority ethnic groups to be targeted, the current stock of skills within the business, the degree of competition and barriers to entry, the availability of suitable bilingual ethnic personnel available for employment, the relative importance (strategically or otherwise) of the ethnic market in the overall market, the resources available to the business and more. Clearly the contextual embedding of the business needs to be taken into account.

Cultural knowledge management

One major issue that businesses may need to consider is cultural knowledge management – how the business (as contrasted with individual employees)

Table 10.2   Strategy used for building a relationship with a minority ethnic group

Step 1	Goal setting
Step 2	Planning and staff team development
Step 3	Organizational readiness
Step 4	Outreach
Step 5	Sponsorship and awareness building
Step 6	Business development
Step 7	Evaluation and renewal

Source: Svendsen (1997).

will learn, and how this knowledge is processed and improved upon. This is particularly relevant for market-oriented organizations since cultural sensitivity is now demanded at all levels of the organization. For example, frontline employees (such as security guards, chauffeurs, and receptionists) are the first to greet foreign visitors (Schneider and Barsoux, 2003: 186), and a lack of behavioural consistency with that of sales personnel is bound to create cognitive dissonance, checking the cultural approximation.

According with the marketing concept, it is the organization as a whole, rather than individuals, that needs to focus on satisfying customer needs and preferences, subject to meeting business objectives and the societal interest. This is illustrated in a case study by Svendsen (1997), reporting the strategy used by a Canadian financial institution, VanCity Credit Union, for developing a successful relationship with a minority ethnic group, the Filipino community in Vancouver. The study describes seven steps in building a relationship with a minority ethnic group, compiled in Table 10.2.

In Step 1, goal setting (such as increasing the customer base, raising awareness and credibility) may involve assisting community-based organizations through employee volunteering, sponsorship of important community events, and financial information and advice through community media and seminars. Step 2 refers to planning and staff team development. This encompassed involving Filipino employees, particularly those speaking Tagalog. Most of these staff members already knew community leaders and were members of community organizations. Staff contributed cultural knowledge, sensitivity and enthusiasm. Organizational readiness, in Step 3, focuses on ensuring that the whole organization supports and assists relationship building – even in branches remote from the community – as an important means to achieve long-term credibility. Step 4, outreach, involves active participation in community-based organizations. Step 5 refers to sponsorship and awareness building, involving the identification of events and community projects that can be sponsored – such as church and cultural events – and using community newspapers for communications. Finally Steps 6 and 7 consist of business development and evaluation and renewal, respectively.

The process requires attention to three key strategic principles:

1. The business must have long-term goals and accept that it must give to the community before getting.
2. It must demonstrate that it is sincerely concerned about the well-being of the community.
3. The programme must be based on an understanding and appreciation of the community's values, beliefs, aspirations, and fears.

Reportedly, success of the outlined relationship-building process yields a variety of benefits for the business, including:

- increased customer loyalty and support;
- enhanced reputation;
- targeted and effective corporate philanthropy;
- increased employee morale and commitment.

Achieving these benefits justifies that, since 1992, the VanCity Credit Union has successfully implemented similar programmes with the Native American, Chinese, Italian, gay and lesbian, and East Indian communities (Svendsen, 1997: 13).

Functional multilingualism

It is apparent that the development of cultural competencies does not seek to remove the cultural gap; rather its focus is on adaptation, that is, on how to deal with the gap effectively. This is a particularly important point to make because, given the variation in resources available to different businesses, and the environmental dynamism on the group's part to business interactions, it may be crucial for specific businesses to devise an action plan for dealing with the gap.

Functional multilingualism refers to businesses' ability to get messages across in the international arena with whatever language skills they possess (Hagan, 2000). The analysis, however, is clearly transferable to the ethnic marketing situation. A business engaging in ethnic marketing needs to plan for cultural and linguistic differences based on the available resources, to relate better with ethnic minority consumers.

Arguably, the definition of organizational capabilities or competencies, perceived today as fundamental for business success, needs to account for the need to match customers' needs and preferences. While there may be supply-based pressures on the business to standardize its core business activity, sustainable competitive advantage may depend on the attributes that surround that core, including functional multilingualism and, not least important, cultural sensitivity and responsiveness.

In terms of ethnic marketing, homogenization of the core activity may imply that multilingualism, cultural sensitivity and responsiveness are the only attributes that matter. The key is, therefore, to plan for adequately managing the gap. This plan needs to account for:

- levels of existing ethnic language skills;

- spread of competence across languages;

- levels of cultural knowledge of target markets;

- barriers to trade due to missing skills;

- skill gaps/shortages;

- impacts of deficiencies on business with a group;

- strategies employed to overcome skills gaps and other linguistic deficiencies;

- language training being undertaken.

It is an inventory approach in which existing language skill and cultural knowledge deficiencies act as a hindrance to finding and participating in trade opportunities. Identification of the skills gap focuses on the strategies used to overcome these barriers (closing the gap), with particular attention given to training.

References

Beamish, P., Morrison, A. and Rosenzweig, P. (1997) *International Management, Text and Cases*, 3rd edn., Chicago: Irwin.

Bonvillian, G. and Nowlin, W. (1994) 'Cultural awareness: an essential element of doing business abroad', *Business Horizons*, November–December: 44–51.

Breton, J. (2000) 'World Affairs Social Audit', accessed at http://www.world-affairs.com/audit.htm on February 19, 2004, pp. 1–6.

Chapman, J. and McFarland, J. (1995) 'Diversity of the customer base: a business necessity', *Journal of Education for Business*, 71 (Sept./Oct.): 17–18.

Childers, T. and Rao, A. (1992) 'Influence of familiar and peer-based reference groups on consumer decisions', *Journal of Consumer Research*, 19 (September): 198–211.

Cravens, D. W. and Piercy, N. F. (2003) *Strategic Marketing*, 7th edn., Sydney: McGraw-Hill Companies Inc.

Czinkota, M., Ronkainen, I. and Moffett, M. (1994) *International Business*, 3rd edn., Fort Worth, TX: Dryden Press.

Danowski, A. (1993) 'Ethnic markets', *Journal of Bank Marketing*, 25 (November): 65–6.

Dwyer, F., Schurr, P. and Oh, S. (1987) 'Developing buyer–seller relationships', *Journal of Marketing*, 51(2): 11–27.

Fadiman, J. (1986) 'A traveler's guide to gifts and bribes', *Harvard Business Review*, July–August: 122–36.

Hagan, S. (ed.) (2000) *Business Communication across Borders: A Study of Language Use and Practice in European Companies*, London: Centre for Information on Language Teaching and Research.

Haman, A. (1995) '"Nailing the niche", in Chinese market', *Marketing Magazine*, 18 September: pp. 20–1.

Hemphill, H. and Haines, R. (1998) 'Confronting discrimination in your workplace', *HR Focus*, 75(7): S5–S6.

Holliday, K. (1993) 'Reaching ethnic markets', *Journal of Bank Marketing*, Feb.: 35–7.

Hotchkiss, D. (1996) 'Weaving cultural sensitivity into marketing', *Journal of Bank Marketing*, 28 (June): 26–33.

Medcalf, L. (1993) 'A creative mosaic', *Marketing*, 98, 19 July: 13.

Nagy, R. and Lepley, W. (1997) 'Satisfying customers who are members of new ethnic groups', *Journal of Retailing Banking Services*, 19(3): 35–40.

Parissis, M. and Helfinger, M. (1993) 'Ethnic shoppers share certain values', *Marketing*, 98(11): 16.

Pollock, J. (1992) 'Pitching inside to ethnic markets', *Marketing*, 97, 13/20 July: 17 and 31.

Pollock, J. (1993) 'Ethnic marketing: the new reality', *Marketing*, 98, 19 July: 13–19.

Pollock, J. (1997) 'Racial minorities become visible', *Multicultural Marketing*, 3 March: 13.

Schneider, S. and Barsoux, J. (2003) *Managing Across Cultures*, 2nd edn., Harlow: Prentice-Hall.

Schumackler, E. (1995) 'A multiplicity of ethnicity', *Brandweek*, 36, 17 July: 22–8.

Sheth, J. and Parvatiyar, A. (1995) 'Relationship marketing in consumer markets: antecedents and consequents', *Journal of the Academy of Marketing Science*, 23: 255–71.

Svendsen, A. (1997) 'Building relationships with microcommunities', *Marketing News*, 9 (June): 13.

Avon targets black sales reps; Storefront sales and bigger ad push behind attempt to better target ethnic groups

Stephanie Thompson*

Commuters to New York's Grand Central Terminal are seeing Venus and Serena Williams in a giant ad promoting the tennis playing sisters' new Avon jewelry collection. Until recently, Avon's multicultural efforts were limited to occasional brochures targeted to one or another group of ethnic women. From that toe in the water, the direct-selling beauty company will attempt to make a bigger splash among all skin shades with storefront sales – the first time ever at Avon – in high-density Hispanic and African–American markets. It plans to use the Williams sisters in advertising and collateral materials intended to recruit African–American representatives, and has created a position with the title leader of market segmentation, held by Joyce Mullins-Jackson.

C9.1   African–American market

'Our Hispanic reps do very well and we've seen the number of them grow, but growth in African–American representatives has not been as good', Ms Mullins-Jackson said. That reality has prompted efforts to actively recruit with advertising

---

* *Advertising Age*, Sept 1 2003, 74(35): 16

for the first time since the '80s, she said. Venus and Serena Williams have already been used for corporate ads, color cosmetics campaigns and now to launch their line of jewelry. The ads were done in-house.

One of Avon's first steps will be to discontinue specific ethnic-targeted mailings in favor of overhauling its main brochure to reflect 'what this country looks like', she said. That includes featuring a diverse mix of Hispanic, African–American and Asian women in at least 30 per cent of the brochure. The company has also developed an in-house multicultural beauty advisory board of 24 Avon associates who offer input on hair products, skin care, color and fragrances for their various skin tones and will include a new 'Shades of Beauty' column in its representative newsletter.

'Last year, we focused on Hispanics [with a brochure, Avon Es Tu, that featured products including jewelry and statues] and before that we reached out to African-Americans [with a special brochure]', said Ms. Mullins-Jackson. Now, she said, 'we want to make sure we are considering all ethnic groups as part of the whole and really addressing the beauty needs of all women.'

Avon's sales totaled $6.2 billion in 2002 and grew by 8 per cent to $3.14 billion during the first half of 2003. Avon would not disclose how much of the company's sales are from multicultural consumers or how fast those sales are growing.

To reach out to urban minorities who may think Avon's products don't work for them, Avon later this year will test beauty kiosks in storefronts of cities including New York, Atlanta and Chicago where consumers can actually order products directly. Although Ms Mullins-Jackson said there have been Avon Beauty Centers, this will be the first time consumers can order products directly.

The goal is to get ethnic consumers to understand how Avon products apply to them, even those not typically used by their ethnic group. Among the offerings will be the entire array of Avon foundation shades and Double Impact lipstick shades as well as a new skin-care product, Avon Clinical, which will be touted as an alternative to Botox injections. A rollout of the kiosk program next year is planned pending results in the test cities.

Avon will also partner with Latina magazine for a national promotion still in development, and will test a link between its website (avon.com), Univision and a yet-to-be named community organization for its Cellu-Sculpt skin-care product.

QUESTIONS

1. Discuss the advantages of the Avon marketing approach.
2. What do you see are the disadvantages?

CHAPTER 11

Ethnic marketing in practice – communications issues

11.1 Chapter objectives

This chapter discusses the elements that need to be addressed in developing a communication strategy that seeks to target ethnic consumers. The issues are addressed by first outlining a basic model of the communication process. The elements of this process are then linked to marketing communications, a process that needs to be more focused and integrated in the tools it uses than communications as a whole. The sensitivity and focus of these tools in communicating with ethnic minority consumers is then discussed in two parts: how to reach an ethnic market through communications; and how to use communications to help retain ethnic minority consumers.

11.2 Introduction

Successful ethnic marketing 'requires a substantial rethinking of marketing strategies and approaches . . . valuing these segments enough to learn about their needs, attitudes, culture, activities, heroes and lifestyles' (Swenson, 1990: 20). In the light of competitors also acquiring this knowledge, more is needed to sustain a competitive advantage. 'The most successful businesses in coming years will be the ones that make the effort to understand that ethnic and other segmentation – appealing to the tastes and preferences of different groups – is the key to profitability' (Rossman, 1994: 18).

In order to appeal the business must develop an effective communication strategy to reach the target group. In fact, communication plays an important role in both the attraction and retention of ethnic minority consumers. Communication difficulties (understanding the message) and communication dissonance (discomfort with either the style and/or the means of communication) are common experiences for ethnic minority consumers living in host countries. The targeting of a minority ethnic group requires that the communication strategy addresses how best to reach ethnic minority consumers with information of the value proposition and, after consumption, how to retain the customer.

The importance of addressing cross-cultural communication issues is well recognized by international marketers, who pay considerable attention to cultural differences between countries. Ignoring these differences within a culturally diverse country may be possible but businesses that are culturally sensitive and use an ethnic group's preferred media and etiquette will be offering a superior value proposition than their competitors.

Marketing communications with different minority ethnic groups involves more than just using the preferred language of a group. There are many elements in the ways humans communicate with each other and these elements cohere within a culture to reduce dissonance and to create identity. The means of communication that can be used by a business to reach the group are also plentiful, but some are likely to be far more successful than others. Both the elements of communication style and the communication media are discussed as a prelude to considering how best to attract the attention of ethnic minority consumers and then how to hold them.

An inability to communicate their needs and wants clearly may lead ethnic minority consumers to prefer suppliers that reduce both communication difficulties and dissonance. Firms with this capability have an important resource. Moreover, these firms will still need to communicate their offerings in ways that are meaningful and interesting to the targeted ethnic consumers. The right medium needs to be selected and there is evidence that simple translation of communications across ethnic groups is problematic. This is again a situation where shortcuts can be expected to bring into question the success of ethnic marketing. Marketers also need to elaborate communications programmes that recognize the linkages and interdependence of ethnic consumers with ethnic groups.

11.3 Communication dimensions

The importance of developing a communication strategy for a particular culture is recognized by international marketers, who are aware of the difficulties and pitfalls of communicating across cultural boundaries. Yet, when marketing at home the presumption is often made that mainstream methods of communication will be equally well received regardless of the cultural background of the intended recipient. If a person belonging to a minority ethnic group has adapted to the mainstream culture and under-stands the message, this does not mean that this is the person's preferred way of receiving a message. There may be sufficient dissonance created such that the ethnic minority consumer will be far more receptive to a targeted communication strategy.

The design of a targeted communication strategy needs to take into account all the elements of the communication process depicted in Figure 11.1. This model depicts the communication process as an information-processing activity that, in order to be successful, requires a shared orientation to certain signs or symbols (Schramm, 1971).

The sender or source is the party sending the communication. Both the targeting business and the ethnic consumer targeted are involved in this role at some stage, requiring the targeting business not only to be aware of its role as a sender but also to be aware of the ethnic consumer as a receiver, taking steps to establish a means of communication ethnic consumers are comfortable in using.

The receiver is the party receiving the message. Because the targeting business should be keen to develop a relationship with its targeted group of ethnic consumers, an interactive two-way communication process between the business and the target group will be required. While an individual ethnic consumer may be the recipient, substantiality in segmenting usually

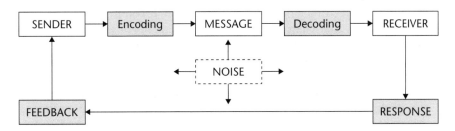

Figure 11.1 Elements of the communication process
Source: Schramm (1971).

requires the business to pay attention to how the ethnic group rather than the individual perceives and receives a message. In turn, the business will need to provide channels and processes for it to receive and acknowledge communications from the group.

Between the sending and receiving of a communication by either party are the message and the medium used. The message is the set of symbols or signs transmitted by the sender. Apart from physical contact (such as a kiss), the message is at some point separate from either sender or receiver. Commonly, the symbols may be words and pictures but sounds and smells are also used. The message is transmitted through a medium or media. The media preferred by mainstream consumers to receive messages may differ from that preferred by ethnic minority consumers because the media itself may be mainstream and not particularly accessible to ethnic minority groups.

Message construction (encoding) and the medium of transmission need to address the sensitivities and preferences of ethnic minority groups. Decoding, the process by which the receiver assigns meaning to the symbols transmitted, must be similar to the encoding process, or else the intended message of the sender is likely to be distorted. Encoding is often ethnocentric, with the sender failing to understand the values and symbols of other cultures, while decoding is inherently within a person's cultural context, providing a fertile field for misunderstanding.

Feedback and response are closely linked. Senders of a message can receive feedback simply from seeing or hearing their own sent message. That may cause them to evaluate the symbols used. Primarily, messages are intended to generate a response from a recipient, such as an action or attitude change. This response feedback is critical to marketers, telling the sender if and how the message is being received.

Message contamination, or noise, is defined as anything in the communication channel that the sender did not intentionally place there. Noise includes competing messages and other distractions that inhibit effective communication, in particular either blocking the intended message or causing its distortion. Noise, therefore, can include distractions to the targeted consumer arising from a difficult accent, poor manners and dress of the message carrier.

In targeting ethnic minority groups within a country, businesses need to understand that complex messages, for example consisting of words and pictures intended to appeal to a heterogeneous audience, are likely to be decoded differently by different groups because of the meanings given to the encoded symbols.

The use of photographs of personal images in a message, for example, can be used to interpret, abstract and activate readers' imaginations (Douglis, 2000). As well as what is photographed, elements such as orientation to the camera, head cant, gestures and smiles become a part of a message that need to be conveyed across cultures, where different meanings may be attached to such depiction. In essence, photographs do not necessarily reflect how people behave but rather how one thinks they behave (Anderson and Imperia, 1992). Both the encoder and decoder undertake their tasks based on their experiences and, unless there is some overlap in experiences, the message received by the decoder is likely to be different from that intended.

Further, in seeking to reach minority ethnic groups with their messages, businesses face considerable noise if they use mainstream media. Ethnic minority consumers can be expected to operate in a noisy communications environment, exposed to both mainstream and ethnic communications media and the pressures of group influence.

While this simple information processing model helps to focus on individual elements of the communication process that need to be addressed by marketers seeking to communicate with ethnic minority consumers, it only hints at the social framework within which all human communications occur. A common understanding of the symbols used is required between sender and receiver. The social context of communications tends to determine whether a communication is private or public, face-to-face or interposed (telephone or mail), assembled or non-assembled. The norms and constraints of society as a whole impinge on the choices. Within a multi-ethnic country, acknowledging the societal rules that govern a minority ethnic group's communications becomes an important part of the communication process.

11.4 Marketing communications and ethnic groups

Businesses use marketing communications to enhance understanding of, association with, attitude and predisposition toward, their brand, service product or organization. Identification of a segment that can be targeted requires attention to the segment's communication behaviour, both in terms of the communication tools, mix and behaviour of the segment (Dhalla and Mahatoo, 1976).

Adapting from Dhalla and Mahatoo (1976), the need to understand the communication behaviour of a targeted minority ethnic group includes:

- their media habits, including readership of representative newspapers and magazines, preference for particular types of television and radio programmes, and favourite time periods for such activity;
- the attention paid to advertising of relevant product categories in various media, the level of confidence in brand advertising and reactions to situational elements in brand advertising;
- the decision-making processes of individuals within the targeted group, including the importance of advertising versus recommendations received by word of mouth or from sales people, the role of opinion

leaders and perceptions of brands and suppliers on such attributes as competence and trust.

On all of these aspects there can be no presumption that ethnic minority consumers are likely to respond in the same way as mainstream consumers.

With such information it is possible to devise a marketing communication strategy – a coordinated programme of activities, often called integrated marketing communication (IMC) (Adcock *et al.*, 1995). The primary objective of an IMC strategy is the unification of all the marketing communication tools a business uses to send target audiences a consistent message that promotes its goals.

Hartley and Pickton (1999) describe three broad fields of IMC: managing consumer contact, marketing communications, and corporate communications, with respective marketing tools in each (refer to Figure 11.2). The boundaries between the three areas are soft, with the possibility of overlap. The need for integrated communication arises because resources spent on isolated activities such as image building and brand building may be wasted and synergies lost in reaching target audiences. The boundaries are soft between the three areas of IMC.

The tools used in IMC vary depending on whether the focus is a group or an individual. The need to adapt a communication strategy to minority ethnic groups becomes apparent by examining some of the tools under each of the headings in Figure 11.2.

Corporate communications that attempt to construct an identity that is perceived the same way by consumers nationally or internationally must ensure the symbols used are interpreted similarly across cultures. Clearly, a lot

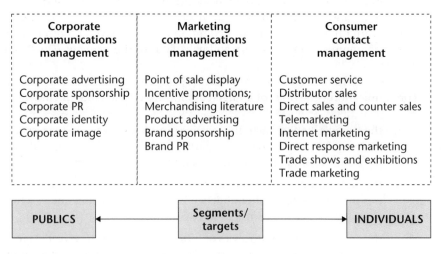

Figure 11.2 Integrated marketing communications instruments
Source: Adapted from Hartley and Pickton (1999).

more than careful language translation is required. Sponsorship of mainstream activities, whether sporting events or festivals, may do little for building corporate image in an ethnic group if it has no association with that activity. Both customer contact instruments (e.g. customer service) and communication (merchandizing materials) will need to be considered for their suitability in reaching a minority ethnic group.

Taking an IMC approach is important in targeting an ethnic group. There can be no presumption that a particular tool works effectively across all cultural groups and an IMC requires audit of tools suitable for particular objectives and particular cultures. To illustrate, Korgaonkar, Karson and Lund (2000) found that Hispanic consumer attitudes to direct marketing in the USA varied according to degree of assimilation, especially between those who had assimilated and those who had more closely maintained their ethnic affiliation.

11.5 Communications to reach an ethnic group

The focus

A multicultural or multiethnic society is based on a collection of different minority ethnic groups alongside a majority 'national' group (Yinger, 1976). This gives rise to many forms of cross-cultural interaction difficulties because the influence of a culture creates a product made out of a residue of behaviours, ideas and beliefs with which people are comfortable and which they consider 'proper' or the right way (Brislin, 1981), although this product may appear overly personal or time inefficient to others. The resulting cross-cultural interaction difficulties ensue from communication complexity, in particular the degree of reliance on non-verbal cues (Weiss and Stripp, 1998). The presence or absence of such cues will influence the capacity of persons from different ethnic groups to appraise information provided by alternative suppliers framed in a different cultural context. Further, after a relationship has developed with a particular supplier, barriers to switching suppliers may be created because communication complexity may discourage further search. Familiarity and perhaps satisfaction with established communication processes increases the perceived risk of switching.

As discussed in previous chapters dealing with consumer behaviour and loyalty, the role of the minority ethnic group in reaching individual ethnic minority consumers must be addressed. This is also the case with the marketing communication strategy. While the aim is to cause a response from an individual decision unit, the strategy targets the group, often using the groups' communication networks. More than these networks, the ethnic group acts as a reference group. The group's endorsement leverages the product to the group's constituency (Macchiette and Roy, 1993). Such a strategy capitalizes on members' goodwill toward the group to which they belong.

Awareness of differences

Hall and Hall (1990) divide all communication into three parts: words, material things and behaviour. Inter-cultural communications are deeper and more complex than spoken or written messages, requiring the right responses rather than sending the right message. Messages can be either fast or slow and the need for the appropriate speed is an important characteristic of human communication. Similar to the discussion by Hofstede (2001: Chapter 9) on how national culture dimension differences can create dissonance between cultures, Hall and Hall (1990) elaborate on the dimensions (of context, space and time) that can create favourable or unfavourable interactions between persons from different cultures. Hence, second and subsequent generation ethnic consumers may have a language proficiency in the dominant language but there are other dimensions of the communication process that hold them to a particular supplier.

Following Hall and Hall (1990: 9–10), context is the information that surrounds an event and is bound up with the meaning of an event. Events and contexts are in different proportions depending on the culture. As a generalization, persons immersed in a low-context culture generally need more information when making a business decision than persons from a high-context culture. Low-context people may be at a loss when high-context people do not provide enough information while high-context people may react to excessive, unsought information. An appropriate level of context is needed for each situation because too much information may lead people to feel they are being talked down to, while too little may alienate them. However, faced with a 'new enterprise' to which they have not been contexted, high-context persons may require more information than low-context persons in order to reach their own synthesis of meaning rather than accepting this synthesis from another foreign party. Hence, within a low-context culture, persons from a high-context culture may be attracted to and retained by a supplier with the most suitable contextual communication strategy.

Space and time can also create dissonance between cultures. Space is perceived by all the senses. Visual, auditory (sound), olfactory (smell), taste and thermal (heat) changes give tone to communication, accent it and may override the spoken word. Time is also structured differently between cultures, ranging from the monochronic to the polychronic, that can influence the customer–supplier relationship (Hall and Hall, 1990). In addition to communication complexity from these elements other differences also operate. These include risk-taking propensity; the bases of trust; concern with protocol; the nature of persuasion (reason or emotion); and whether the form of agreement is implicit or explicit (Weiss and Stripp, 1998).

Communication difficulties and perceived risk

Complementing the cross-cultural communication and decision-making literature, a growing body of consumer behaviour research relevant to ethnic minority consumers (see Cui, 2001) supports a view that persons from a non-dominant cultural background may be attracted to, and stay with, a supplier for different reasons than someone from the mainstream culture. One of these differences arises from the link between communication difficulties and perceived risk. Purchase decisions involve perceived risk. Depending on the consumer's ability and willingness to acquire risk-reducing information, services may involve more risk than goods (Murray, 1991), but here we are concerned with the perceived risk of dealing with a supplier. Interaction between recently arrived ethnic consumers and suppliers depends on the consumers' inexperience in the new marketplace and on the quality of the long-term relationship that their ethnic group, drawing from its collective experience, maintains with suppliers. Individual exchanges are not assessed in isolation but as a continuation of past exchanges likely to continue in the future. Ethnic minority consumers will draw on their ability and ease in communicating with peers, the experiences of similar-others, as a preferred source of market information. This dependence influences the maintenance of customer relationships (Sheth and Parvatiyar, 1995).

'Customers make relationship specific investments of time and effort to identify service providers and develop relationships with them' (Bendapudi and Berry, 1997: 24). These investments involve information, time, effort and money (Shaw and Pirog, 1997), all of which, from an economic perspective, are taken into account by consumers when considering switching suppliers. In the case of ethnic minority consumers, their communication difficulties and dissonance with the communications process can reduce the ability of a business to pass and retrieve information. For products high in interpersonal contact and credence, businesses that customize, personalize and are responsive can further differentiate their value proposition, increasing switching costs, reinforcing customer dependence upon the business and fostering relationship maintenance (Ganesan, 1994). Marketing communications plays a key role in these tasks.

Finally, the ethnic consumer–ethnic group link supports a long-term relationship, provided supply experiences are positive and suppliers remain credible. Inexperienced ethnic minority consumers benefit from the support of the ethnic group through lower perceived risk and because they become important for suppliers through their identification with that group. But continued group membership requires conformance to the group's values and attitudes. Belonging to an ethnic group is not enough; it is necessary to be seen to belong. Hence, in addition to economic costs, social or psychological costs arise for individual members as they become a part of Oliver's 'village envelopment' (see Chapter 6). The social benefits foregone from moving outside the village include the loss arising from the ease and satisfaction of communicating with similar others.

11.6 Communication strategies to hold an ethnic group

Ensuring a message sent is appropriate to a particular ethnic group may increase the likelihood of the desired response, creating awareness and interest, and hopefully trial. Whether ethnic consumers continue to return to the same supplier also requires consideration of communications to be used. Often, it is more than ease or comfort in communication that ethnic consumers may be searching for, and which businesses can provide in their communication strategy.

Acculturation and the adjustment process for a migrant choosing to move to another country was discussed in Chapter 3. Sensory deprivation, arising from the loss of home country language use, the experience of familiar foods and the familiarity of sounds may all contribute to culture shock that reduces over time.

Language is an important facet of communication and a brief review of its contribution to individual well-being helps in understanding the critical role marketing communications can play in holding an ethnic consumer to a particular supplier. A new arrival in a host country, who lacks fluency in the host country language and has limited opportunity to use his or her home country language, faces a loss of familiar benchmarks and may suffer various forms of cultural deprivation, particularly relating to language loss.

Jakobsen (1960) defined six basic functions of language:

1. Referential pleasure – capacity to express precisely and concisely our thoughts.
2. Expressive pleasure – ability to articulate what one feels at any time.
3. Conative pleasure – the effect of own words on the receiving party.
4. Phatak pleasure – ability to start and maintain interaction rituals, all of which have strong cultural contexts.
5. Meta-linguistic pleasure – capacity to elicit, paraphrase, restate and finally to comment and amplify one's own discourse.
6. Poetic pleasure – ability to choose the message, its style, sounds, construction, meanings, images and sensations it conveys.

Communication, encompassing language, is therefore much more than the development of a functional ability to operate in any particular society. Individuals deprived of the opportunity to express fully what they mean may experience deprivation. Hearing or speaking the home country language can provide a pleasurable experience for ethnic consumers and the capacity of a supplier to offer that experience (perhaps because that is where other members of the group also meet) is a strong retention weapon.

Usunier (1998) uses changes in oral pleasure deprivation as an explanatory variable for the adjustment process. The oral pleasure that can be provided by a targeted communication strategy can help retain customers. His explanation of the U curve (see Chapter 3) rests on changing levels of oral pleasure deficiency, including language and culinary elements. Extending the analogy to migrants arriving in a host country with different minority cultures, oral pleasure deficiency will be lessened by learning the behaviours of the ethnically related group. Consistent with the argument that similar others trust, and are more trusted, compared to dissimilar others (Dwyer, Schurr and Oh, 1987), learning the behaviours of similar others reduces uncertainty and the perceived risk of following inappropriate behaviours.

Oral pleasure deficiency is unrelated to the duration of stay (Usunier, 1998). It may persist but on average it is outweighed by positive oral pleasure drawn from life in the host country. Contextual factors such as cultural and linguistic proximity of home and host country are important in determining the adjustment process. The capacity of individuals to manage their transition between complex cultural codes determines the outcome of their experience. Ultimately, their management of this transition is the force that perpetuates the minority ethnic group as a separate cultural entity and explains its continuation, strength and cohesiveness.

Differences between product classes

The effectiveness of a communication strategy in reaching and retaining a targeted ethnic group will vary between different product classes. Research by the authors on the Portuguese community in Australia (Pires and Stanton, 2003) show that differences emerge in terms of the degree of tangibility and the evaluation properties of service-products.

Excepting for service products that can be evaluated through search, if suppliers seek to target ethnic minority consumers they need to reach them using minority ethnic group networks. The importance of the group, specifically the role of other members (similar others), does diminish with the adjustment process. Yet similar others remain by far the dominant information source, joined by an increase in the use of ethnic press, radio and television. Accordingly, not only is it a matter of suppliers developing strategies of information dissemination that specifically operate through the ethnic community to initially attract ethnic minority consumers, but of sustaining this communication over time.

The development of common information strategies for a wide array of service-products that seek to use ethnic information sources is only one element of the targeting process required of suppliers, other than those providing essentially tangible service products. Perhaps the more difficult part of a targeting strategy from the viewpoint of mainstream suppliers is meeting the selection criteria used by ethnic minority consumers to select their preferred suppliers. Classification based on evaluation properties brings out more strongly than a supply-based approach that ethnic minority consumers prefer to retain their original suppliers when service products are difficult to evaluate. To attract and retain ethnic minority consumers requires attention to important elements of ethnicity such as language but also developing a relationship with the minority ethnic group, because, as discussed in Chapter 6, this provides a social context to the consumption that is valued by the individual ethnic consumer. An important part of that social context is the oral pleasure that is provided by the group to its members.

11.7 Summary

This chapter has explained the importance of developing a marketing communication strategy focused on the ethnic group. This importance centres on both functional elements of communicating and the psychological pleasure that ethnic minority consumers may receive from engaging in communications using their home country language.

A process model of communication was used to explain the main elements of communication that need to be addressed by any business seeking to reach a targeted minority ethnic group. The cross-cultural difficulties of ensuring encoder and decoder use symbols with which both are familiar are a minefield for establishing a relationship with the group. In addition, the media accessible to the minority ethnic group and the impacts of noise will also increase the difficulties of businesses in accessing the group.

These problems lead to the need for an integrated marketing communication strategy, the use of particular tools for particular marketing objectives. Market research of the minority ethnic group, in particular concerning its communications behaviour with respect to media habits, advertising responsiveness and the decision-making process, is necessary in order to select the most effective tools.

Communication is an intrinsic part of a culture. The cultural nuances of communication, to reach a minority ethnic group effectively with a message, were discussed. Communications should also be built into the value proposition of the business because it can offer various forms of pleasure to an ethnic minority consumer. As in previous chapters, the target of the communication strategy is the group rather than the individual, mainly because the group acts as a reference and social agent for the individual. Finally, the marketing communication strategy varies with the product classification.

References

Adcock, D., Bradfield, R., Halborg, A. and Ross, C. (1995) *Marketing Principles and Practice*, 2nd edn., London: Pitman.

Anderson, C. and Imperia, G. (1992) 'The corporate annual report: a photo analysis of male and female portrayals', *Journal of Business Communications*, 22(2): 113–28.

Bendapudi, N. and Berry, L. (1997) 'Customers' motivations for maintaining relationships with service providers', *Journal of Retailing*, 73(1): 15–37.

Brislin, R. (1981) *Cross-Cultural Encounters*, New York: Pergamon Press.

Cui, G. (2001) 'Marketing to ethnic minority consumers: a historical journey (1932–1997)', *Journal of Macromarketing*, 21(1): 23–31.

Dhalla, N. and Mahatoo, W. (1976) 'Expanding the scope of segmentation research', *Journal of Marketing*, 40: 34–41.

Douglis, P. (2000) 'Photojournalism: telling it like it is', *Communication World*, 17: 44–7.

Dwyer, F., Schurr, P. and Oh, S. (1987) 'Developing buyer–seller relationships', *Journal of Marketing*, 51(2): 11–27.

Ganesan, S. (1994) 'Determinants of long-term orientation in buyer–seller relationships', *Journal of Marketing*, 58: 1–19.

Hall, E. T. and Hall, M. (1990) *Understanding Cultural Differences*, Yarmouth, ME: Intercultural Press.

Hartley, B. and Pickton, D. (1999) 'Integrated marketing communications requires a new way of thinking', *Journal of Marketing Communications*, 5: 97–106.

Hofstede, G. (2001) *Culture's Consequences*, 2nd edn., Thousand Oaks, CA: Sage publications.

Jakobsen, R. (1960) 'Closing statement: linguistics and poetics', in T. A. Sebeok (ed.) *Style in Language*, Cambridge, MA: MIT Press, pp. 350–77.

Korgaonkar, P., Karson, E. and Lund, D. (2000) 'Hispanics and direct marketing advertising', *Journal of Consumer Marketing*, 17(2).

Macchiette, B. and Roy, A. (1993) 'Affinity marketing: what is it and how does it work?', *Journal of Product and Brand Management*, 2(1): 55–67.

Murray, K. (1991) 'A test of services marketing theory: consumer information acquisition activities', *Journal of Marketing*, 55 (January): 10–25.

Oliver, R. (1999) 'Whence consumer loyalty?', *Journal of Marketing*, 63: 33–44.

Pires, G. and Stanton, J. (2003) 'Information sources and selection criteria used by ethnic minority consumers to choose service providers: does the service classification matter?', in *Challenging the Frontiers in Global Business and Technology*, Global Business and Technology Association Conference, July, Budapest.

Rossman, M. (1994) *Multicultural Marketing*, New York: American Management Association.

Schramm, W. (1971) 'The nature of the communication process between humans', in W. Schramm and D. Roberts (eds) *Process and Effects of Mass Communication*, revised edition, Urbana, IL: University of Illinois Press.

Shaw, E. and Pirog III, S. (1997) 'A systems model of household behavior', *Journal of Marketing Theory and Practice*, Summer: 17–29.

Sheth, J. and Parvatiyar, A. (1995) 'Relationship marketing in consumer markets: antecedents and consequents', *Journal of the Academy of Marketing Science*, 23: 255–71.

Swenson, C. (1990) 'Minority groups emerge as major marketing wedge', *Management Review*, May: 24–6.

Usunier, J. (1998) 'Oral pleasure and expatriate satisfaction: an empirical approach', *International Business Review*, 7: 89–110.

Weiss, S. and Stripp, W. (1998) 'Negotiating with foreign business persons', in S. Niemeier, C. Campbell and R. Driven (eds) *The Cultural Context in Business Communication*, Amsterdam: John Benjamin's Publishing Company.

Yinger, J. M. (1976) 'Ethnicity in complex societies', in A. Lewis *et al.* (eds) *The Uses of Controversy in Sociology*, New York: Free Press.

Surveys point to group differences

Kari van Hoof*

Two 1992 surveys by Yankelovich Partners and Market Development separately questioned 1000 African–American and 1200 Hispanic consumers about their media perceptions and purchasing attitudes. The following tables describe the responses.

Table C10.1 Hispanic media preferences, 1992 (%)

Watch TV (weekday)	95
Proportion of above who watch Spanish language TV	86
Listen to radio (weekday)	84
Proportion of above who listen to Spanish radio	74
Read any newspaper	66
Proportion of above who read any Spanish newspaper	41
Read any magazines	40
Read any Spanish magazines	23

Table C10.2 Hispanics and advertising, 1992 (%)

I would be more inclined to purchase brands that are advertised in Spanish	56
It is preferable to buy brands and products that others are buying	41
One ought to keep up with the latest fads and trends	75
Frequently store brands are better than well-known nationally advertised brands	57
Of the products I know, I prefer to buy products made by well-established firms	74

* *Brandweek*, 18 July 1994

Table C10.3 African–Americans, 1992 (%)

I think most commercials and advertisements on TV, radio and in magazines are designed for white people	58
In advertising, African–Americans should be portrayed as they really are, whether poor or rich	65

QUESTIONS

1. How would the media habits of the Hispanic respondents influence the design of your ethnic marketing communication strategy?

2. How would the advertising responses influence the design of your ethnic marketing communication strategy?

3. Could the perceptions of African–Americans be changed simply by increasing the presence of African–Americans in commercials? Is this all that would need to be changed under 'design'?

A multiplicity
of ethnicity

Eric Schmuckler*

Marketers have been licking their chops for years over the prospect of
a global media village, beaming out unified marketing campaigns to a plugged-
in world. But reality is a little messier than that, if the explosion of ethnic media
outlets in the US is any indication. While no hard numbers are available, over
the last few years ethnic media have blossomed. Eight years ago, Hispanics were
the only ethnic group AT&T targeted; today it attempts to reach out and touch
18 different ethnic groups. In the Russian community, there was just one paper
20 years ago. Today there are 20 papers, two or three television outlets and
three radio stations.

The rise of ethnic media presents both problems and promise. Marketers must
sift through a growing variety of target audiences; translate their message across
cultures or come up with tailor-made ones; and analyze a welter of media
vehicles and buy them efficiently. The reward: you can pinpoint an audience,
talk to it in its own language, create a special bond and perhaps get a jump on
the competition.

Ethnic communities may be small, but they are usually concentrated and
easily targetable. And impact is strong; some direct response runs as high as
10 per cent. The ethnic market, particularly the Hispanic segment, has become
too big a prize to ignore.

Noel Hankin, director of ethnic marketing for Miller Brewing: Miller has three
different Spanish commercials running, set in California, Texas and Miami,
with the same creative message but featuring local music from each area.
Broadcasting dominates Hispanic media, accounting for 84 per cent of all
advertising to Hispanic consumers, versus 45 per cent in the general market.

---

* *Brandweek*, 17 July 1995

Print is the strongest media vehicle in Asian communities; the cultures are highly literate and many papers are high-quality subsidiaries or licensees of major Asian publications. Broadcast in the USA has been hampered by a huge trade in video-cassettes of Asian TV programs. Still, Asian broadcast is growing quickly in the USA, with full time Chinese stations in San Francisco, LA and Honolulu.

The Asian market may be the next great frontier in ethnic media, and illustrates the opportunities of ethnic marketing in a pure form. 'There's a sheer lack of brand knowledge or loyalty among these immigrant communities', said Sullivan. 'This opportunity comes along once a decade. . . . When was the last time a marketer could talk to 10 million people your competitors never spoke to before?'

QUESTIONS

1. What are the problems of developing an ethnic marketing communication strategy given the growth in ethnic media and its diversity?
2. How would you explain the differences in media preferences between groups?

Media unsure whether to target segment in subsets or as part of the mainstream

Joe Mandese*

They are one of the fastest-growing segments of the US population and, perhaps more important, represent some of the most coveted media-buying demos for many top brands, yet Asian–Americans are confounding media planners' attempts to build advertising schedules that can effectively reach them. The main reason, according to a just-released report from a top media agency, is that Asian–Americans comprise distinct subsets, each with its own culture and customs – not to mention different languages.

While the focus on multicultural marketing has been on bigger segments, such as African–Americans and Hispanic–Americans, or even on non-ethnic markets such as gay and lesbian Americans, Asian–Americans have largely been ignored as a distinct media target by many media planners because of their disparate media choices. 'Their growth rate of 61 per cent since 1990 was greater than the growth of the Hispanic–American population', noted Rob Frydlewicz, VP, research director, at Carat Insight, which published the 25-page report *Asian Americans: Great Demos, Growing Numbers*. The problem, Mr Frydlewicz said, is the way that burgeoning population breaks down – 23 per cent Chinese, 17 per cent Filipino, 16 per cent Indian, 11 per cent Vietnamese, 10 per cent Korean, 7 per cent Japanese – and the fact that current media

---

* *TelevisionWeek, 15 Sep 2003*, 22 (37): 11

usage data likely does not reflect the unique usage among those individual groups.

'The syndicated data we work with is not refined enough for us to know exactly how Japanese viewers are different from Chinese viewers. The sample sizes just aren't large enough for us to break that down', Mr Frydlewicz said. As a result, he said planners are left to their own resources and a good measure of intuitive judgment to determine exactly how to target individual groups of Asian–Americans. *'We have a feeling that because Japanese–Americans are more acculturated into American society, that their TV viewing patterns are more like the rest of the population, but we don't have the figures to prove it'*, he said.

That could change over time. While it does not yet have a discrete demographic break for Asian–Americans, Nielsen Media Research has been making a greater effort in its panel recruitment efforts to bring Asian–Americans into its sample.

For the moment, Mr Frydlewicz said planners must rely on crude measures that homogenize Asian–American media usage patterns. Based on Carat's assessment of that data, marketers would do well to stay away from some of the most popular forms of television when targeting people of Asian descent. Instead of top-rated shows such as *Friends* and *CSI*, which index 15 per cent below the US average in reaching Asian–Americans, advertisers would be better off buying animated sitcoms – especially *The Simpsons, King of the Hill* and *Futurama* – which index 16 per cent over the US average. Other good genres for reaching Asian–Americans include fantasy/occult shows such as *Buffy* and *Charmed* or awards shows and beauty pageants.

In terms of individual networks, the study finds that NBC has the greatest weekly reach (43 per cent) among Asian–Americans, but Fox has the best index

Table C12.1 Asian–American viewing by prime-time genre

Genre	Per cent of Asians who view	Index to total US population
Animated sitcoms	15	116
Fantasy/occult	13	110
Awards ceremonies	31	109
Beauty pageants	15	102
Young prime-time shows (18–24)	40	97
Sitcoms	38	91
Prime-time news/interview shows	23	87
Top-rated prime-time shows	41	85
Middle-age prime-time shows (35–54)	43	83
Christmas specials	16	74
Older prime-time shows (55+)	30	73
Dramas	22	71
Reality	12	71
Police/law dramas	20	67

Source: Carat Insight's 'Asian–American: Great Demos, Growing Numbers', based on an analysis of data from Mediamark Research's 2002 Doublebase survey.

(98) relative to the US average. CBS, with a 28 per cent weekly reach and a 69 index to the US average, appears to be the worst place to reach Asians.

Mr Frydlewicz said part of those skews has to do with the overall demographic and geographic nature of those networks. Asian–American households tend to be younger households, which would bias against CBS and in favor of Fox and NBC.

Likewise, they tend to be clustered heavily in a few key markets, especially on the West and East coasts. But Mr Frydlewicz believes the way programmers cast their shows is another key factor influencing the attraction of Asian–Americans to conventional US TV programming. 'I don't think there are any major Asian–American characters on prime-time TV', Mr. Frydlewicz said. 'You'd have to go back to Sulu on *Star Trek* or Margaret Cho's short-run series 10 years ago to find any.'

QUESTIONS

1. Using the table, describe the differences in viewing habits between Asian–Americans and the overall pattern.

2. Why is there a need to target ethnic groups within the Asian–American aggregate?

3. What are the difficulties in reaching ethnic groups classed within the broad Asian–American aggregate and how might these difficulties be approached?

CHAPTER 12

Ethnic marketing in practice – ethics and social responsibility

12.1 Chapter objectives

The identification and targeting of minority ethnic groups within culturally diverse national markets are fraught with difficulties that increase when considerations of ethics and social responsibility are taken into account. On the one hand, communication challenges, limited market knowledge and dependence on preferred suppliers leave ethnic minority consumers open to predatory and other types of unethical business behaviour. Ethnic marketing, therefore, has an ethic dimension that needs to be explored. On the other hand, the difficulties facing businesses and social marketers seeking to identify and target minority ethnic groups may encourage their targeting with mainstream marketing programmes. A further set of ethical consequences needs to be considered in this case.

In this chapter we discuss issues of ethics and social responsibility that may impact upon ethnic marketing, as well as those impacting minority communities from the use of non-ethnic, mainstream marketing programmes. Finally, we look at some methodological issues that may need to be considered in ethnic marketing research.

12.2   What is good?

Ethics has been identified as a category of classical philosophy, together with metaphysics (what is the first principle of things?), epistemology (what is true?), aesthetics (what is beautiful?) and rhetoric (how to persuade or influence others?). Ethics corresponds to 'what is good?' (Seelye and Wasilewski, 1996). Applied to consumer behaviour, 'what is good?' may be expressed as 'what is acceptable behaviour?' The faintest attempt to address this question will inexorably discover the reasoning bedding the popular saying that 'when in Rome, do as the Romans do'.

Culture plays an important role in defining ethics standards because different countries with dissimilar cultures socialize their people differently, according to what is acceptable behaviour (Segal and Giacobbe, 1995). For example, Western ethics involve an epistemological quest for 'objective' reality, the truth. But, to understand Japanese ethics, the underpinnings have to be found in aesthetics, conveyed by social beauty or social harmony (Seelye and Wasilewski, 1996: 165). As much as dissimilar cultures have dissimilar ethics standards (or norms), ethics diversity is linked to cultural diversity.

Cultural diversity is used in the above argument mostly in an international context. However, the marketing relevance of domestic cultural diversity is abundantly demonstrated in this book, justifying inquiry into the marketing ethics and social responsibility issues arising from the targeting of, or the decision not to focus on, individual ethnic minority groups within a national market. Marketing ethics refers to 'the nature and grounds of moral judgments, standards, and rules of conduct relating to marketing decisions and marketing situations' (Vitell, Rallapalli and Singhapakdi, 1993).

12.3   Ethics and marketing

The study of ethics for marketing purposes involves two intertwined conceptual challenges:

1. To define unambiguously what ethics is, as a means to identify unethical marketing behaviour.
2. To distinguish social responsibility issues (what is 'good' for society in general, present and future) from poor business practices.

Ethical marketing behaviour and socially responsible behaviour may involve different requirements in terms of marketing strategies that address customer needs and preferences. Poor business practice may fail to address customer needs and also be socially irresponsible. Figure 12.1 illustrates the need to disentangle these three factors in the overall process of designing a marketing strategy focused on customer needs and preferences.

The figure shows that, while business objectives are generally served by focusing on customer needs and preferences, the competitive environment shapes the competitive requirements that a business must meet in order to compete successfully. Socially responsible behaviour can constrain and/or promote certain behaviours, while the ethical and legal considerations add further constraints.

The ethical challenge becomes clearer if we recognize the need for a firm to simultaneously satisfy its customers' needs as well as societal needs, subject to the firm's objectives, and to remain competitive (hence with the competitive

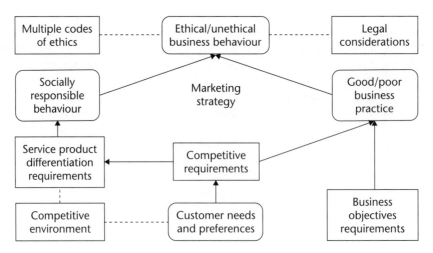

Figure 12.1   Customer needs, social responsibility and poor business practice. Implications for marketing strategy

environment duly taken into account). This market orientation is encapsulated in the marketing concept and consistent with the argument that, while making a profit may be necessary to stay in business,[1] from an ethical perspective firms should neither distort their primary function as providers of a service to their customers, nor overlook that social responsibility has become a salient means of service product differentiation (Macchiette and Roy, 1994; Buchholz and Rosenthal, 2000). In competitive domestic or international environments, businesses need to define a level of 'what is good' that balances own goals, customer needs, and those of society in general. This need is not easily met, notwithstanding ongoing globalization perspectives that pre-empt international market homogeneity. This homogeneity is often taken for granted domestically, negating the need for ethnic marketing.

How important is globalization?

The international environment has been singled out as potentially more difficult for marketers because their 'ethics' parameters may not match the notion of 'good' in the foreign country where they wish to operate (Kotler *et al.*, 1998: 833). That is, there is an ethics gap between the marketer's ethics and the foreign country's ethics. In this case successful international market penetration is compromised, inhibiting a firm's ability to compete (Skubik, 1993).[2] However, rather than obliterating any need for the matching of ethics parameters, the challenges associated with the international environment appear to be gaining in importance because of the current marketing push towards a process of globalization of supply, particularly when this does not correspond to a similarly globalized demand.

Globalization of demand implies sameness across countries. What appears to be happening is a strengthening of cultural differentiation across countries through ethnicity. Ethnicity was expected to disappear as a social force during the twentieth century, effectively ending its social and political importance, and consequently its economic relevance (Bentley, 1981; Hutchinson and Smith, 1996). Instead, the global process by which industrialization, urbanization and mass communications has been transforming society has reinvigorated identity construction and ethnicity (Castles, Cope and Kalantzis, 1992; Cornell and Hartmann, 1998). This is mirrored, for example, in the much heralded strengthening of minority ethnic groups in the United States. The cross-cultural ethics gap may not be getting smaller and it may, in fact, be increasing in complexity, due to consumers' distinct perceptions of ethics issues. A study of ethics perceptions of three consumer groups in the United states – Anglos, strongly identified Hispanics and weakly identified Hispanics – concluded that the less assimilated Hispanics were somewhat more concerned about the magnitude of monetary loss than Anglos, who cared less about the loss and more about the probability of unethical behaviour causing that loss (Shepherd, Tsalikis and Seaton, 2002).

Ethics concerns remain important for businesses, irrespective of the market where they compete; reinvigorated identity construction and ethnicity explain their relevance for ethnic marketing.

12.4 Ethnic marketing ethics

One possible approach to ethnic marketing ethics, understood as ethics applied to marketing practice targeting minority ethnic groups, is to adopt the international paradigm and apply the same procedures that firms use to deal with ethics problems in the international context (Kotler *et al.*, 1998). That is, if dealing with Romans, do as you would in Rome.

Adopt the international paradigm

Consider, for illustration, the proposition often endorsed in the literature that 'bribery is not unethical if it is an accepted practice in the culture where it takes place' (Danley, 1983; D'Andrade, 1985), or 'bribery in ethnic dress' as labelled by Philips (1984: 636). The problem with applying this proposition to ethnic marketing is that, even if discounting the question of attribution (that is, whether the ethics of a bribery action should be assessed from the recipient's or the briber's perspective), the culture of the minority ethnic group is unlikely to replicate either the culture of the majority or that of the country of origin. Indeed, even the closest-knit minority ethnic group is likely to be extensively influenced by the social rules of the host country. It is this that justifies the group's role as a facilitator in the adaptation and socialization of new arrivals to the new market environment, as well as a continued reference for its affiliates.

Overall, the adoption of the international paradigm may prove inadequate because ethnic marketing faces at least four unique environmental problems. These, together with a possible lack of understanding of ethics issues associated with ethnic segmentation and marketing, contribute to the mystification of ethnic marketing, described as a minefield by Blanton (1993). The four problems are outlined in Table 12.1.

The problem of fuzzy boundaries may be solved with more or less difficulty through appropriate market research, as extensively discussed in Chapters 2 to 5. Certainly more challenging is the normative delineation of ethical procedures applicable across minority ethnic groups. A discussion of integrative social contract theory[3] by Dunfee, Smith and Ross Jr. (1999) specifies a loose set of priority rules of behaviour (influenced by concepts underlying principles of international conflicts of law and dispute resolution) that, suitably adapted, may show the way for ethnic marketing. These adapted priority rules are outlined in Table 12.2.

In addition to the need for extensive research on these rules, it is important to understand that they seek to establish an umbrella for ethnic marketing

Table 12.1 Environmental problems facing ethnic marketing

1. The boundaries of the different minority ethnic groups may be fuzzy, even if indicators as simplistic as country of birth or language are used to identify the respective populations. Fuzzy boundaries may result in more than one notion of 'what is good' within the group so defined.
2. The notion of what is 'good' may change from minority ethnic group to minority ethnic group, as it may change from one country to another (Kotler *et al.*, 1998).
3. 'What is good' for one minority ethnic group does not invalidate 'what is good' for any other minority ethnic group (Pruzan and Thyssen, 1990).
4. The application of marketing strategies to accommodate a variety of competing ethics behaviours may ensue while 'ethnic minority consumers from the different minority ethnic groups are potentially in each other's presence'. This has the potential to alienate all parties if an adequate synergy between minority ethnic groups and marketing strategies cannot be reached (Cui, 1998).

Table 12.2 Priority rules of behaviour for ethnic marketing

- Interactions solely within a single community, which do not have significant adverse effects on other humans or communities, should be governed by that community's norms.*
- Community norms for resolving priority should be applied, so long as they do not have significant adverse effects on other humans or communities.
- The more extensive the community that is the source of the norm, the greater the priority which should be given the norm.
- Norms essential to the maintenance of the economic environment in which the interaction occurs should have priority over norms potentially damaging to that environment.
- Where multiple conflicting norms are involved, patterns of consistency among the alternative norms provide a basis for prioritization.
- Well-defined norms should ordinarily have priority over more general, less precise norms.

* 'Norms' are generally understood standards or obligations derived from social contracts, the 'expectations about behaviour that are at least partially shared by a group of decision-makers' (Heidi and George, 1992: 34).

interactions that is likely to remain imperfect, given the uniqueness of individual minority ethnic groups. However, since all ethnic minority groups acculturate, adapt and socialize within the same market environment with its own unique set of norms (whether commercial, civic or civil), the ethics gap may be much smaller for ethnic marketing than for cross-cultural marketing, although variable across minority ethnic groups.

Figure 12.2 illustrates the smaller gap that can be expected to exist between the norms that characterize behaviour by a mainstream group and a minority ethnic group sharing the same territory, as opposed to the larger gap relative to the minority group country of origin. The difference between the gaps represents the extent of the differences between the minority ethnic group norms of behaviour and those of the country of origin, reflecting the dynamic aspect of the acculturation process (discussed in Chapter 3).

Figure 12.2   Acculturation, adaptation and socialization reduce the cross-cultural ethics gap

As an alternative to adopting the international paradigm, a potential solution involves the elaboration of a code of ethics (illustrated by the AMA Code of Ethics in Exhibit 12.1) as a means to facilitate ethical behaviour when marketing to minority ethnic groups and their affiliates.

Develop a code of ethics for ethnic marketing

This can be understood as a system of rules and principles of human conduct that is considered desirable to observe from a moral standing. A quick search of the internet for a code of ethics reveals an enormous variety of such codes, distinguished by type of activity, for example, as well as changes in the codes adopted by organizations.[4] There is also a 'Codes of Ethics Online' site announcing a collection of 850 codes of ethics, as well as guidance on how to write one.[5] There appears to be no code of ethics for ethnic marketing.

A possible explanation for the abundance of codes of ethics may lie with their association with rules for professional conduct, possibly a function of the type of activity and possibly 'enhanced' over time to account for specific conduct problems. The codes target business behaviour, applying universal standards from the supply side without accounting for the uniqueness that may exist in the consumers businesses serve. Consumers' notion of 'what is good' is discarded.

The challenge in accounting for consumers is readily understood when we realize that a business is likely to target a variety of consumer groups. A corresponding variety of codes would be required for the same business, even more when consumer ethnicity is taken into account.

Ethnic marketing ethics seeks to develop a code of ethics that can be applied to marketing practice targeting minority ethnic groups. However, 'written codes and ethics programs do not assure ethical behaviour' (Kotler *et al.*, 1998) and any attempt to globalize a code of ethics needs to be examined for its transferability, given ethnic diversity. It is much like devising a scale of goodness, or ethical intensity, where 'fair' means 'less than ethical' but 'acceptable'. One possible way around this problem may be to apply a contingent approach, keeping the code of ethics general enough to deal with

EXHIBIT 12.1: The American Marketing Association (AMA) Code of Ethics

Members of the American Marketing Association are committed to ethical professional conduct. They have joined together in subscribing to this Code of Ethics embracing the following topics:

Responsibilities of the Marketer

Marketers must accept responsibility for the consequences of their activities and make every effort to ensure that their decisions, recommendations and actions function to identify, serve and satisfy all relevant publics: customers, organizations and society.

Marketers' Professional Conduct must be guided by:

1. The basic rule of professional ethics: not knowingly to do harm;
2. The adherence to all applicable laws and regulations;
3. The accurate representation of their education, training and experience;
4. The active support, practice and promotion of this Code of Ethics.

Honesty and Fairness

Marketers shall uphold and advance the integrity, honour and dignity of the marketing profession by:

1. Being honest in serving consumers, clients, employees, suppliers, distributors, and the public;
2. Not knowingly participating in conflict of interest without prior notice to all parties involved; and
3. Establishing equitable fee schedules including the payment or receipt of usual, customary and/or legal compensation for marketing exchanges.

Rights and Duties of Parties in the Marketing Exchange Process

Participants in the marketing exchange process should be able to expect that

1. Products and services offered are safe and fit for their intended uses;
2. Communications about offered products and services are not deceptive;
3. All parties intend to discharge their obligations, financial and otherwise, in good faith; and
4. Appropriate internal methods exist for equitable adjustment and/or redress of grievances concerning purchases.

It is understood that the above would include, but is not limited to, the following responsibilities of the marketer:

In the area of product development and management:

- Disclosure of all substantial risks associated with product or service usage;

- Identification of any product component substitution that might materially change the product or impact on the buyer's purchase decision;
- Identification of extra cost-added features.

In the area of promotions:

- Avoidance of false and misleading advertising;
- Rejection of high-pressure manipulations, or misleading sales tactics;
- Avoidance of sales promotions that use deception or manipulation.

In the area of distribution:

- Not manipulating the availability of a product for the purpose of exploitation;
- Not using coercion in the marketing channel;
- Not exerting undue influence over the reseller's choice to handle a product.

In the area of pricing:

- Not engaging in price fixing;
- Not practicing predatory pricing;
- Disclosing the full price associated with any purchase.

In the area of marketing research:

- prohibiting selling or fundraising under the guise of conducting research;
- maintaining research integrity by avoiding misrepresentation and omission of pertinent research data;
- treating outside clients and suppliers fairly.

Organizational Relationships
Marketers should be aware of how their behavior may influence or impact the behavior of others in organizational relationships. They should not demand, encourage or apply coercion to obtain unethical behavior in their relationships with others, such as employees, suppliers, or customers.

1. Apply confidentiality and anonymity in professional relationships with regard to privileged information;
2. Meet their obligations and responsibilities in contracts and mutual agreements in a timely manner;
3. Avoid taking the work of others, in whole, or in part, and representing this work as their own or directly benefiting from it without compensation or consent of the originator or owner;

4. Avoid manipulation to take advantage of situations to maximize personal welfare in a way that unfairly deprives or damages the organization of others.

Any AMA member found to be in violation of any provision of this Code of Ethics may have his or her Association membership suspended or revoked.

Reprinted with permission from www.marketingpower.com/live/content 1175.php, published by the American Marketing Association.

inter-ethnic situations yet still dependent on the ethical evaluation of the participants – stakeholders, buyers and sellers. However, this relies on judgement and, arguably, it is this reliance that justifies the need for the code of ethics in the first place.

Contextual embedding

The link between decision-making about ethics and human involvement (and, therefore, judgement) is apparent. Ethical decision-making is seen as part of an individual's character rather than an act to be performed by an individual (Hartman and Beck-Dudley, 1995). This is particularly important because ethical decision-making is often situation-specific, involving an ethical dilemma that needs to be evaluated by its situational content (Jakob *et al.*, 1998).[6] For example, the Ontario Alliance of Career Development Practitioners asserts that, in addition to a code of ethics, practitioners' ethical decision-making requires an understanding of how to use the code, as well as other resources. In developing a framework for ethical decision-making, major importance is given to the nature of the ethical dilemma. In the case of ethnic marketing, ethical decision-making is influenced by culture and ethnicity, both important elements to consider in situations involving different countries, as well as in a multi-ethnic country environment (Sarwono and Armstrong, 1998).

Establishing ethical dimensions for ethnic marketing, whether embodied in a code of ethics or not, is a challenging task. Which strategy is better suited to accomplish this task, however, is a matter tied to developing knowledge about ethnic minority consumers, their relationship to their ethnic group of affiliation, and ethnic marketing itself. Nevertheless, coupled with reflection, the specialized literature identifies related ethics issues, providing some guidance on what those dimensions might be.

12.5 Ethics issues in ethnic marketing

Ethnic minority consumers, particularly during their initial settlement in a new country, may be inexperienced in relation to what is available, where, and how much, as well as being unaware of market dos and don'ts. They compensate for their market inexperience by relying on referral or recommendation by others they trust (eventually their minority ethnic group of affiliation and its resources), particularly when communication difficulties limit the number and range of accessible secondary sources. In doing so, ethnic minority consumers overcome their weakness to reach the mastery stage of the culture shock cycle (discussed in Chapter 3), while groups benefit by becoming stronger and more cohesive. The cooperation of these consumers with their groups can thus be seen as similar to the concept of a strategic partnership, a matter of strength rather than weakness.

Notwithstanding, ethnic minority consumers are perennially perceived as members of sensitive groups, labelled as a minority, disadvantaged, high risk, vulnerable, sensitive and frustrated. Ethics implications for marketing behaviour towards these consumers flowing from such labels may or may not be warranted. The 'minority' label, for example, can be used simply to convey the idea of a comparatively small size, or it may be perceived by marketers to express lesser importance, or even irrelevance, a perception that needs to be questioned.

Being 'special'

Ethnic minority consumers may be perceived as 'special' because they affiliate with a sensitive group, 'a segment of the population generally perceived as being disadvantaged, vulnerable, discriminated against, or involved in social issues which consequently influence their consumer behavior' (Macchiette and Roy, 1994: 58). Within such a scenario, these consumers may be perceived as disadvantaged and in need of 'all types' of help, without considering what is the focus of the disadvantage.

Deception

Disadvantage may ensue from 'too little skill in differentiating between straightforward, informative promotion and puffery' (Davidson, 1995). Arguably this makes ethnic minority consumers more vulnerable to be taken advantage of through deceptive practices (Moore-Shay, 1996; Kotler *et al.*, 1998), such as the abuse of small print, or misrepresentation; or through the taking of unfair advantage of existing infirmities, such as the running of marketing campaigns for alcoholic products targeting groups with higher than average incidence of alcohol-related health problems (Davidson, 1995).

The incidence of deception in marketing is colourfully summarized in a study of ethics in advertising by the Pontifical Council for Social Communications: 'If harmful or utterly useless goods are touted to the public, if false assertions are made about goods for sale, if less than admirable human tendencies are exploited those responsible for such advertising harm society . . .' (Foley, 1997).

Discrimination

Where ethnic minority consumers exhibit visible ethnic elements or features, consumer disadvantage may ensue from racial discrimination (Grier, Williams and Crockett, 1996). In this context, racial discrimination can be understood as an unintended outcome of stereotyping. This is an explanation for the evidence that race and ethnicity are linked, for example, to the under-treatment of pain in the USA. Although there are no differences in the ability to discriminate painful stimuli of a neurosensory basis based on race and ethnicity (Todd, 1996), 'ethnic minority populations are at higher risk for oligoanalgesia, or the ineffective treatment of pain . . . ethnic minority groups often receive different and less optimal management of their health care than white Americans' (Bonham, 2001). Reportedly, the difference in analgesic use relates to a failure by physicians to recognize the presence of pain in patients who are culturally different from themselves. This problem might be heightened by ineffective patient–physician interactions, increasing the influence of physician stereotypes of patients and conveying Bonham's conclusion that patient ethnicity affects decision-making independent of objective clinical criteria.

Less visible issues

Deception and discrimination are clearly important ethics issues involving ethnic minority consumers, if by no means exclusive to ethnic marketing. There are, however, other less visible ethics issues that need to be taken into account.

Cui (1998) sets out to analyse the ethics issues associated with ethnic segmentation and targeted marketing. The study identifies five areas of eventual ethnic segmentation and targeted marketing failure, noting the possible incidence of associated ethical failure: inadvertent stereotypes, biology and genetics, nature of the product, redlining and ethnocentric bias.

Along the argument earlier advanced by Stevenson (1991), 'inadvertent stereotypes' refer to situations where the recognition of a minority ethnic group's importance leads to increased participation by ethnic minority consumers in advertising to other ethnic minority consumers – presumably a good thing – although the actual messages are stereotypical and do not reflect the diversity of the minority ethnic group. 'Biology and Genetics' refer to the use of superficial or exaggerated physical or biological attributes of minority ethnic groups that may suggest that ethnic minority consumers are inferior. The 'nature of the product' refers to the target marketing of ethnic markets with negative, inferior or harmful products. 'Redlining' is the selection or exclusion of markets based on racial lines. Finally, perhaps most important of all in the present context, 'ethnocentric bias' questions whether fundamental marketing principles based on research of the majority

Table 12.3 Possible ethical consequences from target marketing minority ethnic groups with mainstream marketing programmes

- Failure to provide for basic needs. Certain minority ethnic groups may do without needed goods and services, causing harm to their physical or psychological well-being. Similar to Kotler *et al.*'s (1998) principle of meeting basic needs.
- Misallocation of resources, since it does not seek to satisfy 'real' needs and wants, similar to Kotler *et al.*'s (1998) principle of economic efficiency.
- Discrimination against minority ethnic groups by presuming inadequate substantiality. This may involve the deliberate distortion of a firm's primary function of providing a service (Buchholz and Rosenthal, 2000), as well as the potential influence of poor business practices.
- Deliberate overestimation of the targeted mainstream population by including minority consumers with different needs and wants. This may lead to over-marketing resulting in increased costs for consumers in general (Fisher *et al.*, 1999).
- Perpetuation of minority status by promoting continued invisibility of minority ethnic groups.
- Discrimination against minority ethnic groups by providing inadequate, insufficient, misdirected, misinterpretable information. Similar to Kotler *et al.*'s (1998) principle of consumer education and information.
- Small print in contracts and use of jargon may be unfair given the market inexperience of ethnic minority consumers.
- Social responsibility issues such as the failure to translate public interest information in the languages of the minority ethnic groups (e.g. non-smoking campaigns, use of roundabouts).

population can be generalized to minority ethnic groups. Here, the ethical question focuses on both the consequences arising from non-differentiation of ethnic minority groups from the mainstream population and on the consequences from targeting minority ethnic groups with mainstream marketing programmes.

Reflection on this perspective suggests a number of important potential implications, both for ethics and for social responsibility, that are not always easy to separate. These are presented in Table 12.3. Some of the listed possible ethical consequences may result from deliberate actions (such as the intended provision of inadequate, insufficient, misdirected or misinter-pretable information leading to biased decision-making by ethnic minority consumers), while others may not be deliberate.

Mass-designed e-commerce developments may be particularly challenging for ethnic minority consumers, as in the case of online pharmaceutical services. These arguably fulfil some important social functions (such as convenience and accessibility), although the application of safeguards established for the sale of drugs in traditional pharmacies to internet businesses raises ethical questions. This is where inadequate, insufficient, misdirected or misinterpretable information may challenge ethnic minority consumers. For example, 'the treatment of symptoms through online drugs may keep

Table 12.4 Possible consequences from unethical target marketing of minority ethnic groups

- Dumping of lower quality, unsuccessful, defective, untried products. There may be an element of danger. Similar to Cui's (1998) nature of the product.
- Emotional damage to consumers by use of stereotypes, ascription, etc., when consumers are affiliated to the minority ethnic group. Similar to Cui's (1998) 'inadvertent bias'.
- Emotional damage to consumers by use of stereotypes, ascription, etc., when appearance, country of birth, neighbourhood, etc., wrongly suggests affiliation to minority ethnic groups.
- Emotional damage to consumers from assuming no affiliation to a minority ethnic group when affiliation does exist.
- Price discrimination in relation to mainstream prices or prices to other minority ethnic groups (even if price matches perceived net value).
- Alienation of trusted sources, potential gatekeepers to the minority ethnic group, through bribes or similar (Varner and Beamer, 1995).
- Deliberate and deceptive omission or use of small print in contracts.
- Deliberate overpricing or limiting access to services in order to capitalize on lack of market experience and communication difficulties.
- Infringement of consumer privacy, since the right to be left alone includes the right to be free from unwanted marketing solicitations. For example, personal data ethically collected by a marketer into a database – respecting ethnic minority consumers' autonomy as well as their informed consent and freedom to withdraw (Streiner and Norman, 1995) – should not be passed to other marketers (Fisher *et al.*, 1999).
- Racial discrimination – similar to Cui's (1998) redlining.

patients from having the underlying causes properly diagnosed, with potentially serious or even fatal consequences' (Bento, 2000: 433).

Some of the potential ethical consequences listed in Table 12.4 may, on closer situational analysis, result mostly from poor business practices, in which case the resulting ethics/social responsibility issue is still present, but not deliberate. Similarly, the targeting of minority ethnic groups may involve unethical deliberate actions, as well as actions intrinsically unethical. Table 12.4 lists possible consequences from unethical target marketing of minority ethnic groups.

Best practice

Discussion in the previous sections illustrates the need to know more about how marketers can take up the opportunities to target minority ethnic groups without the ethics and social responsibility liabilities. Particularly promising is the development of best practice standards in ethnic marketing that refine and extend the priority rules of behaviour in Table 12.2.

Contrary to engaging in simple translation of existing marketing materials, or the inclusion of minority faces in photographs, a study by the Conference Board of Canada[7] has identified factors that improve on common marketing practice seeking to reach ethnocultural diverse audiences, including the use of multilingual copy, the development of ethnoculturally distinct print advertising, the placing of advertising on multicultural TV and radio stations, the use of point-of-sale displays in ethnic stores, and the development of a diverse and culturally sensitive workforce (an issue further discussed in Chapter 10). Other aspects or factors that may improve on correct ethnic marketing practices have been identified throughout this book, namely in the discussion of the marketing of service-products, but this is an area clearly underdeveloped in ethnic marketing.

In this aspect Canada may be leading the way. The Conference Board of Canada is pursuing a programme of research and education on Best Practices in Maximising the Talents of Visible Minorities, in a consultative process involving major private sector employees, public sector organizations and visible minorities representatives. While this programme seeks to remove the 'glass ceiling' that inhibits the economic advancement of minority individuals rather than focusing on barriers to ethical targeting, ethnic marketing practice has been clearly limited by the ideology that sustains that ceiling. The process of removal of that ceiling, even if limited to visible minorities, may yield valuable information about barriers to ethical ethnic marketing.

12.6 Counteracting unethical behaviour

The vulnerability and exposure to unethical behaviour of ethnic minority consumers may be reduced by natural or artificially induced behaviours. Consumer vulnerability can be reduced by consumers seeking information from a variety of sources (Kotler *et al.*, 1998). This, however, may not always apply to ethnic minority consumers with communication difficulties. As argued earlier, these difficulties may reduce accessibility to secondary sources and may lead to intended and unintended misuse of services, as in the case of online pharmacies, as well as to strong dependence on the minority ethnic group of affiliation.

In terms of consumer exposure to unethical behaviour, the counteracting mechanism may be the development of simple, effective and accessible information and complaint facilities, incorporating Kotler *et al.*'s principle of consumer protection. Examples of these facilities include, in Australia, the Departments of Consumer Affairs and of Fair Trade Practices, and the Better Business Bureau (BBB) organization in the United States. Notwithstanding, these facilities may again be challenging for ethnic minority consumers, and there is evidence that they are not always able to fulfil their purpose. Arguably, 'the causes and implications of third party complaints, such as those filed with the BBB, are not well understood . . . the line between poor business practices . . . and deception or illegal tactics . . . remain unclear' (Fisher *et al.*, 1999: 69).

In fact the ethical dilemma referred to earlier can be reformulated to consider that measures developed for protecting disadvantaged and vulnerable, sensitive ethnic minority consumers may in themselves be unethical if they curtail the consumer's right to make informed choices. As discussed by Sauter and Oretskin (1997), the marketing of potentially harmful products to these consumers may not be to blame, given the legality of the products being marketed.[8] Should market targeting not be allowed at all, or only 'disadvantaged' consumers excluded? If only the latter are excluded, is this not a case of discrimination? There is nothing inherently unethical in targeting. The question that needs to be answered is, who decides that minorities are less able to make rational marketplace decisions (Davidson, 1995)?

Perhaps the solution is to provide additional information to vulnerable consumers in order to compensate for their disadvantage, but this also impinges on the need for all consumers to be provided equal access to market information. The critical factor is the notion of 'equal access', since the equivalence of information provided to ethnic minority consumers may be questionable. This, of course, is an ethnic marketing problem for which Sautter and Oretskin (1997) prescribe four ground rules:

1. that marketers must guarantee that all target markets receive equitable amounts and types of information;

2. that the numbers and types of brands available to various markets should be equivalent, due account given to customer preferences for brands and products;

3. that marketers ensure that equal access is given to information regarding those brands attributes; and,

4. that, if the information involves advertising themes, the marketer ensures that they do not mislead consumers, intentionally or unintentionally.

An apparent problem with these rules is that the information available to consumers is unlikely to be unambiguously attributable to any one supplier, excluding a situation of monopoly. Also, it is unclear how relevant information will be made equally available to distinct segments that have distinct needs and, in all probability, will be targeted by distinct suppliers. Overall, the rules may indicate the way towards ethical and socially responsible marketer behaviour, rather than hard guidelines for that behaviour.

More generally, ethnic marketing ethics and social responsibility issues involve the effects of what marketers do, as well as how they do it. Information about ethnic minorities and an adequate understanding of social rules requires the elaboration of segment profiles and in-depth understanding of groups. Research methods for ethnic marketing are also open to scrutiny.

12.7 Methodological issues

Research ethics involves several key elements that apply equally whether targeting mainstream subjects or applied to ethnic marketing. Informed consent is required from people who are subject to research. They need to be made aware that participation is voluntary, confidential and can be withdrawn at any moment without prejudice or loss. Research also needs to ensure that subjects are not harmed as a result of their participation in the research, including the publication of the research results. The possible problem here is that there may be cases where the research findings can, in an indirect way, result in loss for the participant.

To use an example in the realm of ethnic marketing, consider the case of a loss of funding by a minority ethnic group as an unintended consequence of a survey of ethnic group members, revealing that funding is not warranted. Ethnic minority consumers benefit from community resources, such as the ability of the minority ethnic group to attract public funding, and suffer when that funding is cut. Following Ryan (1996), the thing to do here is for the researcher to make sure that there is no misrepresentation in the report by discussing draft reports with community organizations, and that the implications of publishing materials are fully thought through. While the argument clarifies that the objective is not to 'launder' the research results (Douglas, 1971), it is not clear why the possibility of misrepresentation should be given special attention in this case, rather than being the norm.

Perhaps due to the possibility of unintended consequences such as the one represented above, Ryan (1996) identifies a fundamental ethical tension in respect of the relationship between the institutions associated with a minority ethnic group and researchers, that involves questions about researchers' skills and knowledge versus group needs. Arguably this tension justifies collaboration between researchers and the organizations representing minority ethnic groups, knowledgeable of the issues affecting their members, cultural practices and such. As a caution, the organizations need to recognize their limited research skills and not act as paternalistic gatekeepers, assuming that they can substitute for the group members.

It is important to note the fundamental difference in the role of community groups put forward by Ryan, and the role and involvement in the research methodology discussed in Chapter 8. The discussion of methodological issues recommended consultation with community gatekeepers as a means of learning about the issues and group peculiarities relevant to the research in hand, as well as gatekeepers' involvement in the elaboration of the research instrument and consequent distribution. In contrast, Ryan represents community organizations as stakeholders in the research, apparently with vetoing powers, hence true gatekeepers to the community.

It is apparent that there is a pressing need for further work into ethnic marketing research methodology and its ethics and social responsibility

EXHIBIT 12.2: The national workshop on ethics of research in aboriginal health

The National Workshop (NW) on Ethics of Research in Aboriginal Health identifies community structures as the most appropriate mechanisms for determining and monitoring ethical standards. The NW contends that research is frequently undertaken without consultation with communities as to the need for and relevance of research of the communities; often does not provide any benefit to the community being studied; and sometimes does not explicate the theoretical and methodological framework, with a result that the research reproduces the values of the dominant culture (that is, is ethnocentric).

The NW recommends the following procedures in order to promote ethical research:

1. Seek approval of the participant communities and individuals by consulting and negotiating with them the terms, scope and benefits of the proposed project.
2. Clear discussion of the issue of ownership and publication of data.
3. Gender implications, both in respect of focus and benefits, of the research should be explicitly addressed.
4. Employ members of the community to assist the researcher, on advice of the local communities.
5. The assessment process (of research proposals) should begin in the community and resources should be provided for the community for this process.

dimensions, including the role to be played by community organizations. For illustration of the potential role of community organizations, Ryan provides an account of the demands of the Australian Aboriginal community in relation to ethical research procedures (Exhibit 12.2), alerting the reader to the need to attend to the spirit of the demands, rather than considering them as a prescription of what must be done.

12.8 Chapter summary

Attention to ethnic marketing has been increasing although little attention has been devoted to potential ethics implications. Ethics issues associated with differentiated marketing addressed to minority ethnic groups appear not to be amenable to procedures used in the international context. The elaboration of a globalizing code of ethics appears problematic, even if a situation-contingent approach is utilized, arguably because exercise of the code will require judgement to be exercised.

This chapter identified ethics issues for ethnic marketing and explored some of the potential consequences arising from ethnocentric bias, one of five areas of possible ethical failure in ethnic marketing. Some of these consequences may be intrinsic rather than deliberate, suggesting that the ethical implications from marketing behaviour, both identified and yet to be identified, may be augmented by unintended unethical consequences.

While the analysis has not differentiated between marketing situations by the degree of intangibility of the service product, highly intangible activities may justify special attention by researchers and practitioners, given the relative intensity of human involvement. These are important areas for managerial consideration because the targeting of ethnic minority consumers with ethically unsound strategies may lead to alienation of ethnic markets. Careful consideration needs to be exercised before ethnic marketing strategies are developed and implemented.

The unintended unethical consequences of ethnic marketing are not well understood. Further research, starting with the fundamentals of ethnic marketing research methods, particularly the role and involvement of community organizations as gatekeepers to the research, is required. Because different service products may involve different ethics issues, industry-specific studies involving minority ethnic groups will add to our understanding of ethics in ethnic marketing.

Finally, the potential impact of ethnic marketing on mainstream populations and their sharing of one country with a variety of minority ethnic groups can be the basis for building walls between (or segregating) ethnic groups (Yanoov, 1999). The wider societal interest needs to be considered.

Notes

1. The marketing concept does not prescribe profit targets, however necessary they may be over the longer term. Focus is on achieving business objectives, whatever they are.
2. To the extent that international operations are part of an overall competitive strategy (either because of a firm's need to have a presence where its main customers operate, or because the firm must, or needs to follow its competitors) this also can influence a firm's ultimate survival in its domestic market.
3. ISCT is described as encompassing a hypothetical macrosocial contract used as a heuristic device, and actual microsocial contracts based within living communities. These contracts are important for normative judgements in business ethics (Dunfee *et al.*, 1999: 12).
4. For example, the American Psychological Association (APA) Council of Representatives adopted a new Ethics Code effective from 1 June 2003. This new code is available from the APA's website, including a comparison of the new code with the discarded one (www.apa.org/ethics/ visited 27 February 2004).

5. Site of the Center for the Study of Ethics in the Professions, Illinois Institute of Technology (www.iit.edu/departments/csep/PublicWWW/codes/ visited 27 February 2004).
6. The ethical dilemma implies that there may be some question about more than one course of action with differing outcomes or consequences for consumers, involving a concern for the consumer's well-being, or a conflict of interest that questions the appropriateness of an action and whether that action is in the consumer's best interest.
7. The programme of research relies on economic analysis, case studies and, notably, focus groups with visible minorities. Accessed on 27 February 2004, www.conferenceboard.ca/MTVM/Default.htm.
8. A further implication here is that the rights of marketers also need to be protected. Surely the effects of legal social irresponsibility cannot/ought not be owned only by business.

References

Bentley, G. (1981) *Ethnicity and Nationality: A Bibliographic Guide*, Seattle, WA: University of Washington Press.

Bento, R. (2000) 'Side effects: ethical issues in online pharmacies', in *Proceedings*, Seventh Annual International Conference Promoting Business Ethics, St John's University, New York, p. 433.

Blanton, K. (1993) 'Pitfalls in the ethnic ad minefield', *Boston Globe*, 22 August, p. 75.

Bonham, V. (2001) 'Race, ethnicity, and pain treatment: striving to understand the causes and solutions to the disparities in pain treatment', *Journal of Law, Medicine & Ethics*, Spring.

Buchholz, R. and Rosenthal, S. (2000) 'Ethics, economics, and service: changing cultural perspectives', in *Proceedings*, Seventh Annual International Conference Promoting Business Ethics, St John's University, New York, pp. 9–16.

Castles, S., Cope, B. and Kalantzis, M. (1992) 'Australia: multi-ethnic community without nationalism?', extract from *Mistaken Identity* (Sydney: Pluto Press), pp. 139–48. Reprinted in J. Hutchinson and A. Smith (eds) (1996) *Ethnicity*, Oxford: Oxford University Press.

Cornell, S. and Hartmann, D. (1998) *Ethnicity and Race*, London: Sage Publications.

Cui, G. (1998) 'Ethical issues in ethnic segmentation and target marketing', in J. Chebut and A. Oumlil (eds) *Proceedings*, Multicultural Marketing Conference, AMS, Montreal, pp. 87–91.

D'Andrade, R. (1985) 'Bribery', *Journal of Business Ethics*, 4 (August): 239–48.

Danley, J. (1983) 'Towards a theory of bribery', *Business and Professional Ethics Journal*, 2 (Spring): 19–39.

Davidson, D. (1995) 'Targeting is innocent until it exploits the vulnerable', *Marketing News*, 29(19); 11 September: 10.

Douglas, J. (1971) *Understanding Everyday Life: Towards the Reconstruction of Sociological Knowledge*, London: Routledge and Kegan Paul.

Dunfee, T., Smith, N. and Ross Jr., W. (1999) 'Social contracts and marketing ethics', *Journal of Marketing*, 63 (July): 14–32.

Fisher, J., Garrett, D., Cannon, J. and Beggs, J. (1999) 'Problem businesses: consumer complaints, the Better Business Bureau, and ethical business practices', in G. T. Gunlach, W. L. Wilkie and P. E. Murphy (eds) *Proceedings*, Marketing and Public Policy Conference, 9, University of Notre Dame, AMA, pp. 69–72.

Foley, J. (1997) 'Ethics in advertising', in *Communio et Progressio*, Pontifical Council for Social Communications, February 22, Vatican City (accessed at www.Vatican. va/ roman_curia/pontifical_councils/pccs/documents/rc_pc_pccs_doc_22021997_ethics -in-ad_en.html on 27 February 2004).

Grier, S., Williams, J. and Crockett, D. (1996) 'Racial discrimination as a consumer disadvantage? The marketplace experiences of black men', in R. P. Hill and C. R. Taylor (eds) *Proceedings*, Marketing and Public Policy Conference, 6, AMA, p. 131.

Hartman, C. and Beck-Dudley, C. (1995) 'Marketing ethics and the search for virtue', in J. Evans, B. Berman and B. Barak, *Proceedings*, Research Conference on Ethics and Social Responsibility in Marketing, Hofstra University, pp. 1–14.

Heide, J. and George, J. (1992) 'Do norms matter in marketing relationships?', *Journal of Marketing*, 56 (April): 32–44.

Hutchinson, J. and Smith, A. (eds) (1996) *Ethnicity*, Oxford: Oxford University Press.

Jakob, Y., Jou, L., Fonling, F. and Amy, Y. (1998) 'The ethical decision making of marketing professionals in Taiwan', in J. Chebat and A. Oumlil, *Proceedings*, Multicultural Marketing Conference, AMS, Montreal, pp. 24–8.

Kotler, P., Armstrong, G., Brown, L. and Adam, S. (1998) *Marketing*, 4th edn., Sydney: Prentice-Hall.

Macchiette, B. and Roy, A. (1994) 'Sensitive groups and social issues', *Journal of Consumer Marketing*, 11(4): 55–65.

Moore-Shay, E. (1996) 'The lens of economic circumstance: how do economically disadvantaged children view the marketplace?', in R. P. Hill and C. R. Taylor, *Proceedings*, Marketing and Public Policy Conference, 6, AMA, p. 132.

Philips, M. (1984) *Bribery*, New York: Macmillan.

Pruzan, P. and Thyssen, O. (1990) 'Conflict and consensus – ethics as a shared value horizon for strategic planning', *Human Systems Management*, 9: 135–51.

Ryan, L. (1996) 'Researching minority ethnic communities: a note on ethics', in *Proceedings of Minority Ethnic Groups in Higher Education in Ireland*, St Patrick's College, Maynooth, 27 September. Accessed on 27 February 2004 at www.ucc.ie/ucc/ units/equality/pubs/Minority/ryan.htm

Sarwono, S. and Armstrong, R. (1998) 'Cross-microcultural business ethics: ethical perceptions differences in marketing among ethnic microcultural groups in Indonesia', in J. Chebat and A. Oumlil (eds) *Proceedings*, Multicultural Marketing Conference, AMS, Montreal, pp. 80–6.

Sautter, E. and Oretskin, N. (1997) 'Tobacco targeting: the ethical complexity of marketing to minorities', *Journal of Business Ethics*, 16 (10): 1011–18.

Seelye, H. and Wasilewski, J. (1996) *Between Cultures: Developing Self-Identity in a World of Diversity*, Chicago, IL: NTC Publishing Group.

Segal, M. and Giacobbe, R. (1995) 'An empirical investigation of ethical issues in marketing research: Asian perspectives', in J. R. Evans, B. Berman and B. Barak (eds) *Proceedings*, Research Conference on Ethics and Social Responsibility in Marketing, Hofstra University, pp. 110–16.

Shepherd, P., Tsalikis, J. and Seaton, B. (2002) 'An inquiry into the ethical perceptions of sub-cultural groups in the US: Hispanics versus Anglos', *Journal of Consumer Marketing*, 19(2/3): 130–49.

Skubik, D. (1993) 'Ethics and international business', in P. Graham (ed.) *Australian Marketing: Critical Essays, Readings and Cases*, Sydney: Prentice-Hall.

Stevenson, T. (1991) 'How are blacks portrayed in business ads?', *Industrial Marketing Management*, 20: 193–9.

Streiner, D. and Norman, G. (1995) *Health Measurement Scales: A Practical Guide to Their Development and Use*, Oxford Medical Publications, New York: Oxford University Press.

Todd, K. (1996) 'Pain assessment and ethnicity', *Annals of Emergency Medicine*, 2: 421–32.

Varner, I. and Beamer, L. (1995) *Intercultural Communication in the Global Workplace*, Chicago: Irwin.

Vitell, S., Rallapalli, J. and Singhapakdi, A. (1993) 'Marketing norms: the influences of personal moral philosophies and organizational ethical culture', *Journal of the Academy of Marketing Science*, 21: 331–7.

Yanoov, B. (1999) *Celebrating Diversity: Coexisting in a Multicultural Society*, New York: Haworth Press.

CHAPTER 13

Ethnic marketing – challenges and opportunities

13.1 Chapter objectives

This chapter restates the principles underlying an ethnic marketing focus and considers their robustness in a changing political and technological environment. The approach advocated in this book will be challenged for its emphasis on catering for differences based on ethnicity and its advocacy of the disaggregation of broad-based cultural groups. The case for this approach must be placed in the wider context of fundamental issues that marketing theory has failed to address adequately and in the need to account for a changing socio-economic domestic environment in advanced economies that also threatens the irrelevance of marketing nostrums. There are limitations to the universal application of the targeting approach advocated and these also need to be recounted.

In an influential paper, Day and Montgomery (1999) outlined four fundamental issues that marketing needs to address to distinguish it from other fields and disciplines. In arguing for the distinctiveness of marketing in terms of how these issues are addressed, marketing must also confront the lack of universal models available to answer these issues. The need for ethnic marketing can be related to all four issues and current deficiencies in the marketing literature. Five broad trends are cited as likely to shape the direction of marketing, requiring more innovative marketing approaches. The implications of these trends for ethnic marketing are also addressed.

13.2 Fundamental issues and ethnic marketing

The four fundamental issues cited by Day and Montgomery (1999) are:

1. How do customers and consumers really behave?
2. How do markets function and evolve?
3. How do firms relate to their markets?
4. What are the contributions of marketing to organizational performance and societal welfare?

We seek to address these issues in terms of the ethnic marketing approach advocated in this book, contrasted with other approaches.

13.3 How do customers and consumers really behave?

This one broad question raises a plethora of issues that the targeting of ethnic minorities seeks to address, which are essentially glossed over in mainstream marketing, namely the targeting of broad-based aggregates of ethnic minorities. These issues include:

■ *Greater understanding of how consumers narrow the set of alternatives and make their choices*
   This book has rejected the presumption underlying mass-marketing that, for the same product, all consumers narrow the set of alternatives and make their choices using the same criteria. Ethnic marketing pays considerable attention to the information and appraisal difficulties facing ethnic minority consumers and the consequent role of the group

in narrowing the set of alternatives. The minority ethnic group is both a gatekeeper and a part of the consumption environment that creates the 'village envelopment' important for loyalty creation (Oliver, 1999).

■ *Greater understanding of consumers' current, latent and emerging needs*
Cultural diversity is a characteristic of many modern nation-states. In Western economies, this diversity was initially a product of large immigration flows, but rather than assimilation in the discredited version of the American 'melting-pot' (Glazer and Moynihan, 1963), or the French 'crucible' (*Newsweek International*, 2003), many minority ethnic groups have retained their identities, while others are in the process of reawakening. While these identities may change over time, assimilation is not inevitable and these distinct groups also interact with and contribute to changes in the mainstream cultures. Consequently, ethnic marketing rejects the linear assimilation model. In so doing, there can be no presumption that ethnic consumers' emerging needs and wants will necessarily be best satisfied through mainstream offerings.

■ *Developing appropriate models for describing and explaining the processes of search and preference formation that precede choice*
The processes of search and preference formation that precede choice are likely to be different between ethnic minorities and the mainstream. The importance of ethnic network sources in the search process and therefore the need to tailor communications to the group network, is still relatively disregarded by mainstream marketing. Conflicting signs of change are emerging. For example, Verizon, a US telephony provider, has professed to seeking to understand all of the cultural nuances and geographical differences of its customer base, accepting that different minority groups want to communicate differently and have different needs from the mass market. To this end, in New York alone it utilizes eight languages, and its sales and support staff are multilingual. Specific cultural accommodations are also made. Nevertheless, as noted by a rival, Verizon is still offering the same basic services that it offers the mass market rather than acting on the basis that different ethnic communities have different telecom needs (*Telephony*, 2003).

In contrast, driven by cost imperatives, other large organizations have sought to reduce ethnic targeting. Avon has discontinued its specific ethnic-targeted mailings in favour of overhauling its main brochure to reflect 'what this country looks like', that is encompassing multiple ethnicities in one brochure featuring a diverse mix of Hispanic, African–American and Asian women in at least 30 per cent of the brochure (*Advertising Age*, 2003a). Such an approach reverts to the 'melting pot' view of the USA, failing to appreciate the significant cultural differences in communications that occur between ethnic minorities.

With a different rationale, but a similar outcome, Pepsi has also allegedly moved away from an ethnic marketing focus, dropping its advertisements targeting specific 'race-based' groups such as African–American. The claim is that 'race is not the unifier . . . the multicultural mind set is more about your interests, like music, than whether you're Afro American or Latino'. While the professed aim is to cut across cultures, what Pepsi has recognized is that the previous advertisements were too broad-based, encompassing multiple ethnicities, and therefore not well targeted (*Advertising Age*, 2003b). Many other issues arise under this general heading of how customers behave, that are pertinent in distinguishing the behaviour of ethnic minority consumers within a country from the mainstream. These include questions about loyalty, inertia and situational constraints, also addressed in this book. While marketing has generally built on similarities, attention to these differences becomes important when businesses are seeking to develop a competitive advantage.

13.4 How do markets function and evolve?

Resolving segmentation issues lies at the heart of this question, in particular whether segmentation theory and practice has maintained its relevance in an era of increased fragmentation and volatility in competitive markets. Given the prior discussion of differences in consumer behaviour, this book has consistently argued that segmentation based on ethnic minority groups is likely to be effective and rewarding for a particular array of service-products.

The advantages of economies of scale in production, distribution and promotion has been a potent force for mass marketing and for aggregation of ill-fitting ethnic minorities. The 'melting pot' view of acculturation has been an expedient justification to ignore consumer behaviour differences in an environment that was less competitive than today. Replacing it with smaller aggregates based primarily on stereotypical racial groupings is similarly expedient and starting to show its failings. For example, African–Americans have been shown to be less homogeneous in their consumer behaviour by race than by demographics (McKinley, Smith and Marshall, 1998). Segmentation terminology is poorly defined and the label of ethnic marketing used in the USA is different to that used elsewhere. Cui and Choudhury (2002), for example, argue that the trend toward ethnic segmentation and targeted marketing is not unique to the USA, with companies and researchers in other countries also paying more attention to ethnic minority consumers in their own respective markets. But US 'ethnic' marketing programmes target Hispanics, African–Americans and Asian–Americans. These large aggregates contrast with those used elsewhere. It is, therefore, hardly surprising that in the USA 'marketers are wondering whether ethnically tailored programs are effective in fostering greater brand loyalty or if any advantages may be outweighed by the risks of misreading the target markets'. Targeting programmes based on such broad aggregates cannot capture the internal homogeneity and cohesiveness required for effective segmentation.

Because of the costs of targeting ethnic groups, the authors propose a nested hierarchy of segmentation possibilities to determine the suitable segmentation dimension:

- demographic factors (race, language, nationality, income and family composition);
- psychographic factors (values, beliefs, motives and attitudes);
- behavioural factors (media usage, lifestyles, consumption patterns);
- situational factors (occasions, product category);
- personal factors (personality and acculturation).

In this hierarchy, marketing to an ethnic minority differs from targeting an ethnic minority, the focus of this book. Ethnicity in this book is largely through ascription, both self and externally applied. A minority ethnic group has little significance to marketers, in the broadest or macro sense used by Cui and Choudhury (2002), and it is disputable whether it constitutes a group in any cohesive collective sense. The combination of the demographic and the psychographic factors constitute the basis for targeting an ethnic group and their interlinking gives rise to the cohesive behaviour sought by target marketers.

13.5 How do firms relate to their markets?

The strategy underlying the targeting of minority ethnic groups is driven by a significant change in marketing thought. 'There has been a shift from an emphasis on discrete transactions and the acquisition of new customers to relationship and the retention of valuable customers' (Day and Montgomery, 1999). The development of a relationship with ethnic minority consumers will necessarily require a different approach from that used with mainstream consumers and also other minority ethnic groups. This arises from the cultural differences as well as the different problems faced by different ethnic groups in seeking to participate freely in the mainstream economy.

13.6 What are the contributions of marketing to organizational performance and societal welfare?

At first glance, the case for targeting ethnic minority consumers may have little apparent connection with improving macro performance and welfare. That is a blinkered view.

While many Western governments acknowledge the cultural diversity that exists within their national borders, employing varying forms of classification ranging from the sophisticated (Australia) to the naïve (the USA) to collect statistics on ethnic groups, rarely are the potentially positive economic effects of this diversity on the enrichment of the human capital base of a nation explored. Rather than a focus on market opportunities created through diversity of demands, ideas and interacting cultures, there is usually a greater preoccupation on perceived problems (see Stanton, Aislabie and Lee, 1992). A part of this failure by governments and business to focus on market opportunities created by cultural diversity stems from the lack of appropriate business models that account for this diversity in business practice. Business models, including those used in marketing, have an overwhelming reliance on business paradigms that are based on national cultures, unless going abroad. The supremacy of national cultures is reflected in the growth of international management and international marketing knowledge as requiring a cross-cultural focus, while such a focus is considered redundant within a nation. The business implications of cultural diversity within advanced economies remain under-researched and poorly understood.

> As a multicultural society now exists, regardless of future immigration, one might have expected a suitable framework of analysis which includes the multicultural features of population growth. Without an understanding of the overall effects, that is a more general economic framework of economic analysis, policy approaches probably owe more to religious conviction than an understanding of causal relationships. Unrelated to immigration or access and equity issues, there would appear to be a need for an alternative paradigm. This would recognize that the existing population is culturally and linguistically diverse and provide a priori causal links explaining how these characteristics can influence, beneficially or negatively, efficient resource use, the rate and pattern of economic growth and trade.
>
> (Stanton, Aislabie and Lee, 1992: 420)

Although referring to the Australian situation, there is an international failure to address cross-cultural issues within national borders. Such a framework would enable business to focus attention on how a culturally diverse workforce can increase business productivity and garner competitive advantage using the skill and knowledge base arising from cultural diversity. For marketing as a discipline, such a framework can focus attention on the opportunities arising from the diversity of consumption patterns and the cross-fertilization leading to new ideas and products within a culturally diverse economy (Stanton, Aislabie and Lee, 1992). The targeting of ethnic consumers with offers tailored to their preferences increases the array and widens choice. Moreover, it increases ethnic minority participation within the economy.

13.7 Future trends and ethnic marketing

Day and Montgomery (1999) link the issues constituting the domain of marketing to five major changes likely to impact on marketing and therefore to its future directions. While all of these changes will necessarily influence the growth and methods used in ethnic marketing, the opportunities and threats created for ethnic marketing through the operation of such changes are uneven, and only those particularly salient to the arguments developed in this book are addressed here.

Globalization and convergence

The progression from national and sub-national markets to linked global markets provides the drivers for the reawakening of ethnicity, rather than its demise. Succinctly stated:

> Two dramatic and opposing forces are at work in the world today. On the one hand, sophisticated and complex communication and transportation systems move us toward a homogenized existence and identity. Evolving political, economic, and social interdependencies on a global scale enhance this trend toward similarity and uniculturalism. As a powerful countertendency to this homogenization process, however, self- or group identity on the basis of cultural background is on the rise.
>
> (Costa and Bamossy, 1995: vii)

Even when governments in advanced economies do not promote or encourage multiculturalism and permanent migration is tightly controlled, economic and cultural globalization tendencies may trigger a search for community identity. Technological change, improving communications and the growing integration of markets encourages the pursuit of difference, whether in terms of individual lifestyles, group cultural identity, or assertion of national uniqueness (Castles *et al.*, 1992). This argument echoes Melucci (1989), for whom the strengthening of ethnicity is a response to the increasing complexity of society. The highly differentiated relations typical of complex societies are unable to provide forms of membership and identification to meet individual needs for self-realization, communicative interaction and recognition. The preservation of an ethnic identity offers new or renewed channels of solidarity and identification, a response to the need for collective identity.

Ethnicity is socially constructed, with individuals having the ability to choose from a variety of ethnic heritages (Hutchinson and Smith, 1996). While economic and cultural globalization has tended to reduce ethnicity, recent advances in electronic communications and information technology provide sub-national ethnic groups with dense cultural networks that can sustain interaction in the face of depersonalizing bureaucratic structures.

The contradictory effects of globalization on ethnicity conflict with the belief that globalization of supply ensues from a changing demand that is becoming ever more global and allegedly more homogeneous between countries due to an increasing diffusion of knowledge, technological progress and declining trade barriers. A strengthening of ethnic identity means that, within countries, ethnic minority consumers' needs and wants are not becoming globalized. Hence, the foundations for successful ethnic marketing rest in understanding this growing contradiction between the globalization of supply and the changing political and social conditions operating in liberal democracies that stimulate the permanency of ethnic groups with strong locally constructed identities.

The convergence of supply, with industries losing their defined geographic and user boundaries, also strengthens ethnic marketing. Increasing numbers of potential suppliers empowers minority consumers in terms of their specific demands.

Fragmenting and frictionless markets

The internet 'introduces the possibility of frictionless markets that dictate greater standardization of offerings and weaken long-standing relationships' (Day and Montgomery, 1999: 8). The complexity of change is evident in this statement because the opposite is equally likely to prevail.

While the internet has enabled a new, quasi-economically efficient marketplace that has been characterized as delivering 'perfect information for all', or at least, 'equal access to information about products, prices, and distribution' (Strauss and Frost, 2001: 157–63), Aisbett and Pires[1] (2003) seek to place this 'benefit' in a cultural context. How much information is necessary and expected by consumers? Should it be explicit and direct, or should it be left more implicit? The answers to such questions depend on the target culture, which is often classified as being either *low-context* (exemplified by the 'do it now' North American/Western white male-type audience, with their unique way of defining a business relationship) or *high-context* (exemplified by wanting to build relationships before getting down to business). The point from the marketing perspective is that understanding the target culture is crucial for marketing (e.g. to determine which supplementary benefits should be offered).

The implications of intercultural communication skills for marketing and globalization may be hidden by the technological emphasis on the speed of communications afforded by digital technologies, as if speed guaranteed effective communication. Information and communication technology facilitates the exchange of ideas, and these increase the potential for cultural misunderstandings. This unintended consequence may be facilitated by the sharing of one terminology, but with different intended meaning, when used by technology and business practitioners. Business communication may lack understanding of the fundamental cultural values involved, of the meanings that are not put into words, of the importance of the words that are used, of the way messages are received and transmitted and, ultimately, of what to expect when a stakeholder engages in particular communication behaviour across cultures – whether making a decision, negotiating a sales agreement, writing a legal document, or signing a contract.

A firm needs to know its market and, more precisely, what actual and potential customers consider in their valuations, in order to position itself as the best provider of satisfaction, and in order to control and allocate resources. Globalization and e-commerce have the potential to move business strategies away from niche marketing, towards head-to-head competition in which superior understanding of international consumer behaviour will provide competitive advantage (Pereira, 1998). But to do this requires segmentation of a global market

Global market segmentation (GMS) is the process of identifying specific segments (country groups or individual consumer groups across countries) of potential customers with homogeneous attributes who are likely to exhibit similar buying behaviour, in order to develop, position and sell products across national boundaries (Kumar and Nagpal, 2001). This is not an easy task, given how difficult gathering of information can be even in much smaller local markets. Gathering and exploiting customer information in e-commerce is constrained by technological challenges, lack of experience, privacy concerns and consumers' growing awareness of the value of information, all contributing to making it expensive and elusive (Simcoe, 2001). In fact, there are further complications to GMS because:

- different products are in different stages of the product life cycle at any given time;
- the internet allows for rapid dissemination of information but to different extents across different countries (hence consumer knowledge is variable and rapidly changing across those same countries);
- the above two points challenge effective segmentation due to instability, heterogeneity, measurability and identifiability.[2]

Simcoe (2001) argues that the focus of GMS is on behavioural information, experimenting with product offers to learn about behavioural patterns, and accepting that e-commerce may involve new kinds of buyer–seller interface challenges. Successful companies that have gone online to market themselves and their products globally (e.g. Amazon, DoubleClick, Net perceptions, Personify and Priceline) use the internet as a powerful feedback mechanism that utilizes knowledge of stakeholder behaviours to constantly refine targeted communications with those stakeholders.

While this strategy is argued to resemble neither traditional marketing nor the conventional perception of sophisticated one-to-one, it may be seen as a return to the cognitive models of the 1960s (Nicosia, 1966). Given the difficulties in gathering global information, the strategic shift from niche marketing may give local businesses an advantage; they will at least be more likely to be sought as partners in alliances with foreign firms attempting to enter new markets. On the other hand, it will make it more difficult for small businesses to enter foreign markets. Moreover, marketing theory acknowledges that consumer trust is related to the general propensity to trust of the consumer, to the protection afforded by social and legal structures, to prior interaction with or knowledge of the firm, to expected length of relationship with the firm, and to the interface with the firm being through a knowledgeable salesperson with background identifiable to the consumer (Jarvenpaa and Tractinsky, 1999). One possible consequence is that electronic consumers prefer to purchase from extensions of well-known – often American – retail outlets, and in turn, to prefer goods which have, or appear to have, been manufactured in traditional industrialized countries like Japan, USA and Western Europe (Pereira, 1998).

In summary, the use of the internet for e-commerce potentially enlarges markets and contributes to a more globalized world. Cultural diversity, on the other hand, offers valuable opportunities based on differences. The culturally sensitive marketer can build on characteristic tastes, values and aspirations to create the product message or image most appropriate for a specific community, region or country. Language, time-keeping in business dealings, religion, product packaging, labelling, colour choices and size are only some of many aspects to consider. Reconciling globalization with cultural diversity requires global market segmentation as a prerequisite for developing, positioning and selling products across national boundaries. This should allow culturally sensitive marketers to take advantage of the opportunities from globalization while avoiding cultural clashes and *faux pas*.

The need to target ethnic groups, even if using electronic technologies, is supported by Fletcher (2004). In a review of the impact of culture on website design and content, especially as a promotional tool, Fletcher concludes that practitioners will need to provide specific versions of websites for ethnic groups if they are a target of the promotion. Creation of an effective site for such purposes will require research of the underlying cultural dimensions and the cultural manifestations of the ethnic group if a culturally sensitive website is to be created. Language, content and structure are reviewed for the kinds of cultural changes required. While the new technologies may be able to reach ethnic consumers, effectiveness will require incorporation to the needs of the target group.

Forces of proliferation and fragmentation: towards molecular markets

What emerges from both the dynamics of identity creation, as a response to globalization, and the emergence of new electronic technologies with rapid global applications, is the ability to target smaller market segments. 'No longer will it be safe to assume that markets are predictable and that large segments of the market will behave alike' (Day and Montgomery, 1999: 8). Ethnic marketing can be enhanced through the embrace of electronic technologies.

Demanding consumers and their empowered behaviour

This is another important shift, arising from a coalescence of trends previously discussed. If, as Day and Montgomery (1999) argue, consumers are no longer passive participants in the marketing process and instead show an increasing willingness to search for a better value proposition, then ethnic marketing recommends itself.

13.8   The political environment

This is an issue peculiar to ethnic marketing, perhaps raising more threats than opportunities. Culture and ethnicity are still addressed in the mainstream marketing textbooks as if their only relevance is to an international marketing situation: 'While the issues in markets like the US and Europe are integrating and assimilating minorities into the mainstream, in the Asian-Pacific, African and Latin American markets with strong ethnic history as well as diversity . . . the task is penetrating these markets itself' (Brochure for ESOMAR 2000). This book has challenged this argument throughout.

Liberal democracy and the growth of 'multiculturalism' either *de jure* or *de facto*, allow for the growth and maintenance of ethnic communities. The global and social forces at work in shaping ethnic groups suggest such groups are more likely to strengthen over time (regardless of the level of immigration), and the community elements of such groups, when recognized by marketers, will reinforce their marketing relevance.

The conditions shaping minority ethnic group growth and change in advanced economies do not apply in many less advanced, ethnically diverse economies. It is more likely that the use of a framework of ethnic or multicultural marketing to target individual ethnic groups in such economies will face greater obstacles and may be less successful than in liberal democracies with advanced economies. The impact of the global economy will stimulate the need for groups to seek or maintain collective identity (Melucci, 1989). However, the emphasis on creating a sense of national unity, and the weakness of liberal democratic traditions, will work to foster assimilationist tendencies (sometimes strongly and violently resisted) rather than ethnic group loyalties in less advanced, and often less democratic, economies. That is not to dispute the opportunities for ethnic marketing occurring in many newly industrializing and also post-Soviet Union nations, where permanent ethnic minorities have long coexisted, sometimes very uneasily. Malaysia, South Africa and Russia are prominent examples.

It is also unlikely, following from the social construction and dynamics of ethnic group identity, that a marketing strategy targeting a minority ethnic group within an advanced economy can be used without modification for a related diaspora in international marketing. A minority ethnic group, while linked by perceived common ties to some land of ancestry, may in fact be quite distant in terms of the elements needed to engage in successful communication and trade with this land. To argue that a model of 'international marketing at home' (Wilkinson and Cheng, 1997) can be applied to international marketing abroad ignores the dynamics of group formation and evolution over time.

The optimism of continued tolerance in liberal-democratic societies is being tested and retested. The expansion of the European Union into a pan-union of multiple nationalities and even greater numbers of ethnic groups will provide a rich testing ground for ethnic marketing. There is no indication that language or cultural differences will recede between nations within the union but within nations intolerance of minority ethnic group identity is evident (*Newsweek*, http://msnbc.com/id/3540615/; *Economist*, 2004). As noted in both sources, France has been able to integrate immigrants into a mainstream population in 'a system that was less a melting pot than a crucible'. With a large and growing Muslim minority population, the use of the female headscarf in public schools has been the basis of legislation. Similar issues are being contested in other countries. Nevertheless, such actions do not constrain the use of language, private schooling and other ways of maintaining identity.

Multicultural policies, *de facto* or *de jure*, differ significantly between European countries, with the United Kingdom approach allegedly providing a less repressive contrast to the French (*Economist*, 2004). What has emerged, and is continuing to develop within the UK, is not assimilation but a different pattern of acculturation to that occurring in France. Regardless of the political approach taken, ethnic identity can be predicted to grow because both exclusion and self-inclusion feed its psychological and behavioural roots.

Notes

1. The following paragraphs draw from Aishett and Pires (2003).
2. While these complications point to enormous segmentation challenges, the immense global horizon has been claimed to create 'mirages' of perceived substantiality. Hence segmentation may be viewed as superfluous, although the substantiality test is only possible ex-post (Stanton and Pires, 1999).

References

Advertising Age (2003a) 'Avon targets black sales reps', 74 (1 Sept.).

Advertising Age (2003b) 'Pepsi puts interests before ethnicity', 74 (7 July).

Aisbett, J., and Pires, G. (2003) 'Macro issues in electronic commerce: the cultural divide', *Global Business Economics Review*, 5(2): 369–90.

Castles, S., Cope, B., Kalantzis, M. and Morrissey, M. (1992) 'Australia: multi-ethnic community without nationalism?', reprinted in J. Hutchinson and A. Smith (eds) (1996) *Ethnicity*, Oxford: Oxford University Press.

Costa, J., and Bamossy, G. (eds) (1995) 'Preface', in *Marketing in a Multicultural World*, Thousand Oaks, California: Sage Publications, p. vii.

Cui, G. and Choudhury, P. (2002) 'Marketplace diversity and cost effective marketing strategies', *Journal of Consumer Marketing*, 19: 54–74.

Day, G. and Montgomery, D. (1999) 'Charting new directions for marketing', *Journal of Marketing*, 63 (Special Issue): 3–13.

Economist (2004) 'The war of the headscarves', 7 February: 24–6.

Fletcher, R. (2004) 'The impact of culture on website content, design and structure – an international and a multicultural perspective', UK Academy of International Business Conference, Londonderry, Northern Ireland, April.

Glazer, N. and Moynihan, D. (1963) *Beyond the Melting Pot*, Cambridge, MA: MIT Press and Harvard University Press.

Hutchinson, J. and Smith, A. (eds) (1996) *Ethnicity*, Oxford: Oxford University Press.

Jarvenpaa, S. and Tractinsky, N. (1999) 'Consumer trust in an internet store: a cross-cultural validation': *Journal of Computer-Mediated Communication*, 5(2).

Kumar, V. and Nagpal, A. (2001) 'Segmenting global markets: look before you leap', *Marketing Research: A Magazine of Management and Applications*, Spring: 8–13.

McKinley, L., Smith, J. and Marshall, K. (1998) 'The myth of the monolithic minority: the renewed call for the effective segmentation of African–American consumers', in J. Chebat and A. Oumlil (eds) *Proceedings*, Multicultural Marketing Congress, Montreal, Canada, September, pp. 92–9.

Melucci, A. (1989) *Nomads of the Present: Social Movements and Contemporary Needs in Contemporary Society*, J. Keane and P. Mier (eds), London: Hutchinson Radius.

Newsweek International (2003) 'Generation M', 1 Dec. http://msnbc.msn.com/id/3540615/

Nicosia, F. (1966) *Consumer Decision Processes*, Englewood Cliffs, NJ: Prentice-Hall.

Oliver, R. (1999) 'Whence consumer loyalty', *Journal of Marketing*, 63: 33–44.

Pereira, R. (1998) 'Cross-cultural influences on global electronic commerce', *Proceedings of the AIS*, Baltimore, pp. 318–20.

Simcoe, T. (2001) 'Revenge of the stupid: behavioral marketing and e-commerce', *Focus E-zine*, Cap Gemini Ernst & Young, issue 7: wysiwyg://217/http://www.cgey.com/focus/issue7

Stanton, J. P. and Pires, G. M. (1999) 'The substantiality test: meaning and application in market segmentation', *Journal of Segmentation in Marketing*, 3(2): 105–15.

Stanton, P., Aislabie, C. and Lee, J. (1992) 'The economics of a multicultural Australia', *Journal of Multilingual and Multicultural Development*, 13: 407–22.

Strauss, J. and Frost, R. (2001) *E-Marketing*, New Jersey, NJ: Prentice-Hall.

Telephony (2003) 'Verizon targets minority customer base', 7 April.

Wilkinson, I. and Cheng, C. (1997) 'Multicultural marketing: synergy in diversity', in *Proceedings*, Australia and New Zealand Marketing Educators Conference, Melbourne, December, pp. 1404–14.

The impact of culture on website content, design, and structure – an international and a multicultural perspective

Richard Fletcher*

The extent to which culture will need to be taken into account in design and content of the website will depend on whether the purpose of the site is to merely provide information or whether it is to be used as a vehicle for marketing. It will also be influenced by whether the site is intended to be interactive or passive.

Language is the first issue to be considered. In catering for the needs of different ethnic groups, simple translation from the English is insufficient. This is because a culturally sensitive approach requires that the underlying concepts rather than just the words be rendered in the other language. If this does not occur, then meaning can become distorted and result in offence which is counterproductive, or in hilarity which diminishes the serious attention being given to the message. A related issue is that the patterns of discourse vary from language to language. For example, whereas in one language the main point of the communication may be at the beginning of the sentence and the qualifiers follow, in other languages the qualifiers come first and the main point comes at the end of the sentence. Understanding the pattern of discourse in the language

* University of Western Sydney. Extract from invited paper, presented to the UK Academy of International Business Conference, Londonderry, Northern Ireland, April, 2004

will assist in ensuring that the website is more effective in conveying the desired meaning. Apart from language, there are two other culturally influenced aspects that impact on website design. These relate to structure and content.

As far as structure is concerned, if the relative balance in the English language web page is to be replicated in the foreign language version, the following need to be taken into account:

- In some ethnic groups colours have different images than they do in Australia and greater significance is attached to their auspicious nature. This requires a review of the colours used in the Australian website to ensure that the colours do not detract from the effectiveness of the version of the site in the other language. To illustrate, Table RN13.1 shows meanings attributed to four colours in four different countries.

- A similar situation prevails with the use of numbers. Whilst in many English-speaking countries, negative vibes attach to the number 13, these are insignificant compared for example to the negative vibes attaching to the number 4 in Mandarin. The use of inauspicious numbers on websites, especially in pricing, is to be avoided. Conversely the use of auspicious numbers is positive and in Mandarin, these would be 8, 11, 13, 15, 16, 17, 18, 25, 29, 31, 32 and 39.

Table RN13.1 The differing image of four colours in four countries

Country	Grey	Blue	Green	Red
China	Inexpensive	High quality	Pure Trustworthy Dependable Sincere	Happy Love Adventurous
Sourth Korea	–	Powerful High quality Adventurous Sincere Trustworthy	Pure Adventurous Sincere Trustworthy	Love Good-tasting Adventurous
Japan	Inexpensive	Sincere Trustworthy High quality Dependable	Pure Good-tasting Adventurous	Love Good-tasting Happy Adventurous
USA	Expensive High quality Dependable	Dependable High quality Sincere Trustworthy Expensive Powerful	Good-tasting Adventurous	Love Adventurous Happy Good-tasting Inexpensive

- Different ethnic groups are likely to espouse different values. There needs to be consistency on the website between the symbols employed, the persons (heroes) used to illustrate and the collective or social activities referred to on the one hand and the values that the ethnic group prize on the other.

Religion, ethnicity and acculturation. Generation M

Carla Power and Christopher Dickey*

The debate about where or whether Islam belongs in Europe has become a conversational genre. To ban or not to ban headscarves in schools? Terrorism versus civil liberties? Whither multiculturalism? All worthy questions, you may say, but what do they have to do with charcuterie?

The French simply love it – pork sausages, pigs' feet and ham, but when Mouhad Bourouis, 33, worked at a summer day camp for underprivileged children in the south of France a few years ago, charcuterie posed a problem. Out of 80 kids, 28 were Muslim and the halal restrictions on their diet, like kosher ones for Jewish children, meant they could eat no pork at all. 'The first week I planned 28 meals with no pork, but it was just too expensive and too much of a hassle', Bourouis recalls. 'So the second week, I got all the parents together and told them I would plan meals that would be OK for all the kids. If they really wanted to eat sausage, they could wait to be back at the family dinner table.'

Bourouis, the son of Algerian immigrants and a prosperous attorney in Marseilles, tells the story to show how problems of integrating Muslims into French society can be overcome. But for many in France, and Europe, the tale also poses a deeper question – indeed, an existential one. How much will their societies be changed, willingly or not, by the need to accommodate their

* With Marie Valla in Paris, Friso Endt at The Hague and Elizabeth Nash in Madrid © 2004 *Newsweek*, Inc. Accessed at Newsweek International, http://msnbc.msn.com/id/3540615/

burgeoning Muslim populations? It's not just a matter of bacon and sausage, of course, but of laws, lifestyles, mores, cultures.

The search for an answer, still far from conclusive, has emerged as the most passionately debated issue in European life. Not so long ago, Europe's Muslims were left to wrestle with their own identity issues. Their job, as native Europeans saw it, was to assimilate – or not. That's changed, utterly. Today the spectre of terrorism, fairly or not, looms over the Continent's Islamic communities; last week's bombings in Turkey only intensified the fears and suspicions prevalent in many countries. That makes the question of how to integrate Europe's Muslims both more critical – and far more difficult.

There are now more than 12 million people of Muslim origin in Western Europe, roughly half of them in France. Visiting the city of Marseilles, where nearly a third of the population is Arab, one sees the more familiar dimension of the phenomenon. The youths slouched against walls in the twisting, cobbled streets of the old port are three to five times less likely to have a job than their 'French' counterparts. Whole neighborhoods could easily be in the Maghreb: many have little, if any, contact with the country beyond their walls. Among young men, particularly, Islam has turned from a faith into a rejection of the French system that many feel has failed them.

The real challenge, though, lies not with those who have checked out of the system, but those who want in, on their own terms. That's the role of a new crop of twenty- and thirty-somethings – call them Generation M – who are Europeans in almost every sense of the word. Unlike their forebears, they are mostly born in Europe and claim it as their own society. They do well in school and the workplace and, often, have effectively 'Christianized' their faith by making it a personal matter. 'My religion is something private, something I don't feel like sharing in public', says Delilah Kerchouche, 30, a chic Parisian journalist whose immigrant parents raised her 'as Algerian. But it's definitely part of who I am.' Rather than struggling to 'fit in', these Gen. Mers want Europe to make space for them, and as their numbers grow, Europe needs them to succeed.

In France, Kerchouche is a part of the 'Beurgeoisie', slang for bourgeois Beurs, or successful Maghrebi Arabs. In Britain, she would be a Yummie, or Young and Upwardly Mobile Muslim. They are confident, culturally ambidextrous, second- and third-generation Europeans, aware of their rights as European Union citizens. And critically, they are asserting the right to be both modern and Muslim, both European and Islamic. Swiss-born Tariq Ramadan, whose grandfather founded the revolutionary Muslim Brotherhood in Egypt, encourages these youths to seize their rights as citizens, and to forge alliances with other groups, including the anti-globalization movement. 'Muslims in the West were waiting for answers from the so-called Islamic world', says Ramadan. That's changed. Now girls in Spain and France are going to court to uphold their right to cover their heads in school, while the Arab European League in Belgium is demanding bilingual education for kids who speak Arabic at home.

Such efforts are forcing traditional Europeans to rethink their own ideas of cultural identity – and test the limits of their tolerance. France, for instance, fought a long battle to keep religion, in the form of Catholicism, out of its classrooms. Is it now to permit Muslim girls to wear headscarves? What will the famously laissez-faire Dutch do about ferociously intolerant Muslim preachers who say gays should be slaughtered like pigs? What will they do, a decade or two from now, when the majority of Dutch newborns will be Muslim?

France, with the largest Muslim population, is the great test case. Wave after wave of immigrants have been quietly integrated over the past 100 years by a system that was less melting pot than crucible. It refused to recognize any ethnic, racial or religious distinctions whatsoever among citizens whose right and duty was to share in France's language, its republican values and its historical culture. Until recently the system worked, creating Frenchmen who were black and Frenchwomen who happened to be Jewish, but who didn't threaten France's civilization or identity. American-style multiculturalism, in this context, was considered a recipe for chaos.

That old system is collapsing under the weight of its own contradictions. In the last three months, nearly 100 cases arguing for a girl's right to wear a headscarf to school have been brought before the French Ministry of Education. Earlier this month a multipartisan commission of MPs backed legislation banning all religious symbols from state-run institutions in France, and on October 10 a court upheld the expulsion of Muslim sisters Lila and Alma Levy from a state school in Aubervilliers for wearing hijab. Human-rights campaigners, on the other hand, argue that banning the veil not only contravenes the new European human-rights charter but interferes with French constitutional guarantees of liberty. 'They claim that nobody should force a woman to wear the hijab', says Lila Levy, 18. 'But how can they force us to remove it? If they really cared about our freedom, they should let us be free to decide whether we want to wear it or not.'

Similar battles are playing out elsewhere in Europe. Last February a 13-year-old Spanish immigrant, Fatima Eldrisi, won the right to go to public school in a hijab, after local education authorities agreed that her right to education was more important than what she wore. A parliamentary commission in the Netherlands gloomily observed that 'integration with so-called allochtones [slang for Dutch Muslims] has failed'.

Critics in Britain, which prides itself on its freedom from a state-sponsored cultural identity, are quick to point out the downsides of a more laissez-faire approach – chief among them so-called Londonistan, the network of mosques and meeting halls notorious for harboring Islamic militants. There are many such places, among them a working-class neighborhood of the northern industrial city of Bradford, replete with halal butchers and tandoori restaurants. One 25-year-old man there, bearded with light green eyes, wishes to be identified only as Ahmed. He has a broad Yorkshire accent but says he's an Afghan Pathan. 'If you're Muslim, you're Muslim', he says. 'It doesn't matter if you're Afghan,

British or European. There's only one Islam.' Ahmed says he used to do drugs and hang out in clubs, before rediscovering his religion and getting a job in a factory building tanks and planes. This is his jihad, he says: 'If you want to be a real man, and fight the real fight, you try to be a good Muslim when you're in a place with naked women, with miniskirts, with casinos and guns. The real jihad is when you can control your tongue and your private parts.' In Britain, he notes, he's free to do what he likes as a Muslim. His colleagues and friends are open-minded and tolerant, even reminding him when it's time to pray.

That points toward part of the answer to Europe's Islam question. The fact that most Muslims in Britain were automatically granted citizenship as Commonwealth members produced second and third generations certain of their right to participate in commercial, political and civil life. This is a far cry from some countries in Continental Europe, where state-sponsored secularism and unwillingness to recognize minorities, as in France, or narrow definitions of nationality, as in Germany, left Muslims for many years on the margins of society. To be sure, Britain is also plagued by discrimination. Two-thirds of Muslim organizations reported unfair treatment in state schools and employment compared with other religious groups. Some 80 per cent of Pakistani and Bangladeshi households have incomes at or below the national average, compared with 40 per cent for other ethnic minorities. But at least British Muslims have schools, they've got civil liberties, they've got Muslims in the House of Lords. In Britain Gen. M has undeniably entered the mainstream. Where their parents opened corner shops and halal butchers, they've moved into the civil service, doctors' offices and even that bastion of British culture, the City. BBC Radio's morning religious slot, 'Thought for the Day', features Muslim scholars as well as ministers. British schoolchildren now learn about Islam and Hinduism in religious-education classes. Prince Charles has toyed with changing his title from 'Defender of the Faith' to 'Defender of the Faiths'.

Thirty-year-old Sajid Hussain could be a poster boy for modern Muslim Britain. He's Oxford educated, devout and as comfortable discussing big-bang theory as he is talking about medieval Muslim philosophy. Now he's teaching science at a Bradford secondary school, as well as working to start a new Islamic girls' school that will also welcome Jews and Christians – anyone who is not particularly comfortable with the sex education and liberal atmosphere in Britain's secular schools. It is the ever-moving moral standard, he argues, on issues like dress, premarital sex and homosexuality that unnerves Muslims, just as it does religious Jews and Christians. 'Secularism is not just a problem for Islam, but for all the big religions.'

As Muslims gain the political confidence to assert themselves, and the skills to forge alliances with other groups, their impact on European culture and society can only grow. Even the reluctant French government is realizing that life in a globalized world may mean that Muslims – and, indeed, religion itself – cannot be kept in purdah. Nor can the broad cultural identities associated with religion and ethnicity simply be denied. The devout and the doubting, the radical and the secular, all may think of themselves as 'Muslim', and more and more they will assume their rightful place in the arts and the media, in parliaments and on village councils, in board rooms and on military promotion lists.

Generation M is changing Islam from a foreign faith into a dynamic force for change that cannot be resisted any more than it can be predicted. Asma, a pretty green-eyed 16-year-old student at Averroes, France's first Muslim school, in Lille, recalls having to remove her hijab when she went to her former high school. At Averroes, she can wear it – and no longer must hide herself behind the traditions of French secularism. It remains to be seen whether, when it comes time for her own daughter to decide to wear the hijab or not, that tradition may itself be gone. Along, perhaps, with charcuterie?

DISCUSSION AND QUESTIONS

1. Is Generation M a possible segmenting criterion?
2. Explain the differences between the French and British government approaches to the acculturation process.
3. How are these differences likely to influence marketing strategies?
4. Given the possible divisiveness of a strategy targeting ethnic groups in the French political climate, is it ethical for marketers to proceed?

Index

Page numbers in *italics* refer to tables, figures and exhibits: page numbers in **bold** refer to main discussion.